ARABS IN AMERICA

The Contributors

SHARON MCIRVIN ABU-LABAN is Assistant Professor of Sociology at the University of Alberta.

ISMAEL AHMED is a teacher and community organizer.

ALEX AJAY is a member of the Middle East Research and Information Project.

MAHFOUD BENNOUNE is a member of the Department of Anthropology at the University of Michigan.

MARY BISHARAT is a writer and social worker.

CARLO CALDAROLA is Associate Professor of Sociology at the University of Alberta.

KAREN FARSOUN is a member of the Middle East Research and Information Project.

SAMIH FARSOUN is a member of the Middle East Research and Information Project.

DAN GEORGAKAS is an author and journalist.

L. M. KENNY is Professor and Chairman of the Department of Islamic Studies at the University of Toronto.

JAMES A. MCCLURE is a United States Senator from Idaho.

AYAD AL-QAZZAZ is Associate Professor of Sociology at California State University, Sacramento.

EDWARD W. SAID is Professor of Comparative Literature at Columbia University.

ELIAS SAM'O is Associate Professor of Political Science at Central Michigan University.

FAYEZ A. SAYEGH is a diplomat and member of the Palestine National Council.

MICHAEL W. SULEIMAN is Professor and Chairman of the Department of Political Science at Kansas State University.

JANICE J. TERRY is Associate Professor of History at Eastern Michigan University.

AAUG Monograph Series: No. 5

ARABS IN AMERICA
MYTHS AND REALITIES

edited by
Baha Abu-Laban
Faith T. Zeadey

THE MEDINA UNIVERSITY PRESS INTERNATIONAL
WILMETTE, ILLINOIS
1975

First published in the United States of America in 1975 by
The Medina University Press International
P.O. Box 125
Wilmette, Illinois 60091

Baha Abu-Laban is Professor of Sociology at the University of Alberta.

Faith T. Zeadey is Instructor of Sociology at Worcester State College.

CONTENTS

FOREWORD

As an educational organization dedicated to the dissemination of information concerning issues of importance to the Arab world as well as the Arab-American community, the Association of Arab-American University Graduates, Inc., has been active in a variety of ways. Of major importance has been the AAUG publication program, which has so far resulted in the production of significant information papers, books, bibliographies, and audio-visual educational material. As part of this program, the AAUG has customarily published the proceedings of its annual convention.

The papers in this volume were first presented at the Seventh Annual Convention of the AAUG, which was held in Cleveland, Ohio, October 25-27, 1974. The theme of the convention was "Arabs in America: Dynamics of a Challenge." Approximately fifty papers were presented; as in the past, it was decided to publish only a portion of them owing to practical as well as technical considerations.

The central concern of the essays included in this volume is the problematic relationship that currently exists between the Arab-American community and the larger society. Just as the challenges facing Arab Americans were intensified in the aftermath of the 1967 June War, so too those challenges were intensified, perhaps even more so, in the aftermath of the 1973 October War, the energy crisis, and the oil embargo. Not coincidentally, the themes of the 1968 and 1974 AAUG conventions were similar. However, the monographs resulting from these two conventions differ significantly, reflecting the steady movement of the AAUG and its membership toward certain important goals. The focus of the first monograph (*The Arab Americans: Studies in Assimilation,* edited by Elaine Hagopian and Ann Paden) is on the historical, demographic, and socioeconomic processes associated with community formation and the adaptation of Arab immigrants to the American environment. This volume, in contrast, focuses on the biased and unfavorable treatment of Arabs in the mass media of communication, in school textbooks, in church publications and teachings, and in the workplace. The topic of this volume is timely and of urgent importance to Arab Americans as well as to the larger society.

As the seventh President of the AAUG, I wish to acknowledge with thanks the contributions made by the editors of this volume, the authors whose essays are presented here, and the other participants at the convention who presented papers, appeared on panels or participated in forums, or served as panel chairpersons or commentators. A special note of thanks is also due to the following persons without whose work the convention could not have been the success that it was: Charles Abookire, Jr., Joyce Aruri, Flora Azar, Martha Bisharat, Georgine Cooper, Pierre Gabriel, Minor H. George, David Harami, Labib Hishmeh, Hassan Husseini, Nazik Kazimi, Joanne Fedor McKenna, and Mary Macron.

H. S. HADDAD

Professor of History
St. Xavier College

PREFACE

Arabs in the United States and Canada are one of the least studied and yet perhaps one of the most disparaged of all ethnic and minority groups. The few existing studies of Arab Americans deal primarily with the history of their migration to North America, their sociocultural and demographic characteristics, their religious organizations, their economic adjustment to American life, their acculturation or assimilation. While there is a need for more research on these topics, there is an even greater need for studies focusing on majority group attitudes and reactions toward Arabs, for with few exceptions this research area has been entirely neglected. This collection of essays represents an attempt to meet this need.

The contributors to this volume examine the structuring of information about Arabs in the mass media of communication and in religious and educational institutions, and discuss, more specifically, the treatment of Arab workers in selected American and European settings. Significantly, these essays agree that the Palestine question and the Arab-Israeli conflict are important factors in the frequently displayed bias against Arabs in newspapers, magazines, books, radio, and television. Aided by favorable social and political conditions, Zionist propaganda in America and elsewhere has very frequently succeeded in defining the Palestine problem and the Arab-Israeli conflict in ways that favor Israel, that inhibit a better understanding of the fundamental issues in the conflict, and that adversely influence the image and the treatment of Arabs. In an attempt to clarify relevant issues, the last two essays deal with recent American and international developments concerning the Palestine question and the Arab-Israeli conflict.

Not all accounts of Arabs in the North American and Western European mass media are biased or unfavorable. Several essays in this volume agree to this. Nor are the different media equally guilty of biased reporting. Janice Terry's paper reveals differences in treatment of relevant issues among American and Western European newspapers. Similarly, as can be seen in the study by Karen Farsoun, Samih Farsoun, and Alex Ajay, the degree of bias displayed in the media may change over time. In a content analysis of publications of the American Left, these authors note that whereas the Old Left was sympathetic toward Israel and Zionism, the New Left, essentially a product of the 1960s, has come to view Zionism as a tool of capitalism and imperialism, and Israel as a settler state. Janice Terry also finds a perceptible change in Western press coverage of the Middle East before and after the Arab-Israeli war of October 1973.

Although the studies of the media presented in this volume are not exhaustive, it is significant that they agree that the mass media in general have been grossly biased in reporting news items concerning Arabs and the Arab-Israeli conflict. Michael Suleiman denounces the mass media for reiterating stereotypical beliefs and myths concerning Arabs. And Elias Sam'o remarks that although the media inevitably are subjective, this kind of bias "goes beyond the expected failings of human beings." Indeed, one might argue that this bias may well reflect a traditional, albeit variable, pattern of Western hostility toward Arabs and the Arab culture.

The nuances of biased reporting are manifold. In written accounts (newspapers, magazines, etc.), bias is found in the use of loaded or valuative words, misleading or emotional titles, "carefully selected" size of type for titles and subtitles, and incomplete and/or erroneous stories, as well as in the placement of articles. With reference to Arabs and Palestinians, some aspects of this bias were well identified by Anna Patterson in a letter published in the July 9, 1974, issue of the *Christian Science Monitor*.

> Why is it that when individual Palestinians kill, the news media term it "slaughter" or a "massacre," but when the Israeli government kills or bombs, the news media term it a "reprisal" or "retaliation" or say it is "understandable"? Why is it not a massacre when the Israeli government shoots down a Libyan airliner killing 108 innocent people? Is it "understandable" when the Israeli government bombs Palestinian refugee camps or Lebanese apartment buildings killing men, women, and children? Is it not a slaughter when the Israeli government bombs Palestinian homes—if one can term tents and shanties homes?
>
> It is amazing that the news media can "understand" these acts when Dr. Israel Shahak, an Israeli who is head of the Israeli League of Human and Civilian Rights, testified on April 4 before a House Committee and said that he could not understand his government's policies of

bombing civilian targets, deporting Arabs from their homes, and blowing up Arab homes for no reason. Dr. Shahak also cannot understand how he can "be for the right of Soviet Jews to come to Haifa and be against the right of Palestinians to come back to Haifa."

Finally, how can anyone not understand that the Palestinians want what every American and every person in the world wants—peace and the right to live in their homes with democratic rights? Is it not understandable that if someone took away your homes and your rights you would want them back—even 25 or 50 years later?

The problem of bias against Arabs is not limited to the news media. The "discourse of Orientalism" is probably a standard source of information about the Arabs and Islam for American students at all levels. Edward Said exposes some of Orientalism's "facts" about Arabs and Islam for what they really are: myths garbed in the protective cover of what appears to be "scientific" analysis. Other scholars at the convention underlined structural factors associated with the perpetuation of serious deficiencies in the Orientalist perspective and in regional studies programs whose focus includes the Middle East, the Arabs, and Islam. With disappointment, these scholars pointed to the entrenchment of Orientalism in American educational and political institutions.

The articles by Ayad Al-Qazzaz and L. M. Kenny are concerned with the treatment of Arabs and the Middle East in elementary, junior high, and high school social science textbooks. These textbooks share with the mass media the dubious distinction of creating, reiterating, and perpetuating certain stereotypical beliefs and myths about Arabs. With reference to the Arab-Israeli conflict and current events in the Middle East, the textbooks surveyed tend to give Israel preferential treatment and thereby contribute to the formation of unfavorable attitudes toward and prejudices against Arabs and Palestinians.

With regard to another potent agency of socialization, namely, the church, the contributions by Carlo Caldarola and Sharon Abu-Laban reveal significant denominational similarities and differences in the treatment of Middle East peoples and the Arab-Israeli conflict. Caldarola's essay examines the fundamentalist approach to Israel and Jews, while Abu-Laban's study compares the treatment of Middle East peoples in the Sunday school textbooks used in two "conservative" and two "liberal" programs. Both authors note that those denominations which adhere to a literal interpretation of the Bible view Israel as the fulfillment of biblical prophecy. Abu-Laban found that although the liberal denominations tend to be less imprisoned by religious dogma than their fundamentalist counterparts, liberal church textbooks, in varying degrees, treat Arabs unfavorably and view Jews as "the Chosen People," Palestine as "the Promised Land," and Islam as an alien religion.

The essays by Mary Bisharat and Mahfoud Bennoune are concerned with the exploitation of immigrant Arab workers under the capitalist system of production. Sharing a similar concern, the papers by Ismael Ahmed and Dan Georgakas specifically address the role of ethnicity in the treatment of Arab workers in Detroit's automobile plants. It is clear that Arab workers are doubly jeopardized. On the one hand, because of their minority status they suffer, as do black workers, from employers' manipulative and exploitative practices. On the other hand, Arab workers are subjected to further disparagement and ill-treatment because they represent the "unpopular" side of the Arab-Israeli conflict.

The final essays focus on recent developments concerning the Arab-Israeli conflict and the question of Palestine. Sen. James A. McClure draws attention to what he believes to be an American awakening vis-à-vis the rights of the Palestinian people and the role of the Palestine Liberation Organization. Fayez Sayegh's essay draws attention to a new level of international awareness of the national rights and aspirations of the Palestinian people. Both of these writers agree on the importance of the role of the United States in the resolution of the Middle East conflict. Whether or not the American awakening to which Senator McClure refers will encompass a genuine change of U.S. government policy, including the hitherto "unlimited" congressional support for Israel, remains to be seen. So far, as Sayegh correctly notes, the United States has not been in tune with the realities that recent events have brought to the fore. Among other things, the U.S. government has yet to recognize the national rights and aspirations of the Palestinian people.

Important as it may be, a genuine change of U.S. government Middle East policy is not sufficient to eradicate prejudice against Arabs. The papers included in this book clearly show that such prejudice is a product of several interactive and mutually reinforcing elements in the institutional structure of American society. In that sense, Arab Americans face essentially the same difficulties as do other minority groups. But, unlike members of these groups, Arab Americans face further disparagement and stigmatization because of the Arab-Israeli conflict—a conflict of cardinal significance in the United States. In

this conflict, the Arab side is made to appear "wrong." A major
concerted and sustained fight against ignorance and all sources of
bias and prejudice against the Arab-American minority group is needed
to rectify this situation.

BAHA ABU-LABAN
FAITH T. ZEADEY

PART I: IMAGES IN THE MASS MEDIA

Janice J. Terry

THE WESTERN PRESS AND THE OCTOBER WAR: A CONTENT ANALYSIS

DID THE 1973 OCTOBER WAR and the Arab oil boycott transform Western attitudes regarding the Middle East? Many observers are convinced that the Arab military successes, coupled with the message that the Arab nations, through their oil resources, had the power to bring Western industry and life-styles to a crashing halt, significantly altered U.S. and European opinions of Israel and the Arab nations. This study examines three U.S. and two European newspapers during a four-month period before the war, the month of the war itself, and a four-month period following the war in order to ascertain in quantitative terms whether or not the media did, in fact, significantly modify its Middle East coverage.

METHOD

The *New York Times,* the *Washington Post,* and the *Detroit Free Press* were selected as the U.S. newspapers to be analyzed; the *Times* (London) and the French *Le Monde* were selected as representative of leading European newspapers.

Articles pertaining to the Middle East, although not those containing speeches or government statements, were coded on IBM coding forms

This paper appears also in *Middle East Crucible: Studies on the Arab-Israeli War of October 1973,* ed. Naseer Aruri (Wilmette, Ill.: Medina University Press International, 1975).

on a scale from one to ten.[1] In each case, the title of the newspaper, the date, the type of article, and the attitudes revealed in it were coded. The general attitude toward the conflict and breakdowns on attitudes toward the United Nations, specific Arab nations, the Palestinians, and the Arab oil boycott were included on the coding form. Whether or not the coverage linked the conflict to the superpower rivalry between the United States and the U.S.S.R. was also noted. For the European press, attitudes toward Continental détente with the Arab nations and opinions regarding U.S. policies in the Middle East were coded.[2] Finally, articles were classified as news articles, editorials, features, or cartoons.[3] Only major articles were coded; when the coverage was massive, as during the war, news items grouped under one headline were coded as one article.

The attitudes were coded as being either for or against Israel or Arab nations. An article was considered to be for one side if its attitude toward the actions of that side was favorable or if it described that side in favorable terms. An article was coded as being against one side if it displayed hostility toward the actions of that side or described that nation or its leadership in unfavorable terms. In cartoons, caricatures with racially derogatory features or disparaging stereotypes were coded as negative. An article was coded as neutral if it lacked value-laden adjectives, presented both sides of the case, or merely provided information or news coverage of events.

Once all of the articles had been coded, the information was transferred to IBM punch cards. The computer was then fed the data and was programed to tally the number of articles and types of attitudes

1. For previous studies of the same U.S. newspapers from 1948 to 1973, see Janice Terry, "A Content Analysis of American Newspapers," in *The Arab World: From Nationalism to Revolution,* ed. Abdeen Jabara and Janice Terry (Wilmette, Ill.: Medina University Press, International, 1971); Janice Terry and G. Mendenhall, "1973 U.S. Press Coverage on the Middle East," *Journal of Palestine Studies,* vol. IV, no. 1 (Autumn, 1974). Data from earlier years cited in the present study are from these two earlier papers. Gordon Mendenhall assisted in the computer programing for the present study.

2. The statistical data for 1973 concerning the superpowers are somewhat blurred owing to the détente between the former cold war rivals, although to some extent the 1973 war exacerbated many of the old antagonisms. Support for the détente softened the formerly strident U.S. editorial stance against Soviet policies in the Middle East, but after the October war more negative articles again appeared. European coverage differed notably from U.S. coverage on this issue.

3. It is somewhat difficult to distinguish between editorials and features in *Le Monde.* For purposes of this study, items classified in *Le Monde* as "Viewpoints" ("Points de Vue") were coded as editorials.

revealed, and to provide statistics comparing the coverage in the five newspapers by type of article. Tabulations were obtained on the frequency of occurrence of those articles dealing with the Arab-Israeli conflict, the United Nations, the Palestinian refugees, and the commandos. Percentages of occurrence were also tabulated. Secondly, tabulations were obtained on those items dealing with attitudes as dependent variables, using the type of article and newspaper as the independent variables. Comparisons were then obtained for coverage prior to the war (June–September 1973), during the war (October 1973), and after the war (November 1973–February 1974). In this manner a statistical picture of any differences in coverage before and after the war could be quantitatively noted. Differences among the newspapers, and between the U.S. and the European media, are clearly evident.

The volume of material, with 2,616 articles coded, offers numerous possibilities for further grouping and analysis. The nuances of some articles and cartoons are necessarily lost because of the broad categories that are demanded by the volume of the material. This methodological problem can only be overcome by a complex and expensive word tabulation. This study does, however, clearly document the press coverage in terms of volume and general attitudes for these five newspapers—both in the United States and in Europe. In addition, it reveals some significant differences among Western newspapers.

GENERAL RESULTS

A total of 2,616 articles were coded (see Table 1). The data on the *New York Times* are somewhat deceptive, as news articles under one headline were coded as one article. As a consequence the number of news articles coded for the *New York Times* is not indicative of the number of column inches devoted to Middle East news; in terms of space allotted, the *New York Times* coverage was, in fact, more extensive than the statistics indicate.

The extensive coverage in *Le Monde* is notable because, unlike the other newspapers coded, it does not publish a massive Sunday edition, but rather a joint Sunday and Monday edition. Thus *Le Monde* has only six days of publication to the seven for the other newspapers. As with the *New York Times*, many articles under one headline were coded as one article, indicating that *Le Monde*'s Middle East coverage is the most extensive of any of the papers analyzed.

In the nine-month period of time covered, both *Le Monde* and the *Washington Post* each published over 600 articles on the Arab-Israeli conflict and the oil boycott as it pertained to the Middle East and the West. This is a massive increase in total coverage in comparison with that of previous years. For example, in 1968 the *Washington Post* published only 49 articles, while the *New York Times*, the *Washington Post*, and the *Detroit Free Press* collectively published only 275 articles—less than one-third what the *Post* singly published in the months before and after the 1973 war. In 1948, another peak year of coverage, articles in the same newspapers totaled 1,140; these figures, of course, more closely approximate the 1973 data. Unfortunately, no comparable statistics are available for the European press, but it seems likely that its volume of coverage has increased similarly.

In all of the newspapers most of the news coverage was neutral. As might be expected, opinions and attitudinal biases became more apparent in editorials and features. In its total coverage, the *New York Times* contained 7.1 percent pro-Israeli and 2.1 percent anti-Arab material for a total of 9.2 percent favoring Israel (see Table 2). This compares with 0.8 percent pro-Arab, 0.5 percent anti-Israeli, and 1.1 percent pro–Palestinian refugee coverage, which totals 2.4 percent pro-Arab material. Similarly, the *Washington Post* coverage was 5.8 percent pro-Israeli and 2.3 percent pro-Arab; the *Detroit Free Press*, 6.8 percent pro-Israeli and no pro-Arab material; the *Times*, 2.7 percent pro-Israeli and 2.3 percent pro-Arab; and *Le Monde*, 2.5 percent pro-Israeli and 2.5 percent pro-Arab. Thus the European newspapers were more nearly balanced in their total coverage than were the U.S. newspapers.

The figures also indicate a marked drop in pro-Israeli/anti-Arab editorial coverage (see Table 3). In 1948, 31 editorials in the *New York Times* (57.4 percent of total editorial coverage in that paper) favored Israel; in 1968, 6 editorials (37.5 percent) did so; and in the period of this study, 11 editorials (10.9 percent) favored Israel. Similar declines are found in the other U.S. newspapers.

In features, the pro-Israeli stance of the U.S. press becomes more pronounced. The *New York Times* issued 23 features favorable to Israel (23.7 percent of total feature coverage in that paper), the *Washington Post*, 17 (16.0 percent), and the *Detroit Free Press*, 8 (17.7 percent). At the same time, the *New York Times* published 6 pro-Arab features, (6.2 percent), the *Washington Post*, 9 (8.5 percent), and the *Detroit Free Press*, none. In other words, there were approximately twice as many pro-Israeli features as pro-Arab ones. In spite of this bias, the feature coverage has become more balanced, for pro-Arab features were almost totally absent in pre-1973 coverage.

Le Monde had 7 pro-Israeli features (4.6 percent) and 8 pro-Arab (5.2 percent), while the *Times* had 12 pro-Israeli (14.1 percent) and 7 pro-Arab (8.2 percent).

The data indicate that mention of the Palestinians as a separate entity in press coverage has become quite frequent. In the U.S. media this is not a *re*appearance of the Palestinian entity, but its first quantitative appearance. In 1948 the Palestinians were mentioned in the three U.S. newspapers in 12 articles, and in 1968 in only 23. In this study the Palestinians were mentioned specifically in 541 articles: 191 in the *New York Times*, 96 in the *Washington Post*, 42 in the *Detroit Free Press*, 91 in the *Times*, and 122 in *Le Monde* (see Table 17). For the U.S. press alone this is a startling increase of over 1000 percent! There was an indication that while there may be growing sympathy for or at least awareness of the Palestinian case, there is also growing hostility to most commando activities. There were 2 *New York Times*, 2 *Washington Post*, 4 *Times*, and 5 *Le Monde* features indicating sympathy for the Palestinians (see Table 3). In contrast there were 10 *New York Times*, 2 *Washington Post*, 3 *Detroit Free Press*, 4 *Le Monde*, and no *Times* features criticizing the commandos (see Table 4). Editorials in these newspapers also reflected this attitude.

The European attitudes with regard to the oil issue contrast considerably with those of the U.S. press. To a great extent this reveals the greater dependency of Europe on Arab oil, and the determination of European leaders not to alienate the Arab states (see Tables 5–8). Consequently, the *Times* published only 1 editorial criticizing the Arab embargo and *Le Monde* published 5, whereas there were 12 anti-Arab editorials in the *New York Times* and 15 in the *Washington Post*. The U.S. editorials, as well as features, tended to stress the "blackmail" aspects of the boycott, a theme completely absent from the European press coverage.

Finally, the two European newspapers occasionally criticized U.S. policies in the Middle East (1 news article, 1 feature, and 1 editorial in the *Times*, and 1 editorial in *Le Monde*; see Table 9). *Le Monde* reflected the independent French policy in international affairs and stressed the best interests of Europe in 1 news article, 7 editorials, and 4 features. However, both newspapers were unanimous in praising the efforts of Henry Kissinger in the Middle East. The *Times* printed 5 editorials and 2 features lauding Kissinger. Even the generally less pro-U.S. French press picked up the trend; *Le Monde* issued 3 editorials, 4 features, and 3 cartoons commending Kissinger's diplomacy.

THE OCTOBER WAR: BEFORE AND AFTER

Not surprisingly, press coverage was at its peak during the October war, and at times equaled or surpassed the total coverage in the four months preceding the outbreak of hostilities. In the four months following the war, the extent of coverage remained at least 10 to 20 percent higher than in the period prior to October. This indicates a continuing interest in Middle East news, in the possibility of a resolution of the Arab-Israeli conflict, and in the Arab oil embargo. The total coverage in the five newspapers after the war was more than twice that of the months prior to it (see tables 10-13). The distribution among news articles, features, editorials, and cartoons remained fairly consistent, indicating an increase in coverage in all types of articles (see Table 14). Interestingly, the European newspapers had a somewhat higher level of coverage prior to the war than the U.S. newspapers. The European media, therefore, evidence a continuing interest in Middle Eastern affairs, while the U.S. press tends to be more "crisis oriented."

Editorial coverage of the war and its aftermath tended to favor the Israeli position; however, there were some pro-Arab editorials, whereas there had been few if any in the years before 1973 (see tables 15-16). There were also some anti-Israeli editorials, although these were outnumbered by pro-Israeli editorials four to one. The war also strained the U.S.-U.S.S.R. détente. Although there were no editorials criticizing Soviet policies in the Middle East before the war, during the war U.S.S.R. actions in the Middle East were criticized several times. Editorials also stressed a certain sympathy for the Palestinian refugees, who were generally depicted as victims.

Mention of the Palestinians as a separate entity did not increase during the war or afterward, but remained fairly constant (see Table 17). This seems to support the hypothesis that notice of the Palestinian entity emerged after the 1967 war when the Palestinian commandos forced world attention to face the reality of Palestinian grievances. During the war, mention of the Palestinians actually dropped slightly; this was probably owing to the focus on institutionalized polities and the military confrontations among internationally recognized governments. Articles continued to reflect opposition to commando activities (see Table 18).

Certainly the most notable change in coverage concerned the issue of the oil embargo, which became a major news item during and after the October war (see tables 19-23). Only 78 articles were published on oil and the Middle East prior to the war; after the war 368 such articles were published. Editorial coverage more than tripled, with a number of editorials merely discussing the problems and complexities posed by the Arab embargo. There were very few pro-Arab articles, most of them appearing in the European press.

Tables 24 and 25 primarily indicate an increase, following the October war, in the volume of coverage of the Arab-Israeli conflict, but do not reveal any important changes in attitudes toward the Arabs or the Israelis. However, neutral coverage did increase slightly, and this may be indicative of the beginning of changing attitudes. On the other hand, it may also merely represent an attempt by the press to include more balanced material from both Israeli and Arab sources. The European newspapers had fewer pro-Israeli articles both before and after October 1973 than did the U.S. press. They also issued fewer anti-Arab articles. Thus the European press had begun to alter its coverage, or to reach a greater balance in its coverage, prior to the war.

Table 1

Number of Articles on the Middle East, June 1973 - Feb. 1974

Newspaper	No.	%
New York Times	462	17.7
Washington Post	662	25.3
Detroit Free Press	292	11.2
Times	508	19.4
Le Monde	692	26.4
TOTAL	2,616	100.0

Table 2

Attitude toward the Arab-Israeli Conflict

Attitude	New York Times No.	%	Washington Post No.	%	Detroit Free Press No.	%	Times No.	%	Le Monde No.	%	Total No.	%
Neutral	329	86.6	498	88.8	236	90.1	451	94.0	607	94.4	2,121	91.1
Against both	2	0.5	13	2.3	7	2.7	5	1.0	4	0.6	31	1.3
Pro-Israeli	27	7.1	30	5.3	15	5.7	12	2.5	16	2.5	100	4.3
Pro-Arab	3	0.8	6	1.1	-	-	1	0.2	4	0.6	14	0.6
Anti-Israeli	2	0.5	3	0.5	-	-	4	0.8	3	0.5	12	0.5
Anti-U.S.S.R.	5	1.3	4	0.7	1	0.4	-	-	-	-	10	0.1
Anti-U.S.	-	-	-	-	-	-	-	-	-	-	-	-
Anti-Arab	8	2.1	3	0.5	3	1.1	1	0.2	-	-	15	0.6
Sym. for refugees	4	1.1	4	0.7	-	-	6	1.3	9	1.4	23	1.0
TOTAL	380		561		262		480		643		2,326*	

*Total here is less than total on Table 1 because not all articles mention the Arab-Israeli conflict.

Table 3

Pro-Israeli/Anti-Arab and Pro-Arab/Anti-Israeli Coverage *

Type of coverage and attitude	New York Times No.	New York Times %	Washington Post No.	Washington Post %	Detroit Free Press No.	Detroit Free Press %	Times No.	Times %	Le Monde No.	Le Monde %
Total editorials	101		61		30		52		65	
Pro-Israeli	6	5.9	11	18.0	5	16.7	1	1.9	9	13.8
Anti-Arab	5	4.9	1	1.6	-	-	-	-	-	-
TOTAL	11	10.9	12	19.7	5	16.7	1	1.9	9	13.8
Pro-Arab	-	-	2	3.3	-	-	-	-	4	6.1
Anti-Israeli	1	.9	2	3.3	-	-	2	3.8	3	4.6
Sym. to refugees	-	-	-	-	-	-	2	3.8	4	6.1
TOTAL	1	.9	4	6.6	-	-	4	7.6	11	16.9
Total features	97		106		45		85		152	
Pro-Israeli	21	21.6	15	14.1	7	15.5	11	12.9	7	4.6
Anti-Arab	2	2.0	2	1.9	1	2.2	1	1.2	-	-
TOTAL	23	23.7	17	16.0	8	17.7	12	14.1	7	4.6
Pro-Arab	3	3.1	5	4.7	-	-	1	1.2	3	1.9
Anti-Israeli	1	1.0	2	1.9	-	-	2	2.3	5	3.3
Sym. to refugees	2	2.1	2	1.9	-	-	4	4.7	8	5.2
TOTAL	6	6.2	9	8.5	-	-	7	8.2		
Total cartoons	2		19		21				15	
Pro-Israeli	-	-	4	21.0	2	9.5	-	-	-	-
Anti-Arab	-	-	-	-	-	-	-	-	-	-
TOTAL	-	-	4	21.0	2	9.5	-	-	-	-
Pro-Arab	-	-	1	5.3	-	-	-	-	-	-
Anti-Israeli	-	-	-	-	-	-	-	-	-	-
Sym. to refugees	-	-	-	-	-	-	-	-	-	-
TOTAL	-	-	1	5.3	-	-	-	-	-	-

*Details may not add to total owing to rounding.

Table 4

Attitude toward the Commandos

	Pro No.	Pro %	Anti No.	Anti %	Neutral No.	Neutral %	Total No.
New York Times							
News articles	1	0.8	1	0.8	124	98.4	126
Editorials	-	-	15	88.2	2	11.8	17
Features	-	-	10	62.5	6	37.5	16
TOTAL	1	-	26	-	132	-	159
Washington Post							
News articles	-	-	-	-	65	100.0	65
Editorials	-	-	10	90.9	1	9.0	11
Features	-	-	2	16.7	10	83.3	12
TOTAL	-	-	12	-	76	-	88
Detroit Free Press							
News articles	-	-	1	3.1	31	96.8	32
Editorials	-	-	3	75.0	1	25.0	4
Features	-	-	3	60.0	2	40.0	5
TOTAL	-	-	7	-	34	-	41
Times							
News articles	-	-	4	6.1	61	93.8	65
Editorials	-	-	9	69.2	4	30.8	13
Features	3	27.3	-	-	8	72.7	11
TOTAL	3	-	13	-	73	-	89
Le Monde							
News articles	-	-	-	-	68	100.0	68
Editorials	2	15.4	9	69.2	2	15.4	13
Features	1	6.2	4	25.0	11	68.7	16
Cartoons	-	-	1	100.0	-	-	1
TOTAL	3	-	14	-	81	-	98

Table 5

Attitude on Oil Embargo in News Articles

Attitude	New York Times	Washington Post	Detroit Free Press	Times	Le Monde
			No. of news articles		
Neutral	181	126	44	66	99
Pro-Arab	-	-	1	-	-
Anti-Arab	-	-	-	-	-
Russia benefit	-	-	2	-	-
Pro-U.S.	-	-	-	-	-
Oil as good for U.S./Arabs	-	-	-	-	-
Oil as good for Europe	-	-	-	-	1
Oil as good for Europe/Arabs	-	-	-	-	-
Anti-oil companies	-	-	-	-	-

Table 6

Attitude on Oil Embargo in Editorials

Attitude	New York Times	Washington Post	Detroit Free Press	Times	Le Monde
			No. of editorials		
Neutral	37	2	4	15	4
Pro-Arab	-	-	-	-	3
Anti-Arab	12	15	2	1	5
Russia benefit	1	6	-	-	-
Pro-U.S.	-	-	-	-	-
Oil as good for U.S./Arabs	3	1	1	1	-
Oil as good for Europe	-	-	-	-	3
Oil as good for Europe/Arabs	-	-	-	-	-
Anti-oil companies	1	-	-	-	3

Table 7

Attitude on Oil Embargo in Features

Attitude	No. of features				
	New York Times	Washington Post	Detroit Free Press	Times	Le Monde
Neutral	33	10	7	14	14
Pro-Arab	2	2	2	2	-
Anti-Arab	22	13	12	1	-
Russia benefit	-	-	-	1	-
Pro-U.S.	1	6	3	-	-
Oil as good for U.S./Arabs	4	2	1	1	-
Oil as good for Europe	-	-	-	-	9
Oil as good for Europe/Arabs	-	1	-	-	-
Anti-oil companies	-	-	2	-	-

Table 8

Attitude on Oil Embargo in Cartoons

Attitude	No. of cartoons				
	New York Times	Washington Post	Detroit Free Press	Times	Le Monde
Neutral	1	-	2	-	2
Pro-Arab	-	5	7	-	-
Anti-Arab	-	1	1	-	-
Russia benefit	-	-	-	-	-
Pro-U.S.	-	-	1	-	-
Oil as good for U.S./Arabs	-	-	-	1	-
Oil as good for Europe	-	-	-	-	1
Oil as good for Europe/Arabs	-	-	-	-	-
Anti-oil companies	-	-	-	-	-

Table 9

European Attitude toward U.S. Policies in the Middle East

Newspaper and attitude	No. of articles			
	News articles	Editorials	Features	Cartoons
Times				
Pro-U.S. support for Israel	1	1	1	–
Anti-U.S. support for Israel	1	–	–	–
Neutral	–	–	–	–
Pro-U.S., anti-Arab	–	–	–	–
Pro-U.S., pro-Arab	–	5	2	–
Pro-Kissinger	–	–	–	–
Pro-Europe	–	–	–	–
Le Monde				
Pro-U.S. support for Israel	–	1	–	–
Anti-U.S. support for Israel	–	1	–	–
Neutral	–	–	–	–
Pro-U.S., anti-Arab	–	–	–	–
Pro-U.S., pro-Arab	–	3	4	3
Pro-Kissinger	–	7	4	–
Pro-Europe	1	–	–	–

Table 10

Number of News Articles on the Arab-Israeli Conflict before and after the October War

Newspaper	June-Sept. 1973		Oct. 1973		Nov. 1973-Feb. 1974		Total
	No.	%	No.	%	No.	%	No.
New York Times	86	33.3	30	11.6	142	55.0	258
Washington Post	83	17.5	122	25.7	269	56.7	474
Detroit Free Press	22	11.2	57	29.0	117	59.7	196
Times	95	25.4	94	25.1	185	49.5	374
Le Monde	147	32.0	99	21.6	213	46.4	459
TOTAL	433		402		926		1,761

Table 11

Number of Editorials on the Arab-Israeli Conflict before and after the October War

Newspaper	June-Sept. 1973		Oct. 1973		Nov. 1973-Feb. 1974		Total
	No.	%	No.	%	No.	%	No.
New York Times	19	18.8	25	24.7	57	56.4	101
Washington Post	11	18.0	14	22.9	36	59.0	61
Detroit Free Press	1	3.3	8	26.7	21	70.0	30
Times	12	23.1	15	28.8	25	48.1	52
Le Monde	12	18.5	20	30.8	33	50.8	65
TOTAL	55		82		172		309

Table 12

Number of Features on the Arab-Israeli Conflict before and after the October War

Newspaper	June-Sept. 1973		Oct. 1973		Nov. 1973-Feb. 1974		Total
	No.	%	No.	%	No.	%	No.
New York Times	19	19.6	14	14.4	64	65.9	97
Washington Post	9	8.5	30	28.3	67	63.2	106
Detroit Free Press	7	15.5	12	26.7	26	57.8	45
Times	12	14.6	35	42.7	35	42.7	82
Le Monde	31	20.4	28	18.4	93	61.2	152
TOTAL	78		119		285		482

Table 13

Number of Cartoons on the Arab-Israeli Conflict before and after the October War

Newspaper	June-Sept. 1973		Oct. 1973		Nov. 1973-Feb. 1974		Total
	No.	%	No.	%	No.	%	No.
New York Times	2	66.7	-	-	1	33.3	3
Washington Post	1	5.3	5	26.3	13	68.4	19
Detroit Free Press	1	4.8	4	19.0	16	76.2	21
Times	-	-	-	-	-	-	-
Le Monde	-	-	5	33.3	10	66.6	15
TOTAL	4		14		40		58

Table 14

Percentage Distribution of Articles on Middle East Conflict before and after the October War

	June-Sept. 1973	Oct. 1973	Nov. 1973-Feb. 1974
New York Times			
News articles	68.3%	43.5%	53.8%
Editorials	15.1	36.2	21.6
Features	15.1	20.3	24.2
Cartoons	1.6	-	0.4
Washington Post			
News articles	79.8	71.3	69.9
Editorials	10.6	8.2	9.4
Features	8.7	17.5	17.4
Cartoons	1.0	2.9	3.4
Detroit Free Press			
News articles	71.0	70.4	64.8
Editorials	3.2	9.9	11.5
Features	22.6	14.8	14.8
Cartoons	3.2	4.9	8.8
Times			
News articles	79.8	65.3	75.5
Editorials	10.1	10.4	10.2
Features	10.1	24.3	14.3
Cartoons	-	-	-
Le Monde			
News articles	77.4	65.1	61.1
Editorials	6.3	13.2	9.4
Features	16.3	18.4	26.6
Cartoons	-	3.3	2.9

Table 15

Editorial Coverage of Arab-Israeli Conflict before and after the October War

Attitude	No. of editorials			
	June-Sept. 1973	Oct. 1973	Nov. 1973-Feb. 1974	Total
Neutral	24	41	87	152
Against both	3	6	4	13
Pro-Israeli	3	11	18	32
Pro-Arab	1	2	1	4
Anti-Israeli	5	2	1	8
Anti-U.S.S.R.	—	3	1	4
Anti-U.S.	—	—	—	—
Anti-Arab	—	1	5	6
Sym. to refugees	1	2	5	8

Table 16

Feature Coverage of Arab-Israeli Conflict before and after the October War

Attitude	No. of features			
	June-Sept. 1973	Oct. 1973	Nov. 1973-Feb. 1974	Total
Neutral	45	70	175	290
Against both	—	5	1	6
Pro-Israeli	10	15	36	61
Pro-Arab	—	2	7	9
Anti-Israeli	—	1	3	4
Anti-U.S.S.R.	3	3	—	6
Anti-U.S.	—	—	—	—
Anti-Arab	2	—	4	6
Sym. to refugees	3	2	8	13

Table 17

Mention of the Palestinians

	No. of articles		
	June-Sept. 1973	Oct. 1973	Nov. 1973-Feb. 1974
News articles			
New York Times	56	13	84
Washington Post	29	10	30
Detroit Free Press	6	4	24
Times	24	5	25
Le Monde	40	11	21
Editorials			
New York Times	7	3	4
Washington Post	2	1	9
Detroit Free Press	1	-	3
Times	6	5	9
Le Monde	4	10	14
Features			
New York Times	6	4	14
Washington Post	2	2	11
Detroit Free Press	2	1	2
Times	4	5	8
Le Monde	5	6	11

Table 18

Attitude toward Commandos before and after the October War

Newspaper, type of coverage, and attitude	No. of articles		
	June-Sept. 1973	Oct. 1973	Nov. 1973-Feb. 1974
New York Times			
Editorials			
Anti-commando	8	2	5
Pro-commando	-	-	-
Neutral	1	-	1
Features			
Anti-commando	4	1	5
Pro-commando	-	-	-
Neutral	2	1	3
Washington Post			
Editorials			
Anti-commando	2	1	7
Pro-commando	-	-	-
Neutral	-	-	1
Features			
Anti-commando	1	-	1
Pro-commando	-	-	-
Neutral	1	1	8

Table 19

Editorial Attitudes on Oil Embargo before and after the October War

Attitude	No. of editorials			
	June-Sept. 1973	Oct. 1973	Nov. 1973-Feb. 1974	Total
Neutral	6	11	45	62
Pro-Arab	1	1	1	3
Anti-Arab	7	7	21	35
Russia benefit	-	1	6	7
Pro-U.S.	1	1	5	7
Oil as good for U.S./Arabs	1	-	5	6
Oil as good for Europe	-	-	3	3
Oil as good for Europe/Arabs	-	-	3	3
Anti-oil companies	-	-	1	1

Table 20

Feature Attitudes on Oil Embargo before and after the October War

Attitude	No. of features			
	June-Sept. 1973	Oct. 1973	Nov. 1973-Feb. 1974	Total
Neutral	11	15	53	79
Pro-Arab	-	-	7	7
Anti-Arab	4	4	40	48
Russia benefit	-	-	1	1
Pro-U.S.	2	3	5	10
Oil as good for U.S./Arabs	6	-	2	8
Oil as good for Europe	-	-	9	9
Oil as good for Europe/Arabs	-	-	1	1
Anti-oil companies	-	-	2	2

Table 21

Cartoon Attitudes on Oil Embargo before and after the October War

Attitude	No. of cartoons			
	June–Sept. 1973	Oct. 1973	Nov. 1973–Feb. 1974	Total
Neutral	-	3	2	5
Pro-Arab	-	-	-	-
Anti-Arab	1	-	11	12
Russia benefit	-	-	-	-
Pro-U.S.	1	-	-	1
Oil as good for U.S./Arabs	-	-	1	1
Oil as good for Europe	-	-	1	1
Oil as good for Europe/Arabs	-	-	-	-
Anti-oil companies	-	-	-	-

Table 22

Attitude on Oil Embargo in U.S. Press before and after the October War in Features

Newspaper and attitude	No. of features		
	June-Sept. 1973	Oct. 1973	Nov. 1973-Feb. 1974
New York Times			
Neutral	3	6	24
Pro-Arab	3	1	2
Anti-Arab	3	1	18
Russia benefit	-	-	-
Pro-U.S.	-	-	1
Oil as good for U.S./Arabs	3	-	1
Oil as good for Europe	-	-	-
Oil as good for Europe/Arabs	-	-	-
Anti-oil companies	-	-	-
Washington Post			
Neutral	1	1	8
Pro-Arab	1	-	2
Anti-Arab	1	-	12
Russia benefit	1	3	2
Pro-U.S.	1	-	-
Oil as good for U.S./Arabs	-	-	-
Oil as good for Europe	-	-	-
Oil as good for Europe/Arabs	1	-	-
Anti-oil companies	-	-	-
Detroit Free Press			
Neutral	-	1	7
Pro-Arab	-	-	1
Anti-Arab	-	3	9
Russia benefit	1	-	2
Pro-U.S.	1	-	-
Oil as good for U.S./Arabs	1	-	-
Oil as good for Europe	-	-	-
Oil as good for Europe/Arabs	-	-	-
Anti-oil companies	-	-	2

Table 23

Attitude on Oil Embargo in European Press before and after the October War in Features

Newspaper and attitude	No. of features		
	June-Sept. 1973	Oct. 1973	Nov. 1973-Feb. 1974
Times			
Neutral	5	4	5
Pro-Arab			2
Anti-Arab			1
Russia benefit			
Pro-U.S.			
Oil as good for U.S./Arabs	1		
Oil as good for Europe			
Oil as good for Europe/Arabs			
Anti-oil companies			
Le Monde			
Neutral	2	3	9
Pro-Arab			1
Anti-Arab			1
Russia benefit			
Pro-U.S.			
Oil as good for U.S./Arabs			
Oil as good for Europe			9
Oil as good for Europe/Arabs			
Anti-oil companies			

Table 24

Editorial and Feature Coverage of Arab-Israeli Conflict, Not Inclusive
of Oil Issue or Other Items, before and after the October War

Newspaper, type of coverage, and attitude	No. of articles		
	June-Sept. 1973	Oct. 1973	Nov. 1973-Feb. 1974
New York Times			
Editorials			
Neutral	13	14	27
Against both	1	1	-
Pro-Israeli	-	2	4
Pro-Arab	-	-	-
Anti-Israeli	1	-	-
Anti-U.S.S.R.	-	3	-
Anti-U.S.	-	-	-
Anti-Arab	-	1	4
Sym. to refugees	-	-	-
Features			
Neutral	9	7	33
Against both	-	-	-
Pro-Israeli	4	1	16
Pro-Arab	-	1	2
Anti-Israeli	-	1	-
Anti-U.S.S.R.	-	2	-
Anti-U.S.	-	-	-
Anti-Arab	2	-	-
Sym. to refugees	-	1	1
Washington Post			
Editorials			
Neutral	-	1	21
Against both	-	1	1
Pro-Israeli	-	6	5
Pro-Arab	-	-	-
Anti-Israeli	2	-	-
Anti-U.S.S.R.	-	-	1
Anti-U.S.	-	-	-
Anti-Arab	-	-	1
Sym. to refugees	1	-	1
Features			
Neutral	2	10	38
Against both	-	3	1
Pro-Israeli	2	4	9
Pro-Arab	-	1	4
Anti-Israeli	1	-	-
Anti-U.S.S.R.	-	-	3
Anti-U.S.	-	-	2
Anti-Arab	-	-	1
Sym. to refugees	1	-	1

Table 25

Editorial and Feature Coverage of Arab-Israeli Conflict, Not Inclusive
of Oil Issue or Other Items, before and after the October War

Newspaper, type of coverage, and attitude	No. of articles		
	June-Sept. 1973	Oct. 1973	Nov. 1973-Feb. 1974
Times			
Editorials			
Neutral	7	10	15
Against both	1	2	1
Pro-Israeli	1	-	-
Pro-Arab	-	-	-
Anti-Israeli	2	-	-
Anti-U.S.S.R.	-	-	-
Anti-U.S.	-	-	-
Anti-Arab	-	-	-
Sym. to refugees	-	-	2
Features			
Neutral	5	26	19
Against both	-	1	-
Pro-Israeli	-	6	5
Pro-Arab	-	-	1
Anti-Israeli	2	-	-
Anti-U.S.S.R.	-	-	-
Anti-U.S.	-	-	-
Anti-Arab	-	-	1
Sym. to refugees	1	-	3
Le Monde			
Editorials			
Neutral	4	11	11
Against both	-	-	2
Pro-Israeli	2	2	2
Pro-Arab	1	2	5
Anti-Israeli	-	2	1
Anti-U.S.S.R.	-	-	-
Anti-U.S.	-	-	-
Anti-Arab	-	-	-
Sym. to refugees	-	2	2
Features			
Neutral	27	20	72
Against both	-	-	-
Pro-Israeli	-	3	4
Pro-Arab	-	-	-
Anti-Israeli	-	-	-
Anti-U.S.S.R.	-	-	-
Anti-U.S.	-	-	-
Anti-Arab	-	-	-
Sym. to refugees	1	1	3

Michael W. Suleiman

PERCEPTIONS OF THE MIDDLE EAST IN AMERICAN NEWSMAGAZINES

ISRAEL HAS BEEN greatly successful in its efforts to persuade Westerners to view the Middle East and its peoples through Israeli eyes.[1] Consequently the American public *and* its political leaders have accepted the Israeli version of Middle East developments as at once more "objective" or "realistic," *and* more helpful in advancing U.S. interests in the area, than the assessment of the situation advanced by the Arabs. Perhaps the most important result of the 1973 October War between Israel and the neighboring Arab countries has been the "shattering of myths" upon which certain Israeli and Western assumptions have been based.

ISRAELI AND WESTERN ASSUMPTIONS ABOUT THE MIDDLE EAST

While all nationalist movements are in a sense attempts at redefining peoples' images of themselves, Zionism, the Jewish nationalist movement of the past century, can be defined almost solely in those terms. That is to say, the fundamental drive behind the Zionist movement has been a basic desire to change the image Gentiles have of Jews as well as the image Jews have of themselves. Viewed from this perspective, many Zionist and Israeli actions in war, foreign policy, and propaganda become more intelligible.

1. See Michael Suleiman, "National Stereotypes as Weapons in the Arab-Israeli Conflict," *Journal of Palestine Studies*, III, no. 3 (Spring 1974), 109-21.

At first the emphasis was on changing the image of the Jew as a Shylock, a merchant and moneylender. Hence the push for a return to the land, seeking rejuvenation and a chance to prove to the Jews themselves as well as to the Gentiles that Jews are not "different." The image of the Jew as a coward or a nonfighter also had to be combated. Here a great deal of emphasis on "fearlessness" was instilled in the young, sometimes at the expense of other emotions, including love and kindness.[2] Every precaution was taken to be almost completely certain of victory in any contemplated military engagement with the enemy. This involved the practice of outnumbering the enemy forces wherever possible.[3] Then, after the victory, the tactic was to use extensive propaganda to publicize what was termed a David-and-Goliath battle in which the "underdog" won. In this manner, and over a period of time, Israelis and many Jews outside the state began to gain confidence in the fighting ability and prowess of the Israelis.[4] But when this attitude generated overconfidence and arrogance, Israeli leaders began to underestimate the enemy, to ignore possible compromise options, to overestimate the ability of their own forces to respond quickly and effectively in a war situation, and to use flamboyant, exaggerative, and sometimes false statements in addressing their people as well as the enemy—exactly the behavior the Arab leaders manifested in 1948–49 and again in 1967.[5]

Turning specifically to the period immediately preceding the October war, the attitude of the Israelis and their Western, especially American,

2. See Yael Dayan, *Envy the Frightened* (London: Weidenfeld & Nicolson, 1961).

3. For figures on the number of troops of each side in 1948 and 1967, see John Bagot Glubb, *A Soldier with the Arabs* (London: Hodder & Stoughton, 1957), pp. 94–95; Peter Young, *The Israeli Campaign, 1967* (London: William Kimber, 1967); and Edgar O'Ballance, *The Arab-Israeli War, 1948* (New York: Praeger, 1957), and *The Third Arab-Israeli War* (Hamden, Conn.: Archon Books, 1972). For accounts by retired U.N. truce supervisors pertaining to so-called retaliation raids and general Arab-Israeli violence, see E. H. Hutchinson, *Violent Truce* (New York: Devin-Adair, 1956); Carl von Horn, *Soldiering for Peace* (New York: David McKay, 1966), pp. 71–139; and E. L. M. Burns, *Between Arab and Israeli* (London: George C. Harrap, 1962).

4. It is worth noting that while the Israelis are beginning to be seen by some Westerners as "good soldiers" or "militaristic," the same notion does *not* transfer to Jews in general. See Michael W. Suleiman, "The Middle East in American High Schools: A Kansas Case Study," *Middle East Studies Association Bulletin*, VIII, no. 2 (May 1974), 8–19.

5. The same observation was made in "The War That Broke the Myths," *Newsweek*, Oct. 22, 1973, p. 60.

supporters was one of overconfidence. Especially after the 1967 war, the attitude of the Israelis toward the Arabs both within and outside Israel was one of superiority. To them, the Arab was not a good soldier. He was neither effective nor courageous. Furthermore, he was not likely to change for some time—if ever. As I. F. Stone has observed, it is ironic that a people who for centuries have suffered from humiliation, oppression, and persecution as a minority group should, once in the majority as in Israel, begin to develop an attitude of "contemptuous superiority."[6] Far more important than the irony involved is the threat to the peace this attitude has constituted and the price the Israelis themselves have had to pay for such miscalculation.

According to the then prevalent Israeli-Western view, not only was the Arab a poor soldier but the whole Arab fighting machine was an inefficient organization.[7] Allegedly this was due to some deficiency in the Arab psychological make-up whereby the Arabs' pride in and emphasis on "individualism" meant that cooperative work in large organizations was difficult, if not impossible, to sustain for long periods of time. In addition, this view cited the Arabs' sensitivity to criticism, their unwillingness to convey bad news, and the prevalence of primordial (tribe, clan, family) rather than nationalist loyalties as additional "proof" of the inability of the Arabs to put together an efficient fighting force.[8] If such cooperation was difficult to attain within any one Arab state, one could hardly expect the Arab world to act collectively. In other words, it was not possible for the Arabs to be united in their fight against Israel and its supporters regardless of whether the weapon chosen was military or economic. Concerning the possibility of an Arab oil boycott, the United States in particular

6. *In a Time of Torment* (New York: Random House, 1967), p. 438.

7. See Terence Smith, "The October War Changed Everything: The First Israeli Revolution," *New York Times Magazine* (compact edition), Dec. 30, 1973, pp. 120-21, 129-31. Earlier, the same author had written: "More and more [the Israelis] tended to dismiss the Arabs as bumbling soldiers who might gradually improve their equipment but could never mold themselves into an effective fighting force." See "Explosions on Two Fronts," *New York Times*, Oct. 14, 1973.

8. For an exposition of such views, see Sania Hamady, *Temperament and Character of the Arabs* (New York: Twayne, 1960); Y. Harkabi, "Basic Factors in the Arab Collapse during the Six-Day War," *Orbis*, XI, no. 3 (Fall 1967), pp. 677-91; and, to a lesser extent, Morroe Berger, *The Arab World Today* (New York: Anchor, 1964). For a critique of these views and others, as well as the "methodology," see Benjamin Beit-Hallahmi, "Some Psychological and Cultural Factors in the Arab-Israeli Conflict: A Review of the Literature," *Journal of Conflict Resolution*, XVI, no. 2 (June 1972), pp. 269-80.

accepted the Israeli view that Arab oil-producing countries were "conservative" and would not be likely to join the "extremist" Arab states in an embargo against the West. One final element rounds out the old Israeli and Western view of the Arabs, namely, that the Arabs cannot keep a secret. Thus it was argued that even if the other assumptions about potential Arab actions were incorrect, any war preparation on the part of the Arabs would be leaked to the West and the Israelis.[9]

Another faulty assumption—one that perhaps overshadowed all the rest in importance and was even more firmly and unquestioningly held—was the belief that the Arab view of what constituted "rationality" in the Arab-Israeli conflict was the same as the Israeli and Western view. According to the latter, if it is known in advance that a war will result in a definite and major disaster for one side, then that side would be "mad" to start a fight.[10] Hence Israeli leaders were confident that Egypt and Syria would not launch a major offensive. This confidence was expressed in the form of warnings threatening the Arabs with new and untold disasters. The purpose was threefold: (1) to reassure the Israelis of the tremendous military might of the Israeli state—and hence of the security of the inhabitants and forthcoming immigrants, (2) to persuade the West, and especially the United States, that a major war in the area was not likely and therefore there was no reason to pressure Israel into any concession or compromise, and (3) to cow the Arabs into a situation of inaction and avoidance of fighting as a means of regaining some or all of their land.

The Arabs, needless to say, were and are quite sane. Some of their attitudes and their actions, however, differ from those of Westerners—and this has a bearing on the way they behave in a conflict situation. It is indeed a sad commentary on Western scholarship on the Arabs and the Middle East in general that so very many myths have been fostered and/or allowed to persist. It is indeed "logical" and "rational" for a weak person in the West not to pick a fight with a much stronger individual, even when the former feels right and justice are on his side. But this is neither "logical" nor "rational" behavior in the Arab world. Therefore, if a person feels that he has been cheated, mistreated,

---

9. "The War That Broke the Myths," p. 60.

10. This view was repeatedly echoed by Israeli and Western observers before and after the war broke out. For example, according to a dispatch in *U.S. News and World Report* (Oct. 22, 1973, p. 27), "Many military observers questioned the wisdom of Egypt's decision to break the March, 1970, cease-fire that had kept a tenuous peace in the Mideast. *Some called it a 'suicidal impulse'* " (emphasis added).

or generally maligned and humiliated, then honor, duty, and "logic" dictate that he should fight, regardless of the outcome. In other words, in such a situation it is "better"—more "logical" and "rational"—to fight and lose than not to fight at all.[11] If it were otherwise, the Palestinians would have long been suppressed because of the tremendous odds against them. This also explains the failure of the Israeli policy of force as the only language the Arabs understand. It might well be, however, that the so-called Israeli hawks, led by David Ben-Gurion, Moshe Dayan, and Golda Meir, have understood Arab psychology quite well, and that the strategy of "force as the only language" is intended not to end the dispute but to exacerbate it and provide Israel with a chance for further expansion or other advantages.

The Israeli-Western image of the Israeli, the negative mirror image of the Arab, was that of an excellent and heroic soldier. The Israeli military machine was one of the best, if not the very best, not only in the region but in the world. Soldiers and officers worked well together, and no sacrifice was too great for the defense of the homeland. Unlike the Arabs, whose main motivation was hatred of the Israelis, the latter found their source of strength in love of their countrymen and their land.[12] There were no divisions within Israel to weaken the people's resolve. The Israelis (and some outsiders) began to believe themselves invincible.

Apart from conveying the above images of themselves and their enemies to the West, the Israelis had to assure their Western supporters that the latter's interests were being protected and advanced in the area. This was done with the following arguments. First, the Arabs were too weak (and they knew they were too weak) to risk a major

11. This concept appears to be quite "alien" and "illogical" to Westerners. A *Newsweek* reporter refused to accept it as "normal" or "rational," but speculated that "there may have been an element of desperation in the Arab move. Asked if the Arabs could win, Egyptian Foreign Minister Mohammed Hassan el-Zayyat said: 'Frankly, no. But you don't struggle because you are assured of success. You struggle because you are right'" (*Newsweek*, Oct. 15, 1973, p. 41).

12. Herbert Krosney, the *Nation*'s correspondent in Israel, writing in the November 26, 1973, issue of that magazine, quotes an Israeli soldier as saying of the Egyptian soldiers: "They're just poor slobs." Krosney then describes the Israeli soldier as intelligent and "willing to do that job, even at the sacrifice of life, including his own. The depth of the spirit of devotion to country" surprised Krosney. Also, the Israeli soldier, according to this account, "detests war. . . . Perhaps his hatred of war is what pushes him to wage it so well." The last remark makes little sense, even as an apology for what may appear to be "love of war" by the Israelis.

war that might bring about a superpower confrontation—which the West definitely wanted to avoid. Second, U.S. and Western interests were better served by maintaining the (pre-October) status quo: even a partial settlement would result in the opening of the Suez Canal, which would mainly strengthen the Soviet military presence in the area and around the world. Third, Israel (together with Iran) was willing to act in behalf of the United States in opposing or suppressing any "extremist," that is, "anti-Western," movements or regimes in the area. Since the Arabs could not keep a secret, or, put differently, since the Israeli and American intelligence network was virtually fail-safe, any contemplated violence from the Arab side would be nipped in the bud before the issue could be internationalized or constitute a threat to world peace.

Although, in general, European nations, especially because of their greater need for a functioning Suez Canal and their greater dependence on Arab oil, were prepared to pressure the Israelis into some sort of compromise, the Israeli-American view that prevailed saw "Western" interests as indivisible. Those interests definitely included oil. As stated before, the view was that the Arabs were unwilling and/or unable to use the oil weapon effectively; and even if it were used effectively, it would not really hurt the West, especially the United States. As Richard B. Mancke, a staff economist for the U.S. cabinet task force on oil in 1969–70 and professor of law and economics at the University of Michigan, wrote: "In sum it seems to me unlikely that distaste for our Middle East policy would lead to a general embargo of Arab oil sales: both because the U.S. would not be the principal victim and because non-Arab OPEC members would be the principal beneficiaries." [13]

Needless to say, almost as soon as the war started, it became obvious that the United States and its Western allies did not view their interests in the Middle East in quite the same light. Europe could not survive merely on American "assurances." And even the United States came to feel the pinch from the oil boycott.

Prior to the October war the Israelis had succeeded in keeping their Western supporters from making any attempt to break the deadlock and move the situation off dead center. In other words, the Israelis had managed to prevent any changes in the status quo except those that might advance Israeli interests. We have already outlined various parts of the formula the Israelis so successfully followed. Another

13. "Blackmail by Oil," *New Republic*, Oct. 20, 1973, p. 9.

and most important part of that formula was to persuade the Western powers to accept the Israeli view of the nature of the problem in the Middle East. According to this view, the basic question was one of "Arab refugees" and Israeli "security," and every other issue was ancillary or peripheral or artificial. Following this "logic," Golda Meir could announce in London: "There was no such thing as Palestinians. . . . It was not as though there was a Palestinian people in Palestine considering itself as a Palestinian people and we came and threw them out and took their country away from them. They did not exist." [14] If there are no Palestinian people, the Israelis and their supporters need not have a guilty conscience about the dispersion of another people to make room for the Jewish state. If the problem is one of Arab refugees, the solution is to have those refugees resettled among their brethren outside Palestine or Israel. And, since the Palestinians do not constitute a nation, they do not need or deserve a state of their own—a view that the Israeli leadership continues to espouse. [15]

Leaders in all states use "national security" as an excuse or justification for many acts. Among Israelis, however, even by their own admission, "security" has become something of an obsession. In such a situation, outside observers must determine whether or not in any particular instance the leadership is using "national security" as a cover for other, less acceptable objectives—namely, expansionism. It is not important here to determine whether or not Israel's Western friends recognized the presence of an ulterior motive behind the Israeli claim of "national security," for instance, in setting up numerous settlements in different parts of the occupied territories. The important point is that they did little if anything to prevent their establishment. As the moderate Arab states, namely, those that are pro-Western, failed to interest the West, especially the United States, in any reasonable scheme to attain Israeli withdrawal and an equitable settlement, the implications of the Western actions (or lack of them) became clear—that the United States in particular was not willing to effectively challenge the Israeli leaders' view that Israeli occupation of the territory captured from the Arabs in 1967 constituted the best security for Israel and served the best interests of the United States.

14. From Frank Giles's interview with Golda Meir, *Sunday Times* (London), June 15, 1969.

15. See Yitzhak Rabin's first speech to the Knesset as prime minister of Israel, on June 3, 1974, in *Middle East Monitor*, IV, no. 12 (June 15, 1974), 4-6.

AMERICAN OPINION AND THE OCTOBER WAR

It is little wonder, therefore, that both Israel and its Western supporters, primarily the United States, were taken by surprise by the events of early October 1973. It was realized too late that most of the assumptions on which Israeli and U.S. policy were based were erroneous. This is the phenomenon that the American news media have referred to as the "shattering of myths" about the Middle East. It is interesting to note, however, that the American media, reflecting the then prevailing attitudes of the Israeli and American policymakers, presented the Middle East picture from the old perspective for one or two weeks after the war started. They changed only after it became obvious that Israeli casualties were quite high and that a decisive Israeli victory was unlikely. This change in attitude is reflected in the tables at the end of this chapter, which include data on coverage of the Middle East in American newsmagazines. An important item not shown in the tables is the emphasis the American press placed on the Arabs starting the attack. Normally this would not and should not be viewed as unusual or biased. However, when this is compared with the 1967 situation, the pro-Israeli bias becomes obvious. During that conflict, the magazines under review either ignored or muddled the issue of who actually launched the attack.[16] The point is that if who strikes the first blow is important enough to report and emphasize, then this should have been done in both instances.

In general, the tables illustrate the partisanship of the American press in its reporting of the Arab-Israeli conflict over the past two decades.[17] The evidence is clear that 1967 marked the lowest ebb of impartial reporting in these magazines, but that 1973 saw the beginning of a move toward balance.

Looking at each table individually, we find that the Western media have generally ceased to associate the Arabs with nomadic living, a low level of education, and a depressed standard of living (Table 2). Although during the 1973 war references to Arabs as dishonest or unreliable were numerous and their disunity and rivalry were mentioned, in *Time* and, to a lesser extent, *Newsweek,* the "good" qualities of the Arabs were also cited quite often.

16. See Michael W. Suleiman, "American Mass Media and the June Conflict," in *The Arab-Israeli Confrontation of June 1967: An Arab Perspective,* ed. Ibrahim Abu-Lughod (Evanston, Ill.: Northwestern University Press, 1970), pp. 138-54.

17. The methodology followed is detailed in Michael W. Suleiman, "An Evaluation of Middle East News Coverage in Seven American Newsmagazines, July–December, 1956" (M.A. thesis, University of Wisconsin, Madison, 1961).

In 1973 the actions and alleged intentions of the Arabs were reported with greater understanding, if not sympathy, as Table 3 shows. The most important change is to be found in the columns entitled "Arabs' achievements mentioned" and "Arabs' actions justified." With the exception of the *Nation* and the *New Republic,* the weekly magazines surveyed began to show a concern for, and a sensitivity to, the Arab point of view. Arab achievements on the battlefield were amply reported. More significantly, Arab actions or views were adequately justified, placed in context, or explained. This is, of course, what good reporting is all about. However, in the past, as we can see from tables 3 and 5, this was a procedure reserved for reporting on Israel. In 1973 it was applied to both sides.

Turning to American press coverage of Israel, Table 4 shows *Time* as the only magazine studied that emphasized the heroic, self-reliant, hard-working, and efficient characteristics of the Israelis in 1973. However, there was also mention of "bad" Israeli qualities, such as lack of preparation, overconfidence, and underestimation of the enemy. If this is the beginning of a trend that will be followed by *Time* and other newsmagazines, then it is an important and healthy development—and one that accords with the basic objectives of Zionism, namely, to change the image of the Jew and have him or her be treated as a human being. In its zeal, Zionism has, at least in public statements, managed to change the image of the Jew from "subhuman" to "superhuman." This is a very serious error. The problem for Jews and non-Jews alike, in the Middle East and elsewhere, will continue to exist until Jews are treated as other human beings— until they are seen as people with good and bad qualities, capable of greatness but also capable of error, a mixture of strength and weakness, kindness and cruelty, courage and cowardice.

Table 6 reflects the extent of improvement in American reporting on the Middle East in 1973. Thus there was no condemnation of Arab leaders—a marked change from previous years. In the past, of course, President Nasser of Egypt was an easy target of blame for any and all "troubles" in the Middle East. His successor, Anwar Sadat, appears to have avoided antagonizing the Western media. In fact, he came in for some, though slight, praise from certain quarters. What is more significant, perhaps, is that he escaped criticism in the editorial columns of these magazines.[18]

18. Of eleven editorials (five in the *New York Times,* three in the *Nation,* and three in the *New Republic*), only two (in the *New York Times*) were critical of the Arab states. Israel escaped criticism altogether.

The analysis shows that the American media did not by any means stop criticizing or condemning the Arab states. However, at least in the *New York Times*, the amount of pro-Arab reporting came close to the amount critical of the Arabs—a substantial improvement. Also, while it continues to be taboo to criticize Israel, it is clear from our tables that, apart from the reporting in the *Nation*, a definite and significant drop in the pro-Israeli attitude of 1967 took place in 1973. Clearly, the erosion of pro-Israeli bias has not resulted in a pro-Arab gain. Instead, and quite properly, the media have shifted to a more neutral, balanced stance on Middle East issues. This is not to say that the situation is ideal, but that a beginning has been made in the attempt to present the Arabs as human beings—and not merely as the enemies of Israel or as trouble-makers for the United States and the West in general.

REMAINING MYTHS

Much remains to be done before the press fulfills its duties properly. For instance, while the media generally acknowledged the "shattering of myths" about the Middle East, the following important questions were hardly raised, let alone discussed in depth. (1) Who fostered those myths and how? (2) What have been the policy consequences of such erroneous assumptions? (3) What other myths are there that need to be shattered before a major conflict exposes them? (4) Are there new myths developing and gaining popularity? (5) What can be done to stop mythologizing and begin accurate reporting on the Middle East? (6) Shouldn't the political opposition take the administration to task for failing so miserably in its assessment of a dangerous situation in a strategic area?

At least one question (the first) was not asked because the answer was known and quite embarrassing. The media themselves, as we have seen, have been, wittingly or not, a principal agent for propagating myths about the Middle East. Some of these were so shattered by the 1973 war that the media had to take notice of them. But what about the others? Surely the time has come for the American public to be informed of the true nature of the problem in the Middle East. Who are the Palestinians? How did most of them become "refugees"? What is to become of them? Is a solution to the problem in the Middle East unacceptable to them feasible or even desirable? These are questions that have yet to be adequately dealt with in the American press. Also, and despite evidence to the contrary, it is still the popular view in the United States that the "Arab refugees" left their homeland in Palestine of their own accord and/or through exhortation by Arab leaders in the neighboring countries. It is also still generally believed that the Arabs are out to destroy Israel *and* the Israelis. The explanation normally offered—an explanation that is even worse than the assertion itself—is that the Arabs hate the Israelis and are generally anti-Jewish. Since it is not stated that the Israelis hate the Arabs, the implication is that the hatred is one-sided and irrational. Occasionally, however, this alleged Arab hatred of the Israelis is explained in terms of jealousy generated by the lower standard of living of the Arabs and by the presumption (myth) that Palestine was basically desert or arid until the Israelis came along and made it bloom.

The theme that the Arabs do not have much of a case (if they have one at all) in their dispute with Israel is pervasive and one that is presented in various forms. For example, during and after the 1973 war numerous governments in the world expressed their disapproval of Israeli actions either through public statements of criticism or through the recall of diplomatic representatives from Tel Aviv. Almost invariably, the explanation provided in the American press echoed the Israeli claim that such change in policy was due to "blackmail" on the part of the Arab countries. The "reasoning" here is that if any government acts favorably toward the Israelis, it is doing so because it is the proper and right thing to do; but, since the Arabs do not have a case, or are assumed to be in the wrong, any favorable action toward them by third parties must be the result of "immoral," if not illegal, pressure. The legitimate rights of the Arabs and the national interests of third party governments are assumed to be nonexistent or unimportant.

Even as some myths were being shattered, the Israelis were actively spreading new ones intended to bolster their own self-image and to downgrade the enemy. For example, the early setbacks the Israeli forces suffered were supposed to be due to Arab treachery (the surprise attack) and/or American faulty intelligence and/or an Israeli decision not to strike first. This argument, which implied that the Arabs' early successes were atypical and could not be duplicated, was clearly designed to revive or buttress the myth of Israeli invincibility.

On the question of oil, the embargo was presented as a form of blackmail—and the U.S. government, it was argued, should not succumb to it or in any way modify U.S. policy in the Middle East.[19]

19. See *Time*, Nov. 19, 1973, pp. 88-95; and the editorial in the *New York Times*, Oct. 28, 1973.

Furthermore, the boycott idea did not come from the Arabs but from the Soviet Union—and so the United States should intervene and deny the Soviets a victory in the area. Here again the Arabs are assumed to have had no reason to be angry with the United States, but to have merely been doing the Soviets' bidding. Stanley Karnow's remarks are illustrative of this view: "In short the Soviet aim has been to promote Arab unity directed against the U.S. in the expectation that American oil imports would be curtailed." [20]

THE UNITED STATES AND THE MIDDLE EAST—A NEW RELATIONSHIP?

Since we have detected a change in the reporting of Middle East news in American weeklies during the 1973 war, we need to ask what factors brought about the change and whether or not they are transitory or fundamental. [21] There is little doubt that the improved Arab performance in the October war forced the United States, the West in general, and, to some extent, the Israelis to carry out an "agonizing reappraisal" of the situation and of their basic assumptions (myths) concerning it. In other words, they were rudely awakened from their long sleep. This aspect we have already discussed. But apart from the war itself, the attitudes of the Arabs, Israelis, and Americans need to be examined for possible clues.

Following the 1967 war, certain Arab countries (Egypt and Jordan in particular), by agreeing to support U.N. Security Council resolution 242 of November 22, 1967, publicly accepted for the first time the possibility of peaceful coexistence with Israel. This was indeed a major shift in attitude and a significant concession to Israel. Most, though by no means all, Arab countries adopted a wait-and-see attitude to determine whether or not the Israelis would withdraw from the territories occupied in 1967 in return for Arab recognition. Israeli "negativism" on this issue irritated many people, including the leaders of numerous countries. As the Israelis continued to consolidate their hold over the occupied territories—building new roads and new settlements and proposing to allow individual Israelis to purchase

20. "Russian Roulette," *New Republic*, Oct. 27, 1973, p. 13.

21. Discussion of possible reasons for the change in American attitudes appeared in *Time*, Oct. 29, 1973, pp. 52, 54; and *Newsweek*, Nov. 12, 1973, p. 54.

land there—the Israeli contention that "everything is negotiable" rang hollow. Hence an overwhelming number of countries voted to condemn Israel on March 22, 1972 (U.N. Commission on Human Rights), and in July 1973 (U.N. Security Council). U.N. Security Council resolution 242, the plan of U.S. Secretary of State William Rogers, and the Gunnar Jarring mission all failed, as the Israelis showed preference for land over withdrawal, recognition, and peace. When the war broke out and dragged on, many Western journalists pointed out Israel's previous intransigence as one cause. At this time many African countries broke off diplomatic relations with Israel.

Almost concurrent with the above developments, American public opinion, following the traumatic experience in Vietnam, was hardening against any new American military involvement abroad. Though generally sympathetic toward the Israelis, Americans were beginning to fear being dragged into "another land war" in Asia. Besides, there was hardly any doubt that Israel could more than adequately defend itself, and there was no fear of Israel being destroyed or Israelis being "thrown into the sea."

Two other factors seem to have helped in bringing about the change noted in the tables. The first is détente—the policy of accommodation with the Soviet Union so that the two superpowers might cooperate in various economic, political, and even strategic weapons matters. This is the positive response to the fear of a nuclear confrontation between the two countries over a "problem" area such as the Middle East. Consequently, many Americans began to adopt the view that Arab-Israeli differences, squabbles, or even violent confrontations should not be allowed to escalate into a nuclear war, and began to support a peaceful compromise—a compromise that would include the Palestinians and one that would necessitate concessions Israel was reluctant if not unwilling to accept. Hence the irritation by and criticism of Israeli actions. The policy of détente also helps explain the fact that enthusiasm and support for Israel in 1973 came mainly (almost solely) from the American Jewish community—in marked contrast to the situation in 1967, when political, economic, emotional, and symbolic support came from almost all sectors of American society.[22] The second factor that has played a part, although an uncertain one, in changing public attitudes is oil. This factor has been more influential, however, in changing governmental policies both in the United States and the West generally.

22. See *Time*, Oct. 29, 1973, pp. 52, 54–56.

SUMMARY AND CONCLUSIONS

The thesis of this paper is that Western countries, particularly the United States, by accepting the Zionist-Israeli view of the Arabs, the Israelis, and the nature of the problem in the Middle East, found themselves formulating policies based on erroneous assumptions (myths). Because of their misreading of the situation, they failed to enact policies that might well have prevented the fourth round of Arab-Israeli fighting. During the October war, many of the previously accepted assumptions were declared "shattered." Unfortunately, however, it is not certain that these "shattered myths" have been completely removed from the consciousness or, more appropriately, subconsciousness of Western policymakers and journalists. Furthermore, even though numerous assumptions were found to be erroneous, no over-all attempt was made to determine what other Western assumptions about the Middle East might be incorrect. Various factors combined to make American attitudes toward Middle Eastern peoples and American reporting about the Middle East less partisan (that is, less pro-Israeli). Some of these factors will continue to influence policymakers to adopt a more "evenhanded" approach to Arab-Israeli differences. However, policymakers act within certain constraints, including public opinion, and public opinion on the Middle East continues to be shaped to a great extent by the propagation of pro-Israeli views. Therefore, the attempt to seek a more balanced presentation of facts on the Middle East should be applied to all the media of communication: the press, radio, television, the movies, textbooks, popular fiction, and so on.

Table 1

Number of Items on the Middle East in Certain American Magazines
July–Dec. 1956, May–June 1967, Oct.–Nov. 1973

Magazine	'56	'67	'73
New York Times	187	26	45
U.S. News and World Report	100	43	31
Nation	31	5	7
New Republic	41	6	8
Newsweek	103	27	41
Time	95	10	47

Table 2

Characteristics Attributed to Arabs in Certain American Magazines
July–Dec. 1956, May–June 1967, Oct.–Nov. 1973

Magazine	Nomadic living			Low standard of living			Low standard of education			Undemocratic orientation			Dishonesty, unreliability			Disunity, rivalry			"Good" Qualities		
	'56	'67	'73	'56	'67	'73	'56	'67	'73	'56	'67	'73	'56	'67	'73	'56	'67	'73	'56	'67	'73
New York Times	12	15	–	17	1	–	5	1	–	2	3	–	–	18	1	12	24	1	4	5	3
U.S. News and World Report	41	3	1	42	15	4	31	–	2	10	–	–	16	15	5	20	41	6	–	5	–
Nation	3	–	–	10	–	–	7	–	–	6	–	1	4	2	1	1	1	–	8	–	–
New Republic	–	–	–	16	2	5	4	–	–	5	–	–	8	11	11	2	9	2	–	–	–
Newsweek	24	2	2	16	–	3	1	–	–	2	3	2	–	20	25	18	10	5	–	10	10
Time	18	5	15	9	–	–	2	–	–	1	–	3	10	–	1	5	3	–	5	12	42
TOTAL	98	25	18	110	18	12	50	1	2	26	6	6	38	66	44	58	88	14	17	32	55

Note: Figures indicate number of times mentioned.

Table 3

Treatment of Arabs and Arab States in Certain American Magazines
July–Dec. 1956, May–June 1967, Oct.–Nov. 1973

Magazine	Refugees Mentioned			Arabs' desire for peace and security mentioned			Arabs' achievements mentioned			Israeli "mistreatment" of Arabs mentioned			Arabs' actions justified		
	'56	'67	'73	'56	'67	'73	'56	'67	'73	'56	'67	'73	'56	'67	'73
New York Times	5	19	3	–	–	1	2	–	10	36	4	2	9	4	13
U.S. News and World Report	1	1	2	–	2	–	–	–	12	–	8	3	–	*	20
Nation	3	5	2	–	–	–	5	–	–	4	1	1	1	1	–
New Republic	2	3	1	–	1	–	–	–	2	3	7	6	2	*	–
Newsweek	2	13	5	–	–	2	–	–	24	6	31	8	–	*	2
Time	1	14	24	–	–	14	4	–	46	17	1	–	3	8	27
TOTAL	14	55	37	0	3	17	11	0	94	66	52	20	14	12	62

Note: Figures indicate number of times mentioned.
  * Not reported.

Table 4

Characteristics Attributed to Israelis in Certain American Magazines
July-Dec. 1956, May-June 1967, Oct.-Nov. 1973

Magazine	Modern, high standard of education			Heroism, self-reliance, capacity for hard-work, efficiency			Honesty, no envy			Democratic and Western-like orientation			"Bad" qualities		
	'56	'67	'73	'56	'67	'73	'56	'67	'73	'56	'67	'73	'56	'67	'73
New York Times	-	-	-	*	15	1	*	6	-	1	-	-	-	2	1
U.S. News and World Report															
Nation	1	4	-	*	37	2	*	2	3	-	1	-	-	2	-
New Republic	4	-	2	*	7	-	*	-	2	6	-	-	-	-	3
Newsweek	-	5	-	*	4	5	*	5	-	3	3	-	-	-	3
Time	-	9	-	*	17	26	*	4	2	-	-	1	-	3	3
TOTAL	5	18	2	-	81	37	-	17	10	10	4	1	-	7	19

Note: Figures indicate number of times mentioned.
* Not reported.

Table 5

Treatment of Jews and Israel in Certain American Magazines
July-Dec. 1956, May-June 1967, Oct.-Nov. 1973

Magazine	Previous ill treatment of Jews mentioned			Israel's desire for peace and security mentioned			Israel's achievements mentioned			Israel described as strong but small underdog*			Arabs described as intent on Israel's destruction			Arab "mistreatment" of Israel mentioned			Israel's actions justified		
	'56	'67	'73	'56	'67	'73	'56	'67	'73	'56	'67	'73	'56	'67	'73	'56	'67	'73	'56	'67	'73
New York Times	3	-	1	32	24	11	15	30	15	3	11	3	24	18	3	137	47	15	36	58	13
U.S. News and World Report	1	1	3	3	-	7	1	2	1	-	1	3	2	5	1	64	29	15	60	19	17
Nation	12	-	-	21	6	20	24	4	6	19	34	3	50	26	12	25	9	5	23	5	10
New Republic	-	-	4	15	3	12	9	-	4	4	1	4	8	7	2	49	4	4	18	3	5
Newsweek	15	4	1	13	8	4	1	1	27	4	-	1	24	2	5	11	22	20	4	7	39
Time	3	12	14	11	20	17	9	11	37	-	3	7	9	30	17	10	47	41	18	30	36
TOTAL	34	17	23	95	61	71	59	48	90	30	50	21	117	88	40	295	158	100	159	122	120

Note: Figures indicate number of times mentioned.
* This category was designated "among hostile neighbors" in the 1956 study.

Table 6

Item Percentage of All Reporting on the Middle East in Certain American Magazines
July-Dec. 1956, May-June 1967, Oct.-Nov. 1973

Attitude	New York Times			U.S. News and World Report			Nation			New Republic			Newsweek			Time			Average %		
	'56	'67	'73	'56	'67	'73	'56	'67	'73	'56	'67	'73	'56	'67	'73	'56	'67	'73	'56	'67	'73
Pro-Arab leader	–	–	4	2	2	7	–	–	–	6	–	–	1	–	–	1	–	9	0.5	0.8	4.5
Pro-Arab	1	3	11	3	–	3	6	–	–	2	–	–	1	4	15	–	–	2	1.8	1.7	3.9
Pro-Israeli	8	31	16	16	40	16	22	–	57	11	33	13	8	37	–	1	50	17	9.5	35.9	17.3
Pro-Western	6	12	2	18	–	3	18	–	–	15	17	–	14	–	15	10	10	–	10.8	3.4	1.1
Anti-Arab leader	12	31	–	44	30	–	6	60	–	–	33	50	20	44	–	9	10	13	18.0	33.0	–
Anti-Arab	1	12	16	8	26	16	3	20	14	4	17	–	3	7	2	5	50	–	4.0	19.0	16.0
Anti-Israeli	–	–	–	3	2	–	–	–	–	*	–	50	2	15	–	1	–	–	0.7	4.0	0.6
Anti-West	–	4	4	6	9	13	33	40	–	–	33	–	2	4	2	5	10	–	4.5	5.0	1.0
Anti-U.S.S.R.	*	–	4	*	2	23	*	–	29	–	17	13	*	15	–	*	10	–	–	10.0	6.0
Balanced	57	23	29	17	19	23	19	–	14	26	–	–	31	–	42	46	–	23	39.0	6.0	28.5
Neutral	23	8	36	28	19	32	16	20	–	26	–	25	42	11	37	24	–	45	27.5	12.0	36.3

Note: All figures (except those under "Average %") indicate the percentage of number of items of press coverage. If added vertically, total exceeds 100 percent because the same item can be and often is for one party and against another.
* Not reported.

Elias Sam'o

THE ARAB-ISRAELI CONFLICT AS REPORTED BY THE KALB BROTHERS

THE MEDIA ANYWHERE, owing to their nature and mode of operation, are biased. When one speaks of the media, one speaks of an assembly of human beings receiving signals from certain sources, interpreting them, and then relaying them in the form of messages to readers and listeners. The human being is the primary agent of the media, and he is a subjective being. Therefore, bias in the media is not unexpected. In the case of the Middle East conflict, however, and the way it has been covered by the Western media in general and the American media in particular, the bias goes beyond the expected failings of human beings.

Regardless of what inspires this prejudice—some would attribute it to Zionist control of the media, others to ideological, religious, or racial factors—the fact remains that, by and large, the Western media are anti-Arab and pro-Israeli in varying degrees. Although research concerning this matter is not abundant, the findings confirm this contention.

This presentation is a case study of two "star" reporters of the CBS News network, Marvin and Bernard Kalb. In addition to their roles as television "front page makers," the Kalbs are authors, having recently published a book entitled *Kissinger*, which deals with the rise of Henry Kissinger to power and his role in recent international conflicts.[1] Approximately one-fourth of the book is about the conflict

1. (Boston: Little, Brown, 1974).

in the Middle East and concentrates on both the 1970 Palestinian massacre in Jordan and the October war. Although the Kalbs attempt to appear fair and objective in their account of this conflict, there is no mistaking their pro-Israeli, anti-Arab bias—subtle and low-key at times, but most often bold and loud. This bias is demonstrated in their: (1) inconsistency and self-contradiction, (2) distortion, (3) name-calling, (4) condescension, and (5) ridicule.

INCONSISTENCY AND SELF-CONTRADICTION

Two illustrations will demonstrate the Kalbs' inconsistency and self-contradiction. The first concerns the August 1970 cease-fire agreement between Egypt and Israel, which brought Nasser's War of Attrition to an inglorious end. "One provision of the August, 1970, cease-fire was that there was to be no military movement or buildup within a range of 50 kilometers on either side of the canal," note the authors. "In other words," they continue, "it was to be a standstill cease-fire. As it turned out, both Russia and Egypt violated the standstill provision almost from the moment the cease-fire went into effect. They built new missile sites and moved others much closer to the canal." [2] However, the authors further note:

> Sisco has insisted that the Egyptians understood [the standstill] provision very clearly, and that the Russians did, too. But in conversation with Kissinger, Sisco was very reluctant to produce "proof" that the Russians really understood; and Kissinger remained skeptical about the degree to which Dobrynin ever committed himself to the standstill part of the cease-fire. In fact, when Rogers negotiated the cease-fire with the Russians, he was very casual in describing this provision to Dobrynin, and there is a good chance the Russians did not understand it. [3]

Admitting that perhaps the Egyptians and Russians did not understand and/or agree to the standstill provision, the authors nevertheless find them guilty of violating it.

But let us give the Kalbs the benefit of the doubt and assume this provision of the cease-fire agreement was understood and that the Egyptians were violating it by introducing missiles into the canal zone. This would presumably disturb the balance of power in their

2. *Ibid.*, p. 195.
3. *Ibid.*

favor. The Kalbs do not point out, however, that the Israelis were engaged in disturbing the balance of power in their favor by receiving new military aircraft—Phantoms—from the United States. Although the Israeli action may not have constituted a violation of the letter of the agreement, it certainly violated it in spirit. As was noted shortly after the cease-fire went into effect:

> Since Israel's principal means for waging war against the Egyptians is air power, it is therefore possible for her to disturb the balance of forces in her favor by expanding her air force without introducing any additional weapons into the Canal Zone, and thus violate the spirit without necessarily violating the letter of the agreement.
>
> If we accept the thesis that any increase in the number of missiles or military manpower in the Canal Zone by the Egyptians constitutes a cease-fire violation, then we should also accept the thesis that any increase in the capability of the Israeli Air Force constitutes a cease-fire violation.[4]

The second illustration deals with Israeli violations of Security Council Cease-Fire Resolution 338, adopted October 22, 1973. Here again the Kalbs involve themselves in tortured intellectual acrobatics to absolve the Israelis of their violations. This resolution, adopted in the early hours of Monday, October 22, was supposed to go into effect that evening shortly after 6 P.M. According to the authors:

> Apparently what happened was that the commander of the Egyptian 3rd Corps, trapped on the east bank of the canal opposite the Egyptian city of Suez, ignored specific cease-fire orders from Cairo and attempted to break out of Israeli encirclement. The Israelis, still smarting over Egypt's original aggression, beat back that attempt and then intensified their military pressure on both sides of the canal. On the west bank, in particular, the Israelis kept edging toward the strategic prize of Suez

4. Elias Sam'o and Cyrus Elahi, "Cease-Fire: Who Needs It?" *Arab World,* XVI (Nov.-Dec. 1970), 21. Following the cease-fire agreement, the Western media headlined the Israeli allegations of Egyptian violations of the cease-fire standstill provision. I coauthored a letter to the editor concerning this matter in September 1970. Copies of this letter were sent to various American publications: the *New York Times,* the *Washington Post,* the *Detroit Free Press,* the *St. Louis Post-Dispatch,* the *Oregonian, Time,* and *Newsweek.* A copy was sent to the British *Manchester Guardian.* To my knowledge, only one of the American publications, the *St. Louis Post-Dispatch,* published the letter. The copy that was sent to the *Guardian* was published on October 3, 1970.

itself. If the city fell under Israeli control, then there would be no way for the Egyptians to resupply the 3rd Corps.[5]

In the preceding quote the authors assert that the Egyptian Third Corps was "trapped on the east bank of the canal opposite the Egyptian city of Suez" and was encircled by Israeli forces. However, they also note that "the Israelis kept edging toward the strategic prize of Suez itself." The question is, If Suez was under Egyptian control and the supply lines were open, how could the Egyptian Third Corps have been trapped and encircled?

According to the Kalbs, these events were taking place late Monday, October 22. On the following page they state: "By 1 A.M., Washington time, Wednesday, October 24, the second cease-fire went into effect; but moments before the guns were ordered silenced for the second time in forty-eight hours, the Israelis announced that their forces had reached the outskirts of Suez and the 3rd Corps was effectively surrounded." [6] Thus, on Monday the Third Corps was "trapped" and "encircled"; two days later, on Wednesday, it was at last "surrounded."

DISTORTION

The chapter covering the October war begins: " 'OPERATION BADR,' code name for the Egyptian-Syrian attack against Israel . . ." The war is later described as a "well-coordinated Arab assault on the Jewish state." "It was clear," the authors assert, "that Israel was the victim of aggression." They further note that "additional information had convinced the top U.S. officials that Egypt and Syria had broken the cease-fire and that Israel had merely responded to their aggression." The Kalbs conclude triumphantly: "Four times in one generation [the Arabs] had failed in their attempt to drive [Israel] into the sea." [7]

It is useful to compare these remarks with the words of the editor of the *Christian Science Monitor* in the October 16, 1973, issue:

A common assumption during last week was that Egypt and Syria had attacked Israel. We ourselves, in this space, referred to "the Egyptian-

5. Kalb and Kalb, *Kissinger*, p. 487.
6. *Ibid.*, p. 488.
7. *Ibid.*, pp. 450, 452–53, 461, 463, 464.

Syrian attack on Israel." That was a mistake. There was an Egyptian-Syrian offensive against Israeli armed forces. But those Israeli armed forces were in occupation of Egyptian and Syrian territories. Israel has not annexed the Golan Heights, the west bank of Jordan or the Sinai Peninsula. Those are all legally Arab territories taken by armed forces in 1967 and held in defiance of a U.N. resolution and indeed, of the official policies of the United States.

Or perhaps to recall the sardonic, but humorous, words of the *Washington Post* columnist Nicholas von Hoffman: "All kinds of senators are giving every kind of speech about what an international outrage and a violation of civilized law it is for you Egyptians to invade Egypt. They do have a point there, Abdullah. You Egyptians have been occupying Egypt since the time of the Pharaohs, so why not give somebody else a chance?" [8]

NAME-CALLING

The Kalbs resort to name-calling to further demean the Arabs and cast their case in a negative light. It is possible to disregard this tactic, but not when it is used as a substitute for good analysis. The authors state: "Assad had manpower and passion. He was always spoiling for a fight with Israel. The very idea of war strengthened his political position in Damascus." [9]

Arab commentary concerning some former American officials is characterized as a "kind of venomous anti-Semitic propaganda that Egypt, Syria, Iraq and some Palestinian groups had hurled at Arthur Goldberg and Eugene and Walter Rostow." [10] Arab political systems are described as "regimes" that are Russia's "clients"; the Palestinian Resistance Movement as consisting of "terrorists" or "bands of terrorists" engaged in "terrorism." In comparison, the Israeli political system is a "freewheeling democracy," General Rabin is a "dynamic military hero," and Aharon Yariv is "a brilliant Israeli intelligence officer." [11] One would presume that Mr. Yariv, the "brilliant intelligence officer," is the same one who was fooled by the Arabs on October 6.

8. *Washington Post*, Nov. 9, 1973.
9. Kalb and Kalb, *Kissinger*, p. 452.
10. *Ibid.*, p. 188.
11. *Ibid.*, pp. 190, 518.

CONDESCENSION

Thus far the reviews and commentaries concerning this book have emphasized one theme: Kissinger is the Kalb brothers' idol. As noted by Ronald Steel in his analysis of the book, "The Kalbs . . . have trouble wiping the stardust from their eyes in viewing their hero." [12] One would not object to this adulation if it were not built in part on the belittlement and derision of the Arabs. "Here was an American Secretary of State," the authors declare, "a Jew, visibly immersed in Arab culture and devoted to the resolution of Arab problems." [13] It is the height of naïveté to suggest that an American secretary of state, for whatever reasons, is "devoted" to the resolution of "Arab problems," and the height of arrogance to suggest that the Arabs are so helpless as to need an American to solve their problems.

The authors further note that Kissinger "encouraged the emergence of Arab pride, but within a context of realism and responsibility." The unmistakable implication is that without Kissinger, Arab pride would not have emerged or, had it somehow emerged, it would have done so within an unreal and irresponsible context. "Kissinger," they note, "disparaged U.S. intelligence in a gesture to Arab pride." They quote him as having told M. H. Heykal, then editor of *Al-Ahram:* "Our calculations on the size of your concentrations were wrong. Our forecasts as regards your combat capability were also wrong." [14] The authors' bias prevents them from accepting Kissinger's statements as genuine. They consider them as merely "a gesture to Arab pride" in spite of the fact that the Americans and the Israelis have admitted many failures in their intelligence services.

One can almost see Kissinger, through the eyes of the Kalbs, dashing through the sands of Sinai, climbing the heights of the Golan, and singlehandedly saving the wretched Arabs from the mighty Israelis. [15]

12. Ronald Steel, "All about Henry," *New York Review of Books,* Sept. 19, 1974, p. 25.

13. Kalb and Kalb, *Kissinger*, p. 511.

14. *Ibid.*, pp. 501, 512.

15. One is reminded of Oriana Fallaci's interview with Kissinger, in which he is reported to have said: "The main point in the mechanics of my success comes from the fact that I have acted alone. The Americans love this immensely. The Americans love the cowboy, who leads the convoy, alone on his horse, the cowboy who comes into town all alone on his horse and nothing else. Perhaps not even a gun, because he does not shoot. He acts, and that is enough, being in the right place, at the right time. In sum, a Western. This romantic and surprising character suits me because being alone has always been part of my style, or if you wish, of my technique" (quoted in *ibid.*, p. 399).

RIDICULE

The Kalbs, in describing a meeting between Syrian President Assad and Kissinger, note that it "had a 'Mad Hatter tea party quality' to it. Assad seemed to phase in, and then phase out of the mainstream of the discussion: on occasion, he was sharp; at other times, he seemed to drift off into a dreamy reverie twiddling his thumbs, closing his eyes and humming an Arab tune." [16] Those who are familiar with *Alice's Adventures in Wonderland* will recall the Mad Hatter's tea party in which Alice joined the Hatter, the March Hare, and the Dormouse. The scatterbrained behavior of the hosts offended Alice while the conversation ran in circles:

"Why don't you say what you mean?" the March Hare asked.
"I do," Alice hastily replied; "at least—I mean what I say—that's the same thing, you know."
"Not the same thing a bit!" said the Hatter. "Why you might just as well say that 'I see what I eat' is the same thing as 'I eat what I see'!"
"You might just as well say," added the Dormouse, which seemed to be talking in its sleep, "that 'I breathe when I sleep' is the same thing as 'I sleep when I breathe'!"

The authors' insulting analogy leads one to conclude that Assad offended his guest, Kissinger, by his scatterbrained behavior and that the conversation was nonsensical.

While the meeting was in progress, American officials and reporters waited for the secretary in his plane. The meeting lasted longer than expected, and those waiting on the plane speculated about the reasons for Kissinger's delay. The Kalbs give us a sample of the reporters' and officials' remarks: "He's just become the hundred and twenty-eighth Israeli prisoner." "The Syrians kidnapped him." "Maybe he's been assassinated." When the secretary's motorcycle sirens could be heard in the distance, a reporter on the plane remarked, "Well, either he is finally coming, or they're finally coming for us." [17] Perhaps one should not make too much of the authors' attempts at humor. Nevertheless, one cannot help but feel that the "humor" is overshadowed by a pervasive, though subtle, sense of ridicule and contempt for the Arabs. Less subtle, however, is the Kalbs' description of the

16. *Ibid.*, p. 523.
17. *Ibid.*, p. 524.

political forces in Syria as "a murky coalition of religious fanatics, Baathist extremists and communists." [18]

To say that the Kalb brothers are biased is an understatement. In view of what has been said, any further conclusion on my part would be redundant and superfluous. It is tragic that the Arab case has undergone such a tortured transformation on its way to the West. It is unfair not only to the Arabs but also to the West to have the Arab case go through a gross disfiguration that serves the interests of neither and does justice to none. In view of the fact that this distortion of the Arab case reaches millions of well-meaning Americans every evening, one shudders at the dimension of the tragedy.

18. *Ibid.*, p. 523.

Karen Farsoun, Samih Farsoun, and Alex Ajay

MIDDLE EAST PERSPECTIVES FROM THE AMERICAN LEFT

A FUNDAMENTAL REDEFINITION of the attitude of the Left toward Zionism and Israel took place in the 1960s with the emergence of the New Left in the United States and internationally, and the outbreak of the 1967 war. The Old Left had historically shown signs of sympathy to Zionism, a stance which crystallized during the rise of nazism in Germany, the Nazi holocaust, and the Palestine war which led to the creation of Israel. Such sympathies were strengthened by guilt feelings about the ineffective leftist response to Nazi atrocities, and (especially among social democrats) a sense of ideological kinship with the right-wing socialist Israeli establishment. Support for Israel was made easier by the Old Left's frequent adherence to conventional Western perceptions of the conflict. The Arabs of Palestine seem to have been regarded as nonpersons; and the myths and half-truths woven around Israel's existence—those of Israeli democracy[1] and that of Israel being David to the Arabs' Goliath—shut out more serious

This paper first appeared in *Journal of Palestine Studies*, IV, no. 1 (Autumn 1974), 94-119.

1. Israel is better conceptualized as a *"herrenfolk* democracy" (see the definition of this concept in P. van den Berghe, *Race and Racism* [New York: John Wiley, 1967]; pp. 18, 29), in which the democracy of the Jewish Israeli majority is denied to the Palestinian Arab minority. See also S. Jiryis, *The Arabs in Israel* (Beirut: Institute for Palestine Studies, 1969).

questions about the settler-colonial character of Zionism and Israel. Israel's support of the U.S. intervention in Korea, of France in Vietnam and Algeria, its participation in the tripartite colonial attack on Egypt (the 1956 Suez War), and its backing of the United States in the Vietnam War were all relegated to insignificance. Even the refusal to repatriate the Palestinian refugees, and oppressive Israeli treatment of the remaining Palestinian Arab minority, did not seem to diminish the pro-Zionist ardor of the social democratic Left, while communist parties generally followed the Soviet Union in recognizing Israel's right to exist despite these blemishes.

During the 1960s there was an anti-imperialist upsurge within the United States concerning the U.S. role in Vietnam, Latin America, and elsewhere. The acute crisis period generated several radical and protest movements: civil rights and black nationalist movements, the counterculture (the hippies), the student movement (especially Students for a Democratic Society), the peace and antiwar movements, and the women's movement.[2] The June war was the catalyst in producing a revised attitude to Zionism and Israel among the New Left and revitalized sections of the Old Left, a position that eroded the totally pro-Zionist commitment of the intellectuals, left-liberals, and social democrats.[3]

The purpose of this article is to analyze the positions and actions taken by the self-defined leftist organizations in the United States toward the conflict in the Middle East. The study is based on content analysis of their publications—party organs and position papers—and responses to written inquiries.[4]

Almost all the organizations included in the study define themselves

2. The following studies, to name a few, discuss the sources, ideology, and structure of the above movements: J. Boggs, *Racism and the Class Struggle* (New York: Monthly Review Press, 1972); J. Mitchell, *Women's Estate* (New York: Vintage Books, 1971); and M. Miles, *The Radical Probe* (New York: Atheneum, 1971).

3. See Abdeen Jabara, "The American Left and the June Conflict," in *The Arab-Israeli Confrontation of June 1967: An Arab Perspective*, ed. Ibrahim Abu-Lughod (Evanston, Ill.: Northwestern University Press, 1970), pp. 169-91.

4. The method followed is the qualitative analysis of the content of all publications, etc., avaliable from October 1973 to January 1974, a time period in which reportage on and analysis of Middle Eastern politics were at a peak owing to the October war. The focal issues in the analysis are the Palestine-Zionist contradiction, the Arab-Israeli state-to-state conflict, and the role of imperialism and internal class structure in the region. For methodology, see B. Berelson, *Content Analysis in Communication Research* (Chicago: University of Chicago Press, 1952).

as Marxist and anti-imperialist, are formally structured on a national and/or regional scale, and publish official organs. They represent a broad diversity of points of view on the Left, and together comprise nearly all the major formal American leftist organizations currently active. Their attitudes mostly reflect the revitalization and resurgence of the American Left in recent times.

The perspectives reviewed below generally share a materialist conception of history and a fundamental theory of imperialism. They appreciate the world-wide scale of integration that capitalism has achieved in the drive of the Western powers, and now especially the United States, to expand and to dominate the societies of the Third World. Thus, they all see the conflict in the Middle East in terms of the imperialist penetration of the region for economic and strategic purposes. Almost all see Zionism as a product of the forces of capitalism and imperialism, a bourgeois movement, born of the contradictions of European capitalism, that came to play a reactionary role in diverting the Jewish masses from the class struggles in their respective countries. The conflict in the Middle East is seen to be the result of the creation of this colony with the help of the imperialists, and the native Arab, especially Palestinian, people's response to it.

THE COMMUNIST PARTY OF THE UNITED STATES (CPUSA)

Organized out of the left-wing factions of the old Industrial Workers of the World and the Socialist party in the early 1920s, the CPUSA used to be the leading Marxist organization in the United States. Its daily paper, the *Daily World* (formerly the *Daily Worker*), still has the largest circulation of all leftist publications (ca. 20,000).

The political line of the Soviet Union is the prime inspiration of the CPUSA's attitude to foreign affairs: support for détente and peaceful coexistence with the capitalist West is evident in its stances, and recognition is given to the Soviet role in international affairs as a "force for peace"—for example, in getting the October 22, 1973, cease-fire resolution passed by the United Nations.[5] On the other hand, the CPUSA position also voices approval of Soviet support for struggles of national liberation from Western imperialism. In the Middle East especially, Soviet economic and military support for the

5. *Daily World*, Oct. 13, 23, 24, 25, 27, 1973.

Arab countries is viewed as a bulwark against the threat of U.S. imperialism.[6]

The portrait of the October war is that of a just struggle on the part of Syria and Egypt to regain the territories occupied by Israel in 1967.[7] It is thus endowed with the attributes of a limited war of national liberation (which does *not* include Palestinian objectives of regaining the whole territory occupied by Israel in 1948 and after). The blame for the war is placed entirely upon Israel's recent annexationist policies, to which Egypt and Syria are seen as inevitably and justifiably replying with military action.[8]

The former leaders of the governing Israeli Labour party coalition, Meir and Dayan, are considered to head an aggressive military clique which is acting as the agent of U.S. imperialism and the Nixon Doctrine in the Middle East. Its function is to police the area in order to protect U.S. corporate oil interests; it is bent on preventing Arab peoples from achieving national liberation, and on liquidating the just rights of the Palestinians.[9]

Israel and its people are shown to have borne the brunt of the damage from the Meir-Dayan policy, which is wholly destructive of their hopes of peace and prosperity. The high casualty rate in the October war, the world-wide diplomatic isolation of Israel, and the high cost of living due to war expenditures have all made for low morale in the country.

The CPUSA and the U.S.S.R. support and promote the Arab countries because they are undergoing internal struggle and are also fighting for national liberation from imperialism. Egypt, Syria, Iraq, and South Yemen are called progressive countries. Iraq, Algeria, and Libya are complimented for having nationalized their oil industries. Iraq is also applauded for its contribution to the October war and its CP is commended for having formed an alliance with the Ba'ath in a national front. Egypt is especially lauded for its feats in the October war, for demolishing the myth of Israeli invincibility, and for demonstrating

6. The nature of that threat can be seen in the *Daily World* (Oct. 13, 1973) reports of a UPI story about Indian and Chicano Green Berets sent to Jordan in 1970 to assassinate Palestinian leaders, and of the role of the U.S. Sixth Fleet in the suppression of the Palestinians during September 1970. See also *ibid.*, Oct. 26, 28, Nov. 17, 1973.

7. *Ibid.*, Oct. 13, 1973. "Regaining these stolen lands has been the openly-stated objective of the Arab peoples for the past six years" (*ibid.*, Oct. 10, 1973); for the Arabs, "it is a just war to drive the aggressors from their land." See also *ibid.*, Oct. 10, 18, 20, Nov. 7, 1973.

8. *Ibid.*, Oct. 10, 17, 1973.

9. *Ibid.*, Oct. 10, 11, 17, 18, 20, 23, Nov. 2, 17, 1973.

that the "sons" of former feudal peasants can perform well in a modern context.[10]

According to the CPUSA, the only path to peace and to the realization of Israel's true national interest lies in rigorous implementation of U.N. resolution 242 of November 22, 1967.[11] This path would provide for (1) Israeli evacuation of the Arab territories occupied in 1967, (2) recognition of the territorial sovereignty of all the states in the area, including Israel within its pre–June 1967 boundaries (and international guarantees thereof), and (3) fulfillment of the rights of the Palestinians.[12]

The CP upholds the national rights of Israel to the area it controlled prior to June 1967,[13] in line with the Soviet position since 1947 on the partition of Palestine. As an Israeli CP leader expressed this stand to the Knesset on July 18, 1973: "The basis for this decision [partition] was the recognition of the existence of two peoples in the country; the Jewish people and the Arab people of Palestine; their right to self-determination and independent statehood."[14] The CP leader went on: "After establishing recognized, secure and stable frontiers between Israel and the Arab states, there exists the right of the Palestinian Arab people to self-determination—either to establish an independent state, or to live together with Jordan in one state."[15]

The *Daily World* includes reports on Israeli colonization and repression of the populations of the West Bank and Gaza, and the expropriation of Arab properties and attempts to "liquidate the national existence of the Palestinian Arab people" there.[16] But the conflict

10. *Ibid.*, Oct. 17, Nov. 7, 9, 17, 1973.

11. This theme is reiterated consistently in editorials, position statements of CPUSA leaders, articles, and reports on organizations taking some action (demonstrations, speeches, congresses, etc.) to express this view. See *Daily World* editorials, Oct. 10, 13, 17, 1973. See CPUSA leaders' statements in *Daily World*, Oct. 10, 23, 1973, and C. Komorowski's articles, esp. *Daily World*, Nov. 17, 1973. For reports of organizations, see *Daily World*, Oct. 13, 1973 (Federation of Jewish Women's Clubs); Oct. 17, 1973 (Women Strike for Peace); Oct. 18, 1973 (Women's International League for Peace and Freedom); Oct. 20, 1973 (Ad Hoc Committee for Peace with Justice in the Middle East); Oct. 19, 1973 (march on White House); Oct. 20, 1973 (Committee for a Just Peace in the Middle East).

12. See *Daily World* editorial, Nov. 2, 1973. See on the same page a speech expressing a similar stance by Meir Vilner, general secretary of the CPI and Knesset member. See also editorial, Nov. 3, 1973.

13. Interview with British CP leader Solly Kaye in *Daily World*, Nov. 7, 1973.

14. *Daily World*, Oct. 24, 1973.

15. *Ibid.*

16. *Ibid.*, Oct. 13, 16, 17, 23; Nov. 2, 1973.

is seen not as that of a settler-colonial state against the indigenous population it has uprooted; rather, it is considered to derive from the antagonism toward Israel of the neighboring Arab peoples (including the Palestinians of the West Bank) whose territories were occupied in 1967.[17]

The Soviets and American CP members seem to think that the Palestinians themselves are coming around to a "realistic" viewpoint on a peace settlement with Israel. For example, in reporting on the Moscow Peace Conference, the *Daily World* related this vignette:

> In the Middle East commission [discussion group] an elderly man who describes himself as an Israeli gives his ideas—he is for peace but he doesn't see eye-to-eye with the Arabs on a number of issues. A moment afterward a young [unidentified] spokesman for the Palestine Liberation Organization speaks his mind. They do not see eye-to-eye on all questions but they do agree that a political solution to the Mideast problems is preferable to shooting it out to settle differences.[18]

The CPUSA anticipates a relatively bright future for Israel after the negotiations and resolution 242 are fulfilled. It is acknowledged that Israel is a capitalist society with a bourgeois democratic form of government,[19] but little analysis of the class composition or class struggle within Israel is provided. Rather, the economy of Israel is expected to blossom after peace is assured, because of the combination of continued public and private support from the United States, to-be-instituted aid from the reconciled socialist bloc, and the establishment of normal trade relations with the Arab countries. Discussion of the last element explicitly denies that economic cooperation between Israel and Egypt, for example, would be exploitative or neocolonial in nature.[20]

The CPUSA's position on the possibility of social transformation in Israel is expounded in their critique of the American Trotskyist Socialist Workers party's position (see the following section). Tom Foley argues that nonrecognition of Israeli national rights leads to the Arabs' necessity to make a total war of destruction against Israel.[21]

17. *Ibid.*, Oct. 11, Nov. 17, 1973.

18. *Ibid.*, Oct. 30, 1973.

19. *Ibid.*, Nov. 7, 1973 (speech by Solly Kaye, British Jewish CP member).

20. *Ibid.*, Nov. 27, 28, 30, 1973 (a series by Tom Foley, *Daily World* Mideast specialist).

21. *Daily World*, Nov. 12, 1973. See also *ibid.*, Oct. 25, 1973, for the CPI's analysis, "How Israeli Peace Movement Was Kept Weak by Anti-Communism."

This dire threat then gives the Zionists and imperialists the perfect justification for continued aggression. It has the further result of uniting all classes within Israel in defensive nationalism, allowing the covering over of class antagonisms and thus postponing the development of class struggle.

The Socialist Workers Party (SWP)

A second leftist tendency comprises a number of Trotskyist organizations. Of these, the SWP is the oldest and also the largest, at least in terms of the circulation of its party organ, the *Militant*. The SWP originated in the 1920s as a left-Trotskyist split from the CPUSA following the Fourth International. Formally organized as the SWP in the late 1930s, it remains the dominant Trotskyist current. Like nearly all other Trotskyist organizations, it is a cadre party. According to its members, it was composed largely of industrial workers between 1940 and 1960, and since then has widened the class basis of its cadre.

The publications of the Trotskyist organizations are replete with polemics against each other involving organizational and ideological issues (concerning positions on domestic, foreign, and Fourth International matters), and also with attacks on party leaders.[22] The Trotskyists do not support any established socialist state in the world and thus do not have external ideological links. They have been at odds with the Soviet Union ever since the Stalin-Trotsky split, and it is partly this long-standing hostility and suspicion that underlie their current suspicion of Soviet policy and the Soviet position on the Middle East. They are also critical of the People's Republic of China.

While the CPUSA, following the political line of the Soviet Union, concentrates its analysis and commentary on state-to-state relations in the Middle East and sees the need and possibility of a political settlement of the conflict, the SWP emphasizes the role of imperialism, Zionism, and Middle Eastern class contradictions in the permanent conflict in the region.

---

22. One group, the Spartacist League, even attacks Yasser Arafat and George Habbash personally, on their class background, education, prior activities and associations. Nayef Hawatmeh meets with their qualified approval because he criticizes Palestinian nationalism and recommends cross-national (for example, Palestinian-Jordanian and Palestinian-Israeli) mass alliances (*Workers Vanguard*, Nov. 9, 1973).

The Near and Middle East remains of strategic significance to the United States because the area is a political, military and economic crossroads, and because the Middle East is vital to the West. The magnitude of the imperialistic stake in the Middle East is indicated by the fact that 70 per cent of the proven oil reserves are there. . . . the bulk of the oil is owned by five US corporations. Despite all the talk about "Arab blackmail" and the so-called Arab oil weapon, the real situation in the Middle East is that it is dominated economically and politically by imperialism.[23]

The chief instrument (and partner) of Western imperialist domination of the Arabs is Israel.

Israel's permanent mission in the Middle East is to maintain the suppression of the Arab national liberation struggle through military aggression and terrorism.[24]

It is an imperialist beachhead in the Arab world that serves as the spearhead of imperialism's fight against the Arab revolution.[25]

Israel works according to an imperative of striking at any revolutionary or liberational upsurge in the Arab world, and of reducing the Arab world to a state of defeat and demoralization.[26]

However, the counterrevolutionary role of Zionism and Israel is sharply contrary to the interests of the Jewish people. The *Militant* postulates that Zionism does not represent or promote the interests of the Jewish people. "Within Israel, the Zionists lead the Jewish masses into the trap of opposing the national liberation struggle of the Arab people, a just and democratic struggle." [27] The basic interests of the Jewish masses of Israel reside, not with the Zionist state, but in alliance with the Palestinian liberation struggle and in support of the goal of a democratic Palestine.[28]

The distinction between the state and the people or the masses

23. *Militant*, Nov. 30, 1973.

24. *Ibid.*, Oct. 19, 1973.

25. *Ibid.*, Oct. 26, 1973.

26. *Ibid.*, Oct. 19, 1973.

27. *Ibid.*, Oct. 26, 1973. "Zionism is not, as it claims, a national liberation movement. Zionism is a political movement that developed for the purpose of establishing a settler-colonial state in Palestine."

28. *Ibid.*, Oct. 26, 1973.

applied by the SWP to Israel is also used in the analysis of the Arab states. These are conceptualized basically as capitalist countries whose regimes are concerned with their own class survival and are thus opposed to genuine revolutionary mobilization. Hence, the limited aims of the October war are expounded by the *Militant* in emphatic terms:

> The capitalist regimes in Cairo and Damascus are seeking a diplomatic edge through military maneuvers. Their objective is to gain concessions from Israel to oppose the Arab masses.[29]

> As far as Egypt, Syria and the Arab states that are supporting them are concerned, the aim of the war is a compromise between Israel and the Arab regimes that are less unfavorable to the Arab bourgeoisies and military bureaucracies, a compromise that would allow them to contain the mobilization against Zionism and imperialism within limits acceptable from the standpoint of their own economic and political interests.[30]

This vision of the Arab bourgeoisie puts it irrevocably and permanently against the Arab masses. Thus, the Arab revolutionary objectives of national liberation, national economic development, and other democratic tasks can be fully realized and guaranteed only "by the victory of the working class at the head of the toiling masses, chiefly the peasantry, in a revolution against the imperialists, their Israeli agents, the Arab national bourgeoisie, and Arab feudal remnants." [31] It appears that the SWP is posing the necessity of simultaneous national liberation and internal class struggles. It poses no stage theory of revolution—first democratic, then socialist—whereby class collaboration is necessary and desirable in the first stage; instead it apparently visualizes a one-stage socialist revolution energized by the permanent class struggle in the Middle East.[32]

Despite its criticism of the Arab rulers, the SWP, in an article on why socialists should support the Arab side, states that the basic issue in the October war in the Middle East is the struggle of a nationally oppressed people against their colonial oppression. As stated by the SWP candidate for mayor of New York City, Norman Oliver, and reported and noted often in the party paper: "Egyptian and Syrian

29. *Ibid.*
30. *Ibid.*, Nov. 9, 1973.
31. *Ibid.*, Oct. 26, 1973.
32. This is at great variance with the Maoist position discussed below.

troops have entered *their own* territories. The Socialist Workers Party supports the right of the Arab nations to fight to regain the territory seized from them by Israeli aggression." [33] In this struggle, the SWP takes the side of the oppressed Arabs despite differences with their leadership.[34] A victory of the Arabs in a war against Israel is a victory against imperialism and colonialism.[35]

Acrimonious criticism is reserved for the Soviet Union and the CPUSA. Although the Soviet Union is not regarded in Maoist terms as "social imperialist," it is called a Stalinist bureaucracy, reflecting the continuing animosity since the Stalin-Trotsky split. The *Militant* rejects the CPUSA claim that the current move toward settlement in the Middle East is a victory for the people of the area, since this means that the CP is ignoring the Palestinian people.

> The right of the Palestinians to Palestine is central to the divergence between the views of the American Stalinists and their leaders in the Soviet bureaucracy on the one side, and the Palestinian freedom-fighters on the other. The Stalinists support the continued existence of the Israeli settler-state, and thus oppose the Palestinian demands for self-determination.[36]

The SWP ridicules CPUSA and CPSU for their "utopian goal of reconciling the Arab peoples with Israeli colonialism" [37] via U.N. Security Council resolution 242. But the "Stalinists" are seen as even more blameworthy for their acceptance of "peaceful coexistence" and détente.

> Detente is not aimed at bringing peace. Its purpose is to quell the class struggle, to hold back the advance of revolution.
> The point of detente is to weaken and repress revolutionary upheavals when they take place to preserve the agreed-upon global balance of power between imperialist and Soviet spheres of influence.[38]

33. *Militant*, Oct. 19, 1973 (emphasis in original).

34. *Ibid.*, Nov. 2, 1973.

35. "Whatever now happens, the Arabs have won a significant political victory. The imperialists' shock and surprise—a reflection of their racist denigration of the Arabs and their typical imperialist underestimation of the capacity of the oppressed masses to fight back—is itself eloquent testimony to the gains that have been made" (*ibid.*, Oct. 26, 1973).

36. *Ibid.*, Nov. 2, 1973.

37. *Ibid.*

38. *Ibid.*

In the Middle East this agreement includes maintaining Israel as a superior military power . . . and to preserve Israel as an outpost of imperialist aggression.[39]

In contrast to the high-sounding praise the *Daily World* heaped upon the Soviet Union for material, political, and diplomatic assistance to the Arab states, the SWP makes no mention of it at all.

Peace, the party believes, cannot come via superpower settlement, but only by ending Zionist occupation of all Arab land. Since, in the favorite language of the *Militant*, "the very existence of the Israeli state is based on *permanent aggression* against the Palestinian and other Arab peoples, and has been since 1948,"[40] as a result, "the only realistic long-term solution is the overthrow of the Zionist state of Israel and the return of Palestine to the Palestinians, thus eliminating the cause of the aggression."[41] But "the demand for a secular, democratic Palestine is not sufficient by itself. We pose a socialist revolution culminating in the creation of a workers' state as the means of achieving and guaranteeing a democratic secular Palestine."[42]

While strongly supporting the Palestinians, the SWP does not spell out its strategy for accomplishing the liberation of Palestine and the creation of a workers' state there. In particular, apart from denouncing the Geneva Conference, the SWP fails to delineate the action necessary to continue the struggle of the Palestinians at this current phase.

OTHER TROTSKYIST PARTIES

All of the smaller Trotskyist parties agree that the root of the conflict in the Middle East is the Zionist-Palestinian conflict and that Israel is a reactionary colonial-settler state which oppresses the native Arab peoples.[43] There is general accord that Zionism and imperialism are

39. *Ibid.* This is likened to Southeast Asia, where "the central purpose of the Paris accords imposed on the Vietnamese by Washington, Moscow and Peking was to preserve the imperialists' foothold in Saigon" (*ibid.*).

40. *Ibid.*, Oct. 19, 1973 (emphasis in original).

41. *Ibid.*, Oct. 26, 1973.

42. *Ibid.*, Nov. 23, 1973.

43. *Workers Vanguard* (Spartacist League), Nov. 23, 1973; *Class Struggle* (Class Struggle League), Nov. 1973; *Workers Power* (International Socialists), Nov. 2–15, 1973; *Bulletin* (Workers League), Oct. 19, 1973; *Torch* (Revolutionary Socialist League), Nov. 1973.

allied in the Middle East, in that Israel acts as a policeman and agent for the imperialists, primarily the United States.[44] The nature of Israel is seen to be a garrison ghetto (a "prison," a "death trap") for the Jewish masses, but Israeli Jews (the "Hebrew-speaking people") are said to form a legitimate nation *now*, despite their origin, in Palestine.[45]

The ruling groups of the Arab states are generally viewed with disfavor as "bourgeois nationalists." The Spartacist League and the International Socialists perceive them as enemies equivalent to Israel vis-à-vis the Arab masses and especially condemn their containing or crushing the Palestinian movement.[46] The Workers League and the Revolutionary Socialist League criticize the Arab rulers and the truncated state of revolution in their countries, but warn us not to equate Israel and Israeli nationalism (which are racist and reactionary) with the Arab states and Arab nationalism (which have developed as a progressive response to colonialism and Zionism).[47]

In contrast to the SWP, CP, Maoists, *et al.*, three of the five Trotskyist groups (Spartacist League, International Socialists, and Revolutionary Socialist League) rejected the October war outright on the grounds that the Arab leaders' war aims were not progressive but were to accommodate to Israel and to strengthen imperialism in the Middle East.[48] The Workers League at first enthusiastically endorsed the war but then withdrew support for the Arab side in disappointment over the limited goals and fast cease-fire promoted by Sadat.[49] Only the Class Struggle League offered qualified support to the Arab side in the war on the grounds that to liberate any occupied territory is somewhat progressive.[50]

All of the smaller Trotskyist groups agree that the solution to the Middle East conflict is for a proletarian movement including workers from all nationalities to work toward a federation of socialist states

44. *Torch*, Nov. 1973; *Bulletin*, Oct. 19, 1973; *Class Struggle*, Nov. 1973; *Workers Vanguard*, Nov. 9, 1973.

45. *Workers Vanguard*, Nov. 9, 1973; *Class Struggle*, Nov. 1973; *Workers Power*, Nov. 2-15, 1973; *Bulletin*, Oct. 23, 1973.

46. *Young Spartacus* (Youth Group of the Spartacist League), Nov.-Dec. 1973; *Workers Vanguard*, Nov. 9, 1973; *Workers Power*, Oct. 19-Nov. 1, 1973.

47. *Bulletin*, Oct. 19, 23, 1973; *Torch*, Nov. 1973.

48. *Torch*, Nov. 1973; *Workers Power*, Oct. 19-Nov. 1, 1973; *Workers Vanguard*, Nov. 9, 1973.

49. *Bulletin*, Oct. 9, 19, 1973.

50. *Class Struggle*, Nov. 1973.

of the Middle East.[51] They specifically de-emphasize and even denigrate the importance of nationalism as a progressive vehicle (arguing that it is useful only to imperialists to divide the masses among themselves). However, in contrast to the SWP, the Maoists, and many New Left groups, not one of the smaller Trotskyist groups takes up the PLO suggestion of a democratic secular (and socialist) state in which both the peoples of Palestine could live together. Rather, two (Class Struggle League and Revolutionary Socialist League) suggest that the "Hebrew-speaking people" should be treated as a protected minority with full democratic rights,[52] and the other three suggest a binational Palestine with the right of self-determination (including the right to secede) for each national entity.[53]

THE WORKERS WORLD PARTY (WWP)

An early split-off from the SWP, the WWP has moved sufficiently away from the Trotskyist ideology, especially on China and Vietnam, to be seen as a relatively independent third current. Through *Workers World,* the party organ, the party expresses a political conviction which is decidedly anti-Zionist and anti-Western imperialist, but which is critical of both the Soviet Union and China without being committed to the Trotskyist camp—a more eclectic position than any of the other leftist organizations.

WWP considers both the U.S.S.R. and People's China to be sister socialist countries[54] and objects to their appellation as "superpowers," since this usage obscures the differences among such powers (the U.S.S.R. is still a workers' socialist state while the United States is an aggressive imperialist state). The WWP maintains, for instance, that the U.S.S.R.'s "tremendous military and material support" made the development of the Arabs' anti-imperialist resistance possible.[55]

At the same time, the WWP criticizes both the U.S.S.R. and China for their foreign policies of détente and accommodation to the United

51. *Workers Vanguard,* Nov. 9, 1973; *Class Struggle,* Nov. 1973; *Workers Power,* Dec. 21, 1973-Jan. 17, 1974; *Bulletin,* Oct. 19, 1973; *Torch,* Nov. 1973.

52. *Class Struggle,* Nov. 1973; *Torch,* Nov. 1973.

53. *Workers Vanguard,* Nov. 9, 1973; *Young Spartacus,* Nov.-Dec. 1973; *Workers Power,* Oct. 19, Dec. 21, 1973-Jan. 17, 1974; *Bulletin,* Oct. 23, 1973.

54. *Workers World,* Nov. 2, 1973. WWP includes Lenin, Mao, and Trotsky as revolutionary leaders and thinkers.

55. *Ibid.,* Nov. 16, 1973.

States—for example, in their both condemning Israeli aggression without also mentioning U.S. imperialism during the October war—as the WWP believes that no stable détente is possible and that an imperialist-caused war is inevitable.[56] In the same vein, China's post-1970 foreign policy and hostility toward the U.S.S.R. are blamed on the unprogressive ideas of Chou En-lai.[57]

The United States and other Western imperialist countries are at all times held to be the real and ultimate enemy whose interests are to maintain access to oil and to contain and control the Arabs. But the U.S.S.R. also gets a thorough drubbing on both foreign and domestic fronts. Although the U.S.S.R. gives help to the Arabs, it does not give them all that they want and need (for example, offensive weapons) because of the revisionism of Soviet bureaucracy (which seeks to avoid struggle through détente and accommodation to the United States) and its opportunism as regards national liberation and class struggle. That the Soviet Union would agree with the United States to make peace negotiations "without the participation of Palestinian representatives . . . is a gross violation of the right of self-determination of the Palestinian people," and "a betrayal of the principles the Soviet people fought for so heroically under Lenin." [58]

Workers World respects the central position of the Palestinians and Zionism in the Middle East conflict but devotes much more space to the Arab-national-liberation-versus-imperialism level of the conflict. Many articles are spent on describing and evaluating various Arab countries and their ruling regimes. The WWP's analysis of the nature of the Arab regimes allows it to offer them critical support under some circumstances while reserving the right to recognize the limitations of their class-biased rulers.

Given the irreconcilable nature of the contradiction between national liberation and imperialism, it follows that the WWP would reject a U.N.-negotiated settlement.

> The seemingly endless atmosphere of war in the Mideast will not be resolved by any accommodation of the borders. That again will prove to be a temporary measure. Only by ridding the Mideast of the US puppet state of Israel and by establishing a state in which Jews and Arabs can live on an equal footing can lasting peace come to the Mideast.[59]

56. *Ibid.*, Nov. 2, 1973.
57. *Ibid.*
58. *Ibid.*, Nov. 16, 30, 1973.
59. *Ibid.*, Aug. 3, 1974.

THE MAOIST TENDENCY

The group of organizations and their publications here included as Maoist are the weekly *Guardian;* the Revolutionary Union and its monthly, *Revolution;* its student branch, the Attica Brigade, and its monthly, *Fight Back;* and the October League and its monthly, the *Call,* all of whose readers and members are followers of Marxism-Leninism and the thought of Mao Tse-tung. Although they differ among themselves on domestic revolutionary strategy, these groups are all close to the Chinese position on international affairs and are united in their criticism of both the United States and the U.S.S.R. as imperial superpowers. They believe the principal contradiction in the world today to be between imperialism and national liberation, and argue that revolutionary communists must work first and foremost toward building an international, anti-imperialist united front of all Third World countries seeking national liberation from declining U.S. and rising U.S.S.R. imperialism.

Both the United States and the U.S.S.R. are seen as trying to establish or maintain imperial hegemony in the Middle East. Sometimes they are in contention and competition with each other, as in their support for their belligerent clients, but at other times they collude to preserve their common interests and détente.

The imperial interests of the United States revolve around protecting the area for military-strategic purposes, crushing Arab and other national liberation movements, and, of course, keeping the oil flowing: "The US uses Israel as its 'watch-dog' in the heart of the Middle East oilfields, [a revolutionary Union spokesman said]. They want all that oil to keep flowing here at a low price. They have to keep the Mideast weak in order to keep that control. No war—no peace—just turmoil." [60]

Like the United States, the Soviets are believed to be frightened of genuine independence and success by Third World countries, to be competing for control of Middle East resources, especially oil, and to be preserving détente at the expense of smaller nations, as in the joint decision by the United States and the U.S.S.R. to force an unpopular cease-fire resolution (meaning "no war, no peace") through the U.N. Security Council.[61]

While the Soviet Union's policy is to accept, condone, and even

60. *Fight Back,* Nov. 1973. See also *Revolution,* Nov. 1973.

61. *Call,* Oct., Dec. 1973; *Guardian,* Oct. 24, 31, Nov. 28, Dec. 5, 1973; *Revolution,* Nov., Dec. 1973.

reinforce Zionism and the state of Israel, the Maoists argue that it is Zionism and the nature of Israel itself that are at the root of the problem.

The Zionist Israeli state is bound up with aggression, plunder of stolen land. . . . it was created by the Zionists, a movement of some East European Jews, headed by bourgeois forces, with the aid of the imperialist great powers. Israel is an artificial state, a Western settler colony forcibly implanted at the crossroads of the Arab world.[62]

Israel is seen as "the most rapidly expanding state in the world, having trebled its territory in 25 years," "theocratic" in nature, and "the assigned puppet of U.S. imperialism."[63] An informative, historical piece from the Liberation News Service shows how Israel's expansion between 1947 and 1948 was responsible for driving the Palestinians from their homeland.[64] After 1948, the "Zionists quickly demonstrated their role as agents of the U.S. imperialists and have been engaged in expansionist aggression against the Arab peoples ever since."[65]

As with most other leftist groups, the Maoists view Zionism as an ideology that is used against the interests of the Jewish working class. It originally attracted them away from class struggle in the countries where they lived[66] and now "the big business 'friends of Israel' . . . want to prevent the Jewish people in the Mideast from getting the only thing that could guarantee their right to live—a democratic, multi-national state where Jews and Arabs could live together without imperialist control."[67]

The Maoists also critically examine the nature of the Arab countries and their internal conditions and distinguish among them.[68] The *Guardian* argues that current Arab social systems should not be defended:

The Arab countries suffered historical distortions due to colonialism. . . . in some cases semi-feudal and comprador bourgeois classes still dominate the political life of their countries.

---

62. *Revolution*, Nov. 1973. See also *Call*, Dec. 1973.

63. *Guardian*, Oct. 24, 1973; Antioch Attica Brigade Position Paper, *The War in the Mideast: Who Are the Real Aggressors?*, p. 5.

64. *Guardian*, Nov. 14, 1973.

65. *Ibid.*, Oct. 10, 1973.

66. *Revolution*, Nov. 1973.

67. *Fight Back*, Nov. 1973.

68. *Revolution*, Nov. 1973; *Guardian*, Dec. 12, 1973.

But progressive trends are emerging: the independence of the Arab countries and the growing unity of the Arab peoples are also creating more favorable conditions within the Arab countries for the workers' and peasants' movement.[69]

Following from the Chinese formula that "countries want independence, nations want liberation, and the people want revolution," the Maoist strategy for the ultimate victory of the Palestinian and Arab masses is that "the Arab peoples will have to continue developing their struggle along the lines of self-reliance and people's war," since "neither superpower is going to withdraw on its own."[70]

Shorter-term tactical considerations require that the current Arab regimes be brought into a well-defined alliance in the broad anti-imperialist united front. Though they be bourgeois or even feudal and have contradictions among themselves and with their own masses, "at the same time the expansionist nature of the Israeli state places them in contradiction to Zionism and imperialism," and they become "middle forces" fitting into the growing revolutionary trend of small countries wanting independence from and standing up to U.S. and U.S.S.R. domination.[71]

The U.S. Maoists pursue this line in explaining and supporting Chinese foreign policy in general and activity on Mideast affairs in the U.N. in particular. People's China, "which vociferously supports the aspirations of the displaced Palestinian people" and favors "a prolonged struggle to the end," objected to the cease-fire which ended the October war but refused to participate in the vote in the Security Council on the grounds of solidarity with Egypt and Syria and other Arab governments that had taken a minimally progressive stand during the war. China attempts to maintain the anti-imperialist united front by not obstructing the national goals of these countries, even though their governments may not at this time represent the ultimate needs and aspirations of their peoples.[72] The Maoists thus respect the aims of the Arab countries in pursuing the October war but also recognize their limited nature and emphasize more far-reaching aims for the future. They reject both the terms and the principle of the proposed

69. *Guardian*, Oct. 24, 1973.

70. *Ibid.*, Nov. 7, 1973.

71. *Ibid.*, Dec. 19, Nov. 7, 1973.

72. *Ibid.*, Oct. 17, 31, 1973; *Call*, Nov., Dec. 1973.

superpower settlement, as they see it resulting in a net loss to the Palestinians, by assuming, *ipso facto,* that the Zionist state has the right to exist in what was once Palestine.[73]

The Maoists believe that a just and lasting peace in the Middle East cannot be attained unless certain conditions are met. These are: (1) The removal of superpower influence,[74] (2) an end to U.S. military aid and arms to Israel,[75] (3) the return of the land seized by Israel in 1967,[76] and (4) the restoration of the just rights of the Palestinians, defined as national rights to the whole of Palestine to be shared with the Israeli Jews in a democratic secular state.[77]

The Maoists try to achieve two objectives in their reportage and analysis of Middle East affairs. First, they try to follow through on the principles of Marxist-Leninist and Mao Tse-tung thought—that is, the importance of national liberation and the anti-imperialist united front—and apply them to the Palestinian-Zionist and Arab-Israeli conflicts. Second, and something that may not be obvious to the non-American observer on first glance, they are addressing themselves in large part to the not-yet-converted pro-Zionist Left, both Jewish and non-Jewish, in the United States. This is why all their publications present lengthy histories, fact documentations, and class analyses of Israel and Zionism, much of which information was not readily available to the casual young radical before the last few years.[78]

THE PROGRESSIVE LABOR PARTY (PLP)

The biweekly newspaper of the PLP proclaims itself Marxist-Leninist but is radically different in its interpretation of the Middle East conflict from the CPUSA, the Maoists, and the WWP. In brief, the PLP position does not recognize the national question in relation to Palestine, treats no nationalists as respectable (nationalism is referred to as a "trap"),[79] and believes that international proletarian unity

73. *Call,* Dec. 1973.

74. *Guardian,* Dec. 26, Nov. 7, 1973.

75. *Ibid.,* Jan. 24, 1974.

76. *Fight Back,* Nov. 1973; *Guardian,* Oct. 24, 1973.

77. *Guardian,* Oct. 24, Dec. 26, 1973; *Revolution,* Nov., Dec. 1973; *Fight Back,* Nov. 1973.

78. See, for example, *Guardian,* Oct. 10, 24, 1973.

79. *Challenge,* Nov. 2, 1973. For a comprehensive exposition of the PLP's application of these ideas to the Palestine-Israel situation, see their magazine, *Workers' International Newsletter (WIN),* Jan. 1974, pp. 28–50.

and the class struggle should come first and foremost. In the PLP analysis, the Middle East region has no life or dynamic of its own—except insofar as it has a workers' movement similar to those in other areas—but is rather a stage for imperialist confrontation. This is because the Middle East "is strategic geographically and contains two-thirds of modern industry's most important raw material."[80]

Seeing a growing Arab workers' movement as its main worry in the area, in 1947 the US-British imperialists set up the military colony of Israel to: (1) act as a policeman for the oil companies, (2) act as a lightning rod diverting Arab anger away from the oil companies to the Zionist killers, and (3) provide an excuse for the US to arm the reactionary Arab regimes, arms to be used against their own people, to further entrench these pro-US stooges.[81]

Zionism is not seen as a force in its own right but rather as a tool of imperialism. During the most recent war, the

Israeli fascists stand revealed as nothing more than miserable puppets of US imperialism—the US imperialists airlift the most advanced weapons to the Israelis, send agents and "volunteers" to direct the faltering Zionist cause, send money, hold big conferences and pro-Israel rallies, and use their own air force for "reconnaissance" on behalf of their stooges in Tel Aviv.[82]

Other imperialist powers compete with the United States and try to undermine its hegemony in the region. The Soviet Union is harshly criticized for its role here, especially for its promotion of nationalism and downgrading of class struggle. The Soviet Union's tactic is to "abandon revolutionary working class internationalism and ally with some of the most vicious anti-Communist nationalists you can find outside of Israel," and the Soviet Union as well as the United States is accused of wanting to keep "racist-nationalist hysteria" thriving in the Middle East to obscure its own real reasons for being there.[83] This hysteria is maintained by the presence and constant threat of Israel.

80. *Challenge*, Nov. 16, 1973.
81. *Ibid.*
82. *Ibid.*
83. *Ibid.*, Nov. 2, 1973.

The contradiction between Zionism and the Palestinian people, which is focal to the analysis of most of the other groups, is not considered to be primary or even important by the PLP. Similarly, the contradiction between the state of Israel and the Arab nations is not seen as important in its own right but rather as merely a cover for imperialist rivalry. Following this line of reasoning, the PLP does not differentiate the various Arab regimes among themselves (except by which imperialist patron they cling to) and awards them no more credit or respectability than the Israeli regime. All are imperialist stooges despite "a process that saw reactionary pro-US regimes overthrown in Syria, Iraq, Lebanon, Yemen, Libya, South Yemen and Sudan" after the 1952 coup in Egypt.

In a similar manner the October war is not considered a war of national territorial liberation: "This war, like the past two wars, is really caused by ever-sharpening inter-imperialist rivalry—particularly competition between US imperialists on the one hand and Soviet and Common Market imperialists on the other."[84] The military accomplishments of the Arab side are credited to the Soviets more than to the Arabs themselves: "The latest war in the Mideast is a reflection of the growing influence of the Soviet Union in that area, as yet another Arab army—trained, led, and armed by the Soviets—invaded Israel [sic] and won some important military and political gains."[85]

According to PLP analysis, the results of the war cannot be deemed "progressive," since they only serve to entrench the Arab rulers deeper and to enhance Soviet in place of U.S. hegemony. Arab workers are mistaken to view these results as either "liberating" (in the nationalist sense) or "progressive" (in the socialist sense). "Unfortunately, the leadership of the various Arab working class and liberation movements are . . . caught up with the revisionist notions of 'critical support' of enemies of the Arab workers . . . or 'unity [of all classes] in the face of Israeli aggression.' "[86]

The PLP recommends that the primary Palestinian strategy should be, not to liberate Palestine, *but rather to make revolution in the neighboring Arab countries.*

The leaders of the Palestinian Peoples Movement should abandon the self-defeating policy of "critical support" for the reactionary Arab

84. *Ibid.*
85. *Ibid.*, Dec. 13, 1973.
86. *Ibid.*, Nov. 16, 1973.

nationalists and their Soviet mentors. . . . [They] must break resolutely
with the past pro-nationalist policy. . . . And they must work first and
foremost for the defeat and overthrow of the ruling classes of Egypt,
Syria, and Jordan. These are some of the preconditions for eliminating
the menace of Israeli fascism.[87]

If Arab workers must avoid alliances with Arabs of other classes,
then, the PLP suggests, they must seek allies among other workers,
especially in Israel. The only solution that will allow the smashing
of the Zionist ruling clique is Arab-Jewish worker unity—whether
the Arabs are Palestinian or not seems to be irrelevant.[88] This policy
is summed up in the PLP's slogans: Unite to Turn the Guns on
U.S., Soviet, Israeli, and Arab Bosses; and Turn the Imperialist War
into a Class War.

THE AMERICAN BLACKS

Analytically distinct from the above are the organizations and
caucuses of blacks, Puerto Ricans, and other oppressed minorities
in the United States. Since the emergence of the civil rights movement,
these have developed an anti-imperialist ideology and practice in
alliance with oppressed peoples in the Third World, and in support
of their struggles. Black, Puerto Rican, Chicano, Indian, and Chinese-
American (especially I Wor Kuen) liberation movements and organizations were established and/or strengthened in the sixties. As a consequence they came out, in varying degrees, in support of the Palestinian
and Arab liberation struggle and against Zionism, especially after
the 1967 war, when the radical wings of the minority movements
displayed active solidarity with the Palestinian and Arab struggles.

Though it is difficult to estimate, it seems that a fair and increasing
proportion of the black community—whose position we will dwell
on—is in sympathy with the Arab and Palestinian causes. Radical
blacks, Pan-Africans, Third World ideologues, and even Black Muslims
and blacks of other newer American Islamic sects support the Arab
and anti-imperialist struggles.[89] According to a poll conducted by

---

87. *Ibid.*, Nov. 2, 1973.

88. *Ibid.*

89. For example, in Washington, D.C., where 85 percent of the resident population
is black and there are strong American Muslim organizations, one often sees the bumper
sticker: "No Arms to Israel—Muslim League of the USA."

Muhammad Speaks, the organ of the Black Muslims, an overwhelming majority of black Americans support the Arab nations and the Palestinians.

> Polling some 3,200 Black people in Harlem, Bedford-Stuyvesant and East Harlem (New York), the newspaper found that 71 per cent support the Arabs while only 29 per cent sided with Israel or had no view. This marked a significant change in view from 1970 when a similar poll revealed that 40 per cent agreed with the Arabs while 38 per cent were sympathetic to Israel.
> . . . 65 per cent of the Afro-Americans interviewed felt that the Palestinians should have the right to reclaim the land and the property taken from them by the Israeli state.[90]

In contrast, it seems that the black establishment, including its liberal civil rights leadership, is generally supportive of Israel and Zionism (as evidenced by a full-page ad in the *New York Times,* June 28, 1970), while the poor, ghetto, and working-class blacks feel solidarity with the oppressed Palestinians and Arabs—even if the *Muhammad Speaks* pollsters' figures are somewhat exaggerated.

Radical and militant black worker organizations such as the Black Workers Congress (BWC) have been active in support of the Arab cause. On November 28, 1973, black workers and members of the BWC joined Detroit's Arab-American Workers in protesting against United Auto Workers President Leonard Woodcock's purchase of $1 million worth of Israel bonds with union funds. At the rally BWC leaders spoke out strongly against such practices, against Zionism and U.S. imperialism, and in support of the Arab and Palestinian liberation struggle.[91]

The *Black Panther,* organ of the Black Panther party, takes a strong stand against U.S. imperialism in the Middle East conflict but is not as consistently anti-Israeli. The conflict and the tragic loss of

90. See report in *Call,* Jan. 1974, taken from *Muhammad Speaks.* The methodology of the survey and the degree of strictness in the sampling technique are not reported.

91. Interview with one of the BWC leaders who participated in and spoke at the anti-Woodcock rally in Detroit. The demonstration of protest was reported in practically all of the papers studied. It is a significant action on behalf of the growing Arab-American working-class community in Detroit. Some conflicts with the black workers there have already surfaced, as the auto companies use the recent Arab immigrants as strike-breakers and in other ways to split the solidarity of the workers.

life, it writes, are "merely the continuation of the imperialist aggression which began with the European disputes over control of Africa's wealth with World War I and has continued through and included the unsuccessful attempt to conquer or destroy Southeast Asia." [92]

In the October issues concerned with the October war, no mention of Palestine or of the Palestinians is made. In a synopsis of the official position of Ghana, the reader is left with the impression that a peaceful settlement can be achieved in the Middle East by a return to the U.N. resolutions, especially 242, supporting Israeli withdrawal from the occupied territories, leaving Israel intact, and without mention of the rights of the Palestinians. [93]

However, in the November issues there emerges a recognition of and even identification with the Palestinians, while Israel is placed more firmly in a category with reactionaries and imperialists, especially South Africa. In an interview dealing with the role of the Palestinian guerrillas in the October war, Abu Faysal, a representative of the Palestine Liberation Organization (PLO), is referred to as "Brother Faysal," and the PLO is described as a movement "to liberate Palestine from Zionist domination," and as "Arab groups dedicated to the liberation of their homeland." [94]

In November the *Black Panther* also reprinted sections from "Everything You Always Wanted to Know about the Middle East Conflict . . . but Were Afraid to Ask," by the Middle East Coordinating Committee of New York. The reprint concludes with the statement:

> There will be no peace between Israel and her neighbors until occupied Arab lands are returned in accord with UN resolutions and until Israel recognizes the rights of the Palestinians to live in their own homeland in a progressive, democratic state where everyone can live and enjoy equal rights and privileges, regardless of race or religious belief. [95]

Whether the Black Panther party is merely reporting this for informative purposes or endorses *both* parts of this statement is left moot.

92. *Black Panther*, Oct. 20, 1973.

93. *Ibid.*, Oct. 27, 1973.

94. *Ibid.*, Nov. 17, 1973. Abu Faysal states that the Palestinian guerrillas conduct only defensive operations in the Arqub area to protect local peasants from the Israelis and that Palestinian operations within Israel carefully avoid attacking civilians.

95. *Ibid.*, Nov. 7, 1973.

SOCIAL DEMOCRATS AND OTHER PROGRESSIVE GROUPS

Holding socialist ideas to a greater or lesser extent is a wide variety of organizations which may be grouped together for the sake of convenience. To begin with, there are two social democratic parties currently active. The right wing of this tendency is the Social Democratic party (SDP), formerly the Socialist party, under the leadership of Michael Harrington. Organizationally it is a mass party, unlike the Marxist Left cadre parties, and ideologically it emphasizes "freedom and democracy" and is hardly anti-imperialist—it supports the U.S. policy in the Middle East. It is perhaps the only party or tendency left of the liberals which supports Israel unhesitantingly. Since 1967, it has ignored the national rights of the Palestinians. The SDP justifies its position on the ground that Israel is the only democratic nation in the region.[96] The party accepts most Israeli and Zionist propaganda concerning the Middle East conflict and thus reflects the Euro-American social democratic support of Israel.

The left wing of the social democratic tendency, the New American Movement (NAM), has advanced a position on the Middle East which is more progressive. In its national council meetings in early 1974, NAM adopted what it called a minimal resolution:

> Zionism is a distorted form of the need of the Jewish people for emancipation, and an inappropriate method for fighting anti-Semitism. We support the dezionization of the state of Israel.
>
> We support the right of the Palestinian people to national self-determination in Palestinine.
>
> The only way the above goals can be achieved is through their integration with a struggle for a socialist Middle East.[97]

Though somewhat vague, the resolution is a step forward after much deliberation at the meeting on whether to take any position at all on the Middle East.

One of the oldest American socialist organizations is the Socialist Labor party (SLP), which defines itself as Marxist and independent; it is critical of the CPUSA and of the U.S.S.R. but does not refer to either the Trotskyist or the Maoist currents. It is a mass party

96. See party literature and pamphlets. Michael Harrington makes the same point in his speeches, for example, at a lecture attended by the authors at the State University of New York, Albany, in 1970.

97. From NAM, *The Middle East Resolutions at the National Council: A Step Forward,* 1974.

engaging in electoral politics and trade-union organizing. Its paper, the *Weekly People*, attempts to take an "objective" tone in reporting on the Middle East, explicitly supporting neither Israel nor the Palestinians. It sees the parties in the Middle East conflict as puppets of the superpowers, caught up in a tragic play over which they have no control.[98] By this approach, the SLP avoids discussion of the nature of Zionism and Israel, never confronts the problem of the Palestinians or of national liberation, and makes no analysis of the internal structure of the countries involved.

The People's party, a national coalition of both mass and cadre local parties, calls itself anticapitalist but not "specifically socialist or populist."[99] Its member groups work with local units of NAM and the SDP on community projects, and engage in both "electoral and non-electoral (food co-ops, free schools, free health clinics, and other alternative institutions) politics."[100] Their proposed solution[101] for the Middle East conflict is to do away with Israel's theocratic structure and the land of return, and to reconstitute Israel "as a bi-national state, where Jews and Arabs have exactly the same rights as citizens and in the economic and cultural life of the country."[102] All of those who reside there now and who did so prior to 1948, and their descendants, would have rights to citizenship. Although this position does not call for socialism, it does call for U.S. military aid to be withdrawn and for nationalization of U.S. investment there—all in all, an anti-Zionist and anti-imperialist position.

Like NAM and the People's party, the progressive GI organizations had their origins in the antiwar movement of the 1960s and have expanded their opposition to U.S. military intervention in Vietnam to a broader anti-imperialist stand which includes anti-Zionism, without becoming explicitly Marxist. Thus, the *Bond,* organ of the American Servicemen's Union (ASU), in article entitled "GI's: We Must Not Fight in Mideast," argues that Israel was created by the

98. *Weekly People,* Oct. 27, Dec. 8, 1973, Jan. 5, 1974.

99. Letter of principles and information from the national office of the People's party (Washington, D.C.).

100. *Ibid.*

101. Put out by the Michigan Human Rights party, a local member party of the People's party, and which, according to the national office of the People's party, in a private letter dated Jan. 3, 1974, is "for all intents and purposes . . . the national party's position."

102. This "bi-national state" is different in conception from the one proposed by the smaller Trotskyist parties, since the latter provides for the dissection of Palestine anew if either of the constituent "nations" should choose to secede.

Western imperialists to protect their oil interests, at the expense of the Arabs of Palestine, and that Israel's internal structure perpetuates "high unemployment and racist discrimination against dark-skinned Jews." [103] Since Israel did not return the Arab lands occupied in 1967, "the use of warfare [was] the only possible means for Arab nations to regain their land," and anyway, "the very existence of the state of Israel represents *aggression against the Arab nations.*" [104]

Another GI-veterans' publication, *Highway 13,* also condemns U.S. military involvement in the Middle East but is somewhat less consistent on the nature of the Arab nations' response to Israel, seeing both Israel and the Arabs as "victimized puppets of Soviet-American imperialism, and neither as much of an example to progressive-minded peoples." [105] Israel is shown to be a theocratic, expansionist dependent of U.S. imperialism, "in the throes of Zionist fanaticism," while "the Arab States [are] ruled by and serving the interests of either semi-feudal or bourgeoisie classes or oppressive military cliques." [106] The Palestinians, who "continue to serve as a punching bag for everybody," are given no independent role; and the war is seen as having "served the economic and political purposes of the ruling classes on both sides almost as much as it has benefited the imperialist powers who wield the puppet strings." [107] This position is anti-imperialist and anti-Zionist, but pays little attention to the problem of national liberation.

CONCLUSION

The organizations reviewed above generally represent the revitalized and the resurgent Left, the latter being strongly Marxist and having made inroads into the old left-liberal and social democratic tendencies. In terms of their absolute numbers, judging from their membership and the circulation of their publications, the organizations are not large. They have not yet drawn many people away from the dominant bourgeois ideology, nor have they attracted readers away from the

103. *Bond,* Oct. 21, 1973.

104. *Ibid.* (emphasis in original).

105. *Highway 13,* Nov. 1973. But in the December issue, reference is made to the "progressive Arab nations" who have "served notice that the rip-off is over" by making an oil embargo.

106. *Ibid.,* Nov. 1973.

107. *Ibid.*

commercial, liberal, and popular press. However, their influence extends beyond their numbers. On the one hand, they have had a profound impact on leftist intellectuals in general. On the other hand, people with New Left, especially Marxist, perspectives (whether they formally belong to parties or not) promulgate their ideas through a wide variety of social and political activities. They participate in and often lead community-based actions: some examples are setting up and protecting free or inexpensive health clinics; protesting against the break-up of neighborhoods by "urban renewal" or real estate speculators; organizing local political campaigns against corrupt city machines; forming grocery, housing, and child-care cooperatives; and organizing consumers' protests against inflation. They work to build rank-and-file worker movements within the trade-unions to which they belong, and help in organizing drives and supporting boycotts for other progressive trade-unions. Examples include the support for United Farm Workers of America, the Amalgamated Clothing Workers, and the Hospital Workers Union 1199, all of which have current drives to organize the more exploited segments of the labor force not included in unions.

Marxists are also involved in college campus organizations, including anti-imperialist coalitions of American minority and foreign students. They have set up numerous small educational groups studying Marxism and its applications to the current American situation in most urban and university centers. They have been particularly active in the development of the "underground press," a proliferation of local antiestablishment newspapers oriented toward the poor and the proletariat, reporting on and analyzing local struggles (such as the community- and worker-organizing actions cited above) and offering an alternative interpretation of international news.

But one crucial negative aspect of the contemporary Left in the United States must be pointed out: it is fractured and sectarian. The sects are critical of each other and often engage in hostile attacks which at times have even led to physical assaults. This is a debilitating divisiveness and may be a factor in the impotence of the American Left in general. It should thus be clear to the reader that despite the recent dramatic increase in its size, the Marxist Left is still a relatively marginal social force in the country. But the trend that it represents is likely to increase, as the crisis of American capitalism which has revitalized the Left seems to be deepening.

PART II: INSTITUTIONAL BASES OF STEREOTYPES

Edward W. Said

ORIENTALISM AND THE OCTOBER WAR: THE SHATTERED MYTHS

> There is therefore one language, which is not
> mythical, it is the language of man the producer:
> whenever man speaks in order to transform reality
> and no longer to preserve it as an image, whenever
> he links his language to the making of things . . .
> myth is impossible.
>
> Roland Barthes

MYTHS ARE A LANGUAGE: organized, systematic, bearers of a code they articulate but do not either question or fully reveal. There are no innocent, no unideological myths, just as there are no "natural" myths. Every myth is a manufactured object, and it is the inherent bad faith of a myth to seem, or rather to pretend, to be a fact. A myth's first and greatest enemy is analysis and specification, by which its seemingly durable presence—like that of a natural object—is shown to have been created in a specific way, out of specific materials, and for specific reasons. More important, it is the locale of the myth that must be identified. The purpose of this essay is to examine critically, in light of the October war, myths of Arab society which have for

A longer version of this paper appears in *Middle East Crucible: Studies on the Arab-Israeli War of October 1973*, ed. Naseer Aruri (Wilmette, Ill.: Medina University Press International, 1975).

too long been preserved in *the discourse of Orientalism,* that school of thought and discipline of study whose focus includes "the Arabs," Arabism, Islam, the Semites, and the "Arab mind." [1]

It should be pointed out at the outset that Arab society cannot be discussed *in fact,* precisely because the Arabs number over 100 million people and a score of different societies, and because, to my knowledge, there is no truly effective intellectual method for discussing all of them together as a single monolith. Any reduction of this immense mass of history, societies, individuals, and realities to "Arab society" is therefore a mythification. But what can be done is to analyze the structure of thought for which such a phrase as "Arab society" *is* a kind of reality. This structure, as we shall soon see, is a myth, with codes, discourse, and tropes. This structure has a history, albeit a far simpler one than the subject it purportedly treats, and is upheld by a set of institutions that give it whatever power and validity it seems to have. For this myth the October war was a surprise, not because "the Arabs" fought well, but because the Arabs were not supposed to fight at all. The war seemed therefore to be a deviation out of context, a violation of a well-established logic. This is a chorus one can find in many places.

This essay will be divided into three parts. In the first I shall analyze certain myths arising from the Orientalist position. I shall generalize, of course, leaving it to be understood that I will discuss the discourse as a systematic whole, and not every instance of it. Space dictates such a procedure, as well as a conviction that exceptions to the rules of Orientalism as a discourse prove the rules. In the next part I will discuss the modern history of Western scholarship of the Orient and analyze the present institutions that sustain Orientalism. In the final part my concern will be with the ways of dealing methodologically and practically with Orientalism as a myth system and a type of thought.

ORIENTALIST AND ORIENTAL

One of the commonest motifs to appear in discussions of the October war was not that it took place but rather that it took place in the form of a Western and Israeli intelligence failure. On October 31,

1. Much of my discussion of myth is indebted to Roland Barthes, *Mythologies,* trans. Annette Lavers (New York: Hill & Wang, 1972), especially its final section, "Myth Today," pp. 109–59.

1973, the *New York Times* quoted Henry Kissinger as follows: "The gravest danger of intelligence assessments" is in trying "to fit the facts into existing preconceptions and to make them consistent with what is anticipated." The *Times* continued: "This is a judgement widely shared in the intelligence community." Significantly, such a community can exist partly because it speaks a common language of myths for which "intelligence" is possible with regard to the Middle East, and partly because there is a hoard of practical knowledge, historical lore, unshakable convictions ultimately derived from Orientalism. According to Orientalism, Orientals can be observed as possessing certain habits of mind, traits of character, idiosyncrasies of history and temperament, the sum of which inclines Orientals toward certain types of action.

A startling recent piece of Orientalism clarifies the problem with which Kissinger was trying to deal. In its February 1974 issue, *Commentary*, the leading Jewish intellectual journal in the United States, gave its readers an article by Gil Carl Alroy entitled, "Do the Arabs Want Peace?"[2] Alroy's argument is quite predictable: that Arabs want to destroy Israel; that Arabs really say what they mean; that Arabs are as one in their bent for bloody vengeance; and that Arabs are psychologically incapable of peace and congenitally tied to a concept of justice that means the opposite of justice. Because they possess these characteristics, Arabs are not to be trusted and must be fought interminably as one fights any other fatal disease. For evidence Alroy offers a quotation taken from an essay by Harold W. Glidden ("The Arab World," *American Journal of Psychiatry*, February 1972). In this essay, Alroy finds Glidden able to have "captured the cultural differences between the Western and the Arab view" of things "very well." Alroy's argument is therefore clinched— the Arabs are unregenerate savages; and thus an "authority" on the Arab mind has told a wide audience of presumably concerned Jews that they must continue to watch out. And he has done it academically, dispassionately, fairly, using evidence taken from the Arabs themselves—who, he says with Olympian assurance, have "emphatically ruled out . . . real peace"—and from psychoanalysis.

Harold Glidden, it turns out, is a retired member of the Bureau of Intelligence and Research, U.S. Department of State, a Ph.D.

2. Professor Alroy teaches political science at Hunter College and is the author or editor of *Attitudes toward Jewish Statehood in the Arab World* and *Images of the Middle East Conflict,* so he is one who professes to "know" the Arabs, and he is obviously some sort of expert on image-making.

graduate of Princeton, Department of Oriental Languages, and no doubt one of those legendary "Arabists" about whom one has always heard so much. His work is not only naked racism; it is also the poorest sort of scholarship, even though, as we shall soon see, it is essentially a repetition of canonical Orientalist myths. In his article modestly called "The Arab World," which is nothing less than a four-page, double-columned psychological portrait of over 100 million people considered for a period of 1,300 years, Glidden cites exactly four sources: a recent book on Tripoli, one issue of *Al-Ahram, Oriente Moderno,* and a book by Majid Khadduri. The article itself purports to uncover "the inner workings of Arab behavior," which from *our* point of view is "aberrant" but for Arabs is "normal." This is an auspicious start. Thereafter we are told that Arabs stress conformity, that the Arabs inhabit a shame culture whose "prestige system" involves the ability to attract followers and clients, that Arabs can function only in conflict situations, that prestige is based solely on the ability to dominate others, that a shame culture—and Islam itself—makes of revenge a virtue, that from a Western point of view "the only rational thing for the Arabs to do is to make peace . . . [but] for the Arabs the situation is not governed by this kind of logic, for objectivity is not a value in the Arab system."

Glidden continues now, heady with the power of his analysis: "It is a notable fact that while the Arab value system demands absolute solidarity within the group, it at the same time encourages among its members a kind of rivalry that is destructive of that very solidarity." In Arab society only "success counts" and "the end justifies the means." Arabs live "naturally" in a world "characterized by anxiety expressed in generalized suspicion and distrust, which has been labelled free-floating hostility." "The art of subterfuge is highly developed in Arab life, as well as in Islam itself." The Arab need for vengeance overrides everything—otherwise the Arab would feel "ego-destroying" shame. Therefore if "Westerners consider peace to be high on the scale of values" and if "we have a highly developed consciousness of the value of time," this is not true of Arabs. "In fact," we are told, "in Arab tribal society (where Arab values originated), strife, not peace, was the normal state of affairs because raiding was one of the two main supports of the economy." The purpose of this learned disquisition is merely to show how on the Western and Arab scale of values "the relative position of the elements is quite different."

When Alroy was challenged for his use of this shabby work, he replied with the supreme innocence of a man confident in the tradition of his learning that "what is said [in his article and in Glidden's] is about as controversial amongst Orientalists as the multiplication table." [3]

Alroy is useful as a symptom. Anyone who refers blithely to a humanistic tradition whose "uncontroversial" tenets are as irrefutable as the multiplication table can only be expected mindlessly to repeat their underlying code. Neither Glidden nor Alroy disappoints. As with all mythologies, theirs is a structure built around a set of simple oppositions which initiate the distinction between Orientalism and every other form of human knowledge. This, then, is the key reduction. On the one hand there are Westerners and on the other there are Orientals. The former are rational, peaceful, liberal, logical, capable of holding real values, without natural suspicion and distrust, and so forth. The latter are not. These are explicit distinctions. Less explicit is the difference between *us* (Europeans, whites, Aryans) and *them* (non-Europeans, blacks or browns, Semites). The great irony, of course, is that many non-Europeans—Arabs and Jews—are Orientalists who consider themselves part of the European, non-Oriental camp.

One can explain such anomalies by recognizing that a still more implicit and powerful difference posited by the Orientalist as against the Oriental is that the former *writes about*, whereas the latter *is written about*. For the Oriental, passivity is the presumed role; for the Orientalist, the power to observe and to study. As Barthes said, a myth (and its perpetuators) can invent itself (themselves) ceaselessly. The Oriental is given as fixed, stable, in need of investigation, in need even of knowledge about himself. There is no dialectic either desired or allowed. There is a source of information (the Oriental) and a source of knowledge (the Orientalist): in short, a writer and a subject matter otherwise inert. The relationship between the two is radically a matter of power, for which there are of course numerous images.

A large portion of the Orientalist literature involves a very particular kind of compression and reduction. For example, Raphael Patai describes the Middle East as a "culture area." [4] As a result, Patai has eradicated the plurality of differences among the Arabs in the interest of one difference, namely, setting Arabs off from everyone else. Thus reduced, they can be made to permit, legitimate, valorize

3. *Commentary*, LVII, no. 5 (May 1974). This statement was made by Alroy following a letter of mine to *Commentary*.

4. See *Golden River to Golden Road: Society, Culture and Change in the Middle East*, 3d ed. (Philadelphia: University of Pennsylvania Press, 1969), and *The Arab Mind* (New York: Scribner's, 1973).

general nonsense of the sort one finds in works such as Sania Hamady's *Temperament and Character of the Arabs*.

> The Arabs so far have demonstrated an incapacity for disciplined and abiding unity. They experience collective outbursts of enthusiasm but do not pursue patiently collective endeavors, which are usually embraced half-heartedly. They show lack of coordination and harmony in organization and function, nor have they revealed an ability for cooperation. Any collective action for common benefit or mutual profit is alien to them.[5]

The style of this prose tells more perhaps than Hamady intends. Verbs like *demonstrate, reveal, show* are used without indicating to whom the Arabs are demonstrating, revealing, showing. To no one in particular, obviously, but to everyone in general. This is another way of saying that these truths are self-evident only to a privileged or initiated observer, since nowhere does Hamady cite generally available evidence for her observations. Besides, given the inanity of the observations, what sort of evidence could there be? As her prose moves along her tone increases in confidence: "Any collective action . . . is alien to them." The categories harden, the assertions are more unyielding, and the Arabs have been totally transformed from people into no more than the putative subject of Hamady's style. The Arabs exist only as an occasion for the tyrannical observer: the world is *my* idea.

And so it is throughout the work of the contemporary Orientalist— assertions of the most bizarre sort dot his pages, whether it is a Halpern arguing that even though all human thought processes can be reduced to eight, the Islamic mind is capable of only four,[6] or a Berger presuming

5. (New York: Twayne, 1960), p. 100. Hamady's book is a favorite among Israelis and Israeli apologists. Alroy cites her approvingly, and so does Amos Elon, *The Israelis: Founders and Sons* (New York: Holt, Rinehart & Winston, 1971). Morroe Berger (see note 7 below) also cites her frequently. Her model is a book like Edward William Lane's *Account of the Manners and the Customs of the Modern Egyptians* (1833-35), but she has none of Lane's literacy, wit, or general learning.

6. Daniel Halpern's thesis is presented in "Four Contrasting Repertories of Human Relations in Islam: Two Pre-Modern and Two Modern Ways of Dealing with Continuity and Change, Collaboration and Conflict and the Achieving of Justice" (Paper presented to the Twenty-second Near East Conference at Princeton University on Psychology and Near Eastern Studies, May 8, 1973). This treatise was preceded by Halpern's "A Redefinition of the Revolutionary Situation," *Journal of International Affairs*, XXIII, no. 1 (1969), 54-75.

that since the Arabic language is much given to rhetoric Arabs are consequently incapable of true thought.[7] I have called these assertions myth in their function and structure, and yet one must try to understand what other imperatives govern their use. Here one speculates of course. Orientalist generalizations about the Arabs are very detailed when it comes to critically itemizing Arab characteristics, far less so when it comes to analyzing Arab strengths. The Arab family, Arab rhetoric, the Arab character, etc., despite copious descriptions by the Orientalist, appear de-natured, that is, without human potency, even as these same descriptions possess a fullness and depth in their sweeping power over the subject matter. Hamady again: "Thus, the Arab lives in a hard and frustrating environment. He has little chance to develop his potentialities and define his position in society, holds little belief in progress and change, and finds salvation only in the hereafter."[8] What the Arab cannot achieve himself is to be found in the writing about him. The Orientalist is supremely certain of *his* potential, is not a pessimist, is able to define his position, his own and the Arab's. The picture of the Arab-Oriental that emerges is determinedly negative; yet, we ask, why this endless series of works on him? What grips the Orientalist, if it is not—as it certainly is not—love of Arab science,

---

7. Morroe Berger, *The Arab World Today* (New York: Anchor, 1964), p. 140. Much the same sort of implication underlines the clumsy work of quasi Arabists like Joel Carmichael and Daniel Lerner. It is there more subtly in the work of political and historical scholars who include Theodore Draper, Walter Laqueur, and Elie Keddourie. It is strongly in evidence in such highly regarded works as Gabriel Baer, *Population and Society in the Arab East*, trans. Hanna Szoke (New York: Praeger, 1964), and Alfred Bonne, *State and Economics in the Middle East: A Society in Transition* (London: Routledge & Kegan Paul, 1955). The rule seems by consensus to be that if they think at all, Arabs think differently—*not necessarily* with reason, and often without it. See also Adel Daher's RAND study, *Current Trends in Arab Intellectual Thought*, RM-5979-FF (Dec. 1969) and its typical conclusion that "the concrete problem-solving approach is conspicuously absent from Arab thought" (p. 29). In a review-essay for the *Journal of Interdisciplinary History*, IV, no. 2 (Autumn 1973), 287-98, Roger Owen attacks the very notion of Islam as a concept for the study of history. His focus is *The Cambridge History of Islam*, which, he finds, in certain ways perpetuates an idea of Islam (to be found in such writers as C. H. Becker and Max Weber) "defined essentially as a religious, feudal, and antirational system [that] lacked the necessary characteristics which had made European progress possible." For a sustained proof of Weber's total inaccuracy, see Maxime Rodinson, *Islam and Capitalism*, trans, Brian Pearce (New York: Pantheon, 1974), pp. 76-117. There is a useful short account of Orientalist myths militarily in operation before and during the October war in Yassin el-Ayouti, "Al-jabha al-ma 'anawiya fi harb October," *Siyassa Dowaliya*, no. 35 (Jan. 1974), pp. 66-72.

8. *Temperament and Character*, p. 197.

mind, society, achievement? In other words, what is the nature of the Arab presence in the mythic discourse about him?

Two things: number and generative power. Both qualities are reducible to each other ultimately, but we ought to separate them for the purposes of analysis. Almost without exception, every modern work of Orientalist scholarship, especially in the social sciences, has a great deal to say about the family, its male-dominated structure, its all-pervasive influence in society. Patai's work is a typical example. However, a silent paradox immediately presents itself. If the family is an institution for whose general failures the only remedy is the placebo of "modernization," we must acknowledge that the family continues to produce itself and is the source of Arab existence in the world. What Berger refers to as "the great value men place upon their own sexual prowess"[9] suggests the lurking power behind the Arab presence in the world. If, on the one hand, Arab society is represented in almost completely negative and generally passive terms, to be ravished and won by the Orientalist hero, we can assume, on the other hand, that such a representation is a way of dealing with the great variety and potency of Arab diversity, whose source is, if not intellectual and social, then sexual and biological. Yet the absolutely inviolable taboo in Orientalist discourse is that that very sexuality must never be taken seriously. It can never be explicitly blamed for the absence of achievement and "real" rational sophistication which the Orientalist everywhere finds among the Arabs. And yet this is, I think, the missing link in Hamady's, Berger's, Lerner's, and others' arguments, whose main aim is criticism of "traditional" Arab society. They recognize the power of the family, note the weaknesses of the Arab mind, remark the "importance" of the Oriental world to the West, but never say what their discourse implies, that what is really left to the Arab after all is said and done is an undifferentiated sexual drive.

On rare occasions—as in the work of Leon Mugniery—we do find the explicit made clear: that there is a "powerful sexual appetite . . . characteristic of those hot-blooded southerners."[10] Most of the time, however, the belittlement of Arab society and its reduction to platitudes inconceivable for any except the racially inferior, is carried on over an undercurrent of sexual exaggeration: the Arab produces himself, endlessly, sexually, and little else. The Orientalist says nothing about

9. *Arab World*, p. 102.

10. Quoted by Irene Gendzier, *Frantz Fanon: A Critical Study* (New York: Pantheon, 1973), p. 94.

this, although his argument depends on it. "But co-operation in the Near East is still largely a family affair and little of it is found outside the blood group or village." [11] Which is to say that the only way in which Arabs count is sexually; institutionally, politically, culturally they are insignificant.

Just preceding the October war such an image of the Arab seemed to be notably relevant, and it was often occasioned by scholarly discussion of those two recent favorites of Orientalist expertise, revolution and modernization. Under the auspices of the School of Oriental and African Studies there appeared in 1972 a volume entitled *Revolution in the Middle East and Other Case Studies*, edited by P. J. Vatikiotis. The title is overtly medical; one might be expected to think that Orientals were finally being given the benefit of what "traditional" Orientalism had usually withheld: psychosexual attention. In this imposing compilation of studies by noted scholars, the argument is clearly vulnerable. The essays contain distortions, willful slanting of scholarly evidence, and an unbending desire to discredit and debunk the Arabs as a people and as a society. What is interesting in much of the writing is how close to the surface defensive fear of Arab sexuality has come. Having exhausted his time-worn arsenal of racial criticism made with scholarly detachment, the Orientalist now sheds his disguise and attacks the very thing he fears most.

Vatikiotis sets the tone of the collection with a quasi-medical definition of revolution; but since Arab revolution is in his and his readers' minds, the naked hostility of the definition seems acceptable. There is a very clever irony here about which I shall speak later. Vatikiotis' theoretical support is Camus, whose colonial mentality was no friend of revolution or of the Arabs, as Conor Cruise O'Brien has recently shown; but the phrase "Revolution destroys both men and principles" is accepted from Camus as having "fundamental sense." Vatikiotis continues:

> All revolutionary ideology is in direct conflict with (actually, is a head-on attack upon) man's rational, biological and psychological make-up.
>
> Committed as it is to a methodical metastasis, revolutionary ideology demands fanaticism from its adherents. Politics for the revolutionary is not only a question of belief, or a substitute for religious belief. It must stop being what it has always been, namely, an adaptive activity in time for survival. Metastatic, soteriological politics abhors adaptiveness,

11. Berger, *Arab World*, p. 151.

for how else can it eschew the difficulties, ignore and bypass the obstacles of the complex biological-psychological dimension of man, or mesmerize his subtle though limited and vulnerable rationality. It fears and shuns the concrete and discrete nature of human problems and the preoccupations of political life: it thrives on the abstract and the Promethean. It subordinates all tangible values to the one supreme value: the harnessing of man and history in a grand design of human liberation. It is not satisfied with human politics which has so many irritating limitations. It wishes instead to create a new world not adaptively, precariously, delicately, that is, humanly, but by a terrifying act of Olympian pseudo-divine creation. Politics in the service of man is a formula that is unacceptable to the revolutionary ideologue. Rather man exists to serve a politically contrived and brutally decreed order.[12]

Whatever else this passage is, it is nothing less than fascism proclaimed in the name of the human, and a brutal identification of sexuality ("act of . . . pseudo-divine creation") with cancerous disease. Whatever the "human" does according to Vatikiotis is rational, right, subtle, discrete, concrete; whatever the revolutionary proclaims is brutal, irrational, mesmeric, cancerous. Procreation, change, continuity are identified with sexuality and with madness, as well as with abstraction.

Vatikiotis' terms then are weighted and colored emotionally by "rightist" appeals to humanity and decency, and by "anti-leftist" appeals safeguarding humanity from sexuality, cancer, madness, irrational violence, revolution. Since it is Arab revolution that is in question, we are to read the passage then as follows: This is what revolution is, and if the Arabs or the Middle East want it, then that's a fairly telling comment on them, on what kind of inferior race they are.

The scholarly centerpiece of Vatikiotis' collection is Bernard Lewis' essay "Islamic Concepts of Revolution." The strategy here is extremely refined. Most readers will know that for Arabic-speakers today the word *thawra* and its immediate cognates mean revolution; they will know this also from Vatikiotis' introduction. Yet Lewis does not describe the meaning of *thawra* until the very end of his article, after he has discussed concepts such as *dawla, fitna,* and *bughat* in their historical and mostly religious context. The central point there is that "the Western doctrine of the right to resist bad government

12. *Revolution in the Middle East and Other Case Studies: Proceedings of a Seminar* (London: Allen & Unwin, 1972) pp. 8-9.

is alien to Islamic thought";[13] hence, the political attitudes of "defeat-ism" and "quietism." At no point in the essay is one sure where all these terms are being used except somewhere in the history of words. Then near the end of the essay Lewis writes:

> In the Arabic-speaking countries a different word was used for [revolu-tion] *thawra*. The root th-w-r in classical Arabic meant to rise up (e.g., of a camel), to be stirred or excited, and hence, especially in Maghribi usage, to rebel. It is often used in the context of establishing a petty, independent sovereignty; thus, for example, the so-called party kings who ruled in eleventh century Spain after the break-up of the Caliphate of Cordova, are called thuwwar (sing. *tha'ir*). The noun *thawra* at first means excitement, as in the phrase, cited in the Sihah, a standard medieval Arabic dictionary, *intazir hatta taskun hadhihi 'lthawra:* wait till this excitement dies down—a very apt recommendation. The verb is used by al-Iji, in the form of *thawaran* or *itharat fitna*, stirring up sedition, as one of the dangers which should discourage a man from practising the duty of resistance to bad government. *Thawra* is the term used by Arabic writers in the nineteenth century for the French Revolution, and by their successors for the approved revolutions, domestic and foreign, of our own time.[14]

The entire passage reeks of condescension and bad faith. Why introduce the idea of a camel rising as an etymological root for modern Arab revolution except as a clever way of discrediting the modern? One can tolerate this sort of ploy when it is used, say, by Vico in the *New Science* (1744) as he tries to show the etymological relations between the word for "father" and a shriek of fear; Vico's interest is in polemically attacking Cartesian rationalism. One would not know from this slighting account of *thawra* that innumerable people have an active commitment to it in ways too complex even for Lewis' pseudo-Gibbonian sarcasm and scholarship. But it is this kind of essentialized description that is canonical for students and policy-makers concerned with the Middle East. When Lewis' wisdom about *thawra* suddenly appears in a *New York Times* article on modern Libya (by Eric Pace, January 30, 1974) in the throes of revolutionary

13. *Ibid.*, p. 33.

14. *Ibid.*, pp. 38–39. Lewis' study *Race and Color in Islam* (New York: Harper & Row, 1971) expresses similar disaffection with an air of great learning; more explicitly political—but no less acid—is his *Islam in History: Ideas, Men and Events in the Middle East* (London: Alcove, 1973).

agitation, we are comforted to know from Pace that *thawra* originally—
how contemptible is the adverb here—means a camel getting up,
and so all the fuss about Libya and Qaddafi is pretty funny.

Lewis' association of *thawra* with a camel rising, and generally
with excitement, hints much more broadly than is usual for him that
the Arab is scarcely more than a neurotic sexual being. The words
he uses to describe revolution are tinged with sexuality: *stirred, excited,
rise up.* But for the most part it is a "bad" sexuality he ascribes
to the Arab. In the end, since Arabs are really not equipped for serious
action, their sexual excitement (an erection) is no more noble than
a camel's rising up. Instead of revolution there is sedition, setting
up a petty sovereignty, excitement, which is as much as saying that
instead of copulation, the Arab can only achieve foreplay, masturbation,
coitus interruptus. These, I think, are Lewis' implications, no matter
how innocent his air of learning or parlorlike his language. Since
he is so sensitive to the nuances of words, he must be aware, too,
that *his* words have nuances as well. Lewis' quasi philology links
him to a fairly widespread method among contemporary Orientalists,
particularly those specialists in Arab affairs whose work is connected
to government intelligence agencies (Harkabi with Israeli intelligence) [15] or government propaganda machines (Alroy with the Zionist
movement). For such specialists Arabic indicates the nature of the
Arab mentality. Words are unmediated indices of irreducible character
traits, regardless of culture, history, social and economic circumstances.
Arabic words reveal the Arab's obsession with oral functions (note
the sexual motif creeping in again). The words' meanings are instances
of either a malicious hidden significance (proving that Arabs are
innately dishonest) or a fundamental inability to be like the "normal"
Westerner.

The comtemporary *locus classicus* for these views of Arabic is E.
Shouby's "The Influence of the Arabic Language on the Psychology
of the Arabs." [16] The argument he proposes is lamentably simple-
minded, perhaps because he has no notion of what language is and
how it operates. Nevertheless, the subheadings of his essay tell a
good deal of his story; Arabic is "General Vagueness of Thought,"

15. Yehoshafat Harkabi, *Arab Attitudes toward Israel*, trans, Misha Louvish (New
York, 1972). Harkabi is the former chief of Israeli intelligence.

16. *Middle East Journal*, vol. V (1951), reprinted in *Readings in Arab Middle Eastern
Societies and Cultures*, ed. Abdulla Lutfiyya and Charles W. Churchill (The Hague:
Mouton, 1970), pp. 688–703.

"Overemphasis on Linguistic Signs," "Overassertion and Exaggeration." Shouby is frequently quoted as an authority because he speaks like one and because what he hypostasizes is a sort of mute Arab who, at the same time, is a great work-master playing games without much seriousness or purpose. Muteness is an important part of what Shouby is talking about, since during his entire paper he never once quotes from the literature of which the Arab is so inordinately proud. Where then does Arabic influence the Arab mind? Exclusively within the mythological world created for the Arab by Orientalism. The Arab is a sign for dumbness combined with hopeless overarticulateness, impotence with hypersexuality, poverty with excess. That such a result can be attained by philological means testifies to the sad end of a once noble learned tradition.[17]

In everything I have been discussing, language plays the dominant role. It brings opposites together as "natural," it presents human types in scholarly idioms and methodologies, it ascribes reality and reference to objects (other words) of its own making. Mythic language is discourse; that is, it cannot be anything but systematic. One does not make discourse at will, nor statements in it, without first belonging—in some cases unconsciously, but at any rate involuntarily—to the ideology and the institutions that guarantee its existence. These latter are always the institutions of an advanced society dealing with a less-advanced society. This will be discussed in some detail later. The principal feature of mythical discourse is that it conceals its own origins as well as those of what it describes. "Arabs" are presented in the imagery of static, almost ideal types, and neither as creatures with a potential in the process of being realized nor as a history being made. The exaggerated value heaped upon Arabic as a language permits the Orientalist to make the language equal mind, society, history, and nature. Undoubtedly the absence in Arabic of a full-fledged tradition of reported informal personal experience (autobiography, novel, etc.) makes it easier for the Orientalist to let the language as a whole have such uncontrolled significance; thus for the Orientalist the language speaks the Arab, not vice versa. But, as I have been implying, there are historical and cultural reasons for this distortion. I shall now sketch those briefly.

17. See, for example, M. M. Bravmann, *The Spiritual Background of Early Islam: Studies in Ancient Arab Concepts* (Leiden: Brill, 1972).

THE HISTORY OF WESTERN SCHOLARSHIP OF THE ORIENT

Political expediency, coupled with unimaginative intellectual bureaucracy, has, since World War II, confined Orientalism in most
universities and institutes to the culturally decadent thesis of the
regional studies program. In practically all existing programs, the
particularity of literary tradition (which is the way cultures survive,
are transmitted, and exist) has been violated, and countless uninformed
works have masqueraded as "scientific" information about the Middle
East, the Communist world, the Latin American countries, and Southeast Asia. New identities, quite without ontological validity, were
created, each laced with mythical descriptions of the kind I have
just discussed. One striking result is that nowhere in the West today
is there a flourishing school of traditional Oriental philology or is
serious attention paid to literary-humanistic Arabic literature since
the classical period. Very few programs include a study of the traditions
of Orientalism, let alone critiques of Orientalist methodology or rational
examination of what in fact the material of Orientalism is. Area studies
programs hash over and rehash the same sociopolitical clichés about
the Arab mind, Arab nationalism, Islamic institutions, and the Arab-
Israeli conflict. It is only the occasional scholar who seriously asks
why things are this way. Whole generations of Arab and Jewish
students, whose stake in Orientalist theory and practice is very large,
are educated into this corrupt racism, believing themselves to be
gaining the "objective" methods of analysis their teachers have urged
upon them. The result is Jews talking about "the Arab mind" and
Arabs talking about "the Jewish mind": in the long run, both equally
bad.

We are very far from knowing today what price the people of the
Middle East have paid for this kind of knowledge and for the kind
of political action it has prompted. Nevertheless, certain assessments
can be made. First, the study of the Middle East in the West has
not been disinterested. The oil and strategic wealth of the region
as well as its historic importance has made scholarship an act of
acquisition in the grossest way. Second, Orientalism is still far from
the roots of the Middle East problem. Recent attempts to streamline
Orientalism with contemporary techniques, for example, psychoanalysis, have merely increased complicity in the mythology of the
Oriental, his mind, race, and character. What is clearly lacking is
a serious attempt to recognize the dialectic between Orientalist and

Oriental, as well as the restorative dialectic by which the Oriental asserts his actuality over the Orientalist.[18]

The value of such events as the October war, which came as a volcanic surprise after a long period of apparent stagnation and consolidation, is that they run counter to the prevailing, and grossly inadequate, system of ideas. The whole point of the mythology I have been discussing is that in its detail, as much as in its global structure, it denied the Arabs a possibility for any sort of action. Vatikiotis visited Egypt in early 1973 and saw what he wanted to see: a sort of emblem of Oriental despondency. The army, he said, was "in a state of high combat readiness, I would suggest for military *in*action"; the regime was dependent "on the condition of no war no peace." [19] No matter what one thinks of Anwar Sadat's political tactics since the war, there can be no gainsaying the fact that his people moved *from inaction to action.* It is precisely this rupture of continuity which Vatikiotis, Orientalism, and their joint myths, cannot account for.

Until the last third of the eighteenth century, it was uniformly believed that the origin of language and culture was the Middle East. Significantly, proofs for this among Christian scholars and thinkers were linguistic for the most part. The argument was that since the Bible was the Word of God, and since the Bible originated in the Middle East, then Hebrew was the first language, and Adam, Abraham, and Christ the direct genealogical parents of modern man. The human community, barring primitive tribes in Africa and America, was a dynastic result of a first Word, a first place, and a first man. Hebrew and Arabic, along with other Semitic dialects, were connected to each other and with a vague place and time signifying the origin of

18. As Frantz Fanon put it in describing a parallel situation: "It is the white man who creates the Negro. But it is the Negro who creates negritude" (Fanon, *A Dying Colonialism*, trans. Haakon Chevalier [New York: Grove Press, 1967], p. 47). For a more recent analysis of the relationship between Arab and Westerner in common myths, see Sadek G. al-Azm, *Naqd al-thaty ba'd al-hazima* (Beirut, 1969).

19. Vatikiotis, "Egypt Adrift: A Study in Disillusion," *New Middle East*, no. 54 (Mar. 1973), p. 10. See also his hostility to Jacques Berque—stated on the basis of Berque's "ideological" approach, Vatikiotis being of course beyond ideology—in "The Modern History of Egypt Alla Franca," *Middle Eastern Studies*, X, no. 1 (Jan. 1974), 80-92.

knowledge and man.[20] Orientalists were antiquarians and/or biblical scholars like Richard Simon. Thus the Orient (or at least the Near Orient) was, until the late eighteenth century, a religious domain.

In a period of fifty years (1780-1830), a significant change in the intellectual climate of Europe took place. A large part of this change had to do with the discrediting of such notions as that of the first language spoken by men. Also, the discovery of much older and more sophisticated languages than Hebrew—Sanskrit in particular—caused an extraordinary shift in the conception of history and language. During the first twenty years of the nineteenth century, comparative philology was born as a discipline. With the work of Bopp, the two Schlegels, Wilhelm von Humboldt, Grimm, and their disciples, the discovery of the Orient, especially Hindu thought and culture, created a revolution in European knowledge.

This is an enormously complicated change to describe, and no one has done it better and in greater detail than Raymond Schwab in his *La Renaissance orientale*.[21] The change might be described briefly as the replacing of a dynastic idea of human language, culture, and knowledge with a communal, comparative, pluralistic view. Whereas formerly a line could be traced from the language given by God to Adam in Eden, through such events as the building of the Tower of Babel, down to Latin and the European vernaculars, the New Philologists of the early nineteenth century instead distinguished families of languages whose univocal origin, they admitted, could never be discovered. Etymologies of words leading back to Hebrew now seemed like fanciful, unscientific exercises. The New Philologist was interested in the structure of a language, not in the derivation of all words from one Word. Instead of being a religious issue, language became a linguistic issue, properly speaking, and thereafter a political and philosophic one.[22]

The new science of comparative grammar grouped languages into families with very distinct identities. The importance of Sanskrit, moreover, was that it taught linguists that no necessary connection could be assumed between the age and the simplicity of a language.

---

20. This is true of Dante in *De vulgari eloquentia*, which sets forth the canonical view. For the situation in the sixteenth and seventeenth centuries, see D. C. Allen, "Some Theories of the Growth and Origin of Language in Milton's Age," *Philological Quarterly*, XXVIII, no. 1 (Jan. 1949), 5-16.

21. (Paris: Payot, 1950).

22. See Edward Said, "Language as Imagination and Method," in *The Legacy of Structuralism: Polymorphic Criticism*, ed. Carl A. Rubino and Josue Harari (Baltimore: The Johns Hopkins Press, 1975).

Compared with Hebrew or Greek, for instance, Sanskrit was not only older but had a more highly developed grammar and grammatical tradition. Therefore, within the linguistic, and hence the cultural, families, the New Philologist postulated a skeletal *beginning* language—a kind of ideal type—whose structural, phonological, and syntactic features were shared by each individual language in the group. During the space of about thirty years in the early nineteenth century, European philology had identified and described the Indo-European, the Semitic, the Slavic, the Germanic language families. Among these families the Indo-European attracted the most attention, since for the first time it was possible to see the connection between the farther, older Orient and Europe.

Now European scholars vied for the honor of showing how *their* languages carried the Indo-European spirit most faithfully. The burning question of the day, intellectually and politically, was the hierarchy of languages and cultures within and without the great linguistic-cultural groupings. Not only does this question coincide in time with the growing interest in definitions of cultural and national genius; it also corresponds to a moment when the enthusiasm for linguistic discovery allowed such brilliant men as von Humboldt to identify linguistic structure with mental structure. Thereafter the debate about language included such problems as the comparative study of levels of intellect and culture attainable by any given national group, the priority and value accorded one culture and language over another, the attempt to provide typologies of mind based on general characteristics of linguistic structure. Central to those discussions then were theories of *comparative* cultural and linguistic value. Value was now defined, not by temporal priority (Which was the first language?), but by relative and congruent priority (Which language most approaches perfection? and, conversely, Which culture and national character have achieved or may achieve the "highest" development, given the universal laws binding together all human societies and cultures and languages?).

Inevitably such questions led to full-fledged racism. This too is a little-remarked episode in the history of modern regional studies, but it is of major importance. Both before and during the discovery of the Orient the basic anthropological attitude of European writers was staunchly ethnocentric. There is little doubt that Europe was the center of the world, and consequently one finds no sensitivity to the uniqueness of a foreign culture. While learned men appreciated the particular quality of a distant culture, the prevailing feeling was that the Orient constituted a region for Europe to discover, cherish, speculate upon.

The single most impressive work produced as a more or less direct result of the Oriental discoveries of this period, von Humboldt's *Über die Verschiedenheit des menschlichen Sprachbaues und ihren Einfluss auf die geistige Entwickelung des Menschengeschlechts* (1836),[23] exudes an expansive pluralistic air when it comes to mankind and what Goethe had called the concert of nations and civilization. Von Humboldt asserts repeatedly that all languages and civilizations have intrinsic value, since each contributes something to the general good of mankind as a whole. Nevertheless, von Humboldt quite specifically draws an evaluative distinction between inferior and superior kinds of languages and minds. The more impressive, he says, are synthetic languages, which have organic form (Sanskrit, Indo-European generally), whereas the less impressive are agglutinative languages, which merely add and subtract letters (Semitic mainly).[24]

A careful reading of von Humboldt's linguistics suggests that language and mind are interchangeable. Thus, a judgment in favor of one language is also an esteeming of that language's nation and race. Although because of his generous humanism von Humboldt wished to mute or even deny it, such a conclusion could logically be seen in the New Philology that he and a whole generation of European thinkers espoused.

From the point of view of Orientalism the crucial text is Ernest Renan's major philogoical work, the *Histoire générale et système comparé des langues semitiques,* which he wrote in 1847, near the beginning of his career. He states in the 1855 preface that he projected the study as doing for the Semitic languages what Bopp had done for the Indo-European languages. Renan's models were, in addition to Bopp, all those German *philologen* whose ranks included and were to include Wolf, August Boekh, Schleiermacher, Strauss, and Nietzsche. For these men, philology was the study of a language as the synthetic, sympathetic, historistic total of an entire culture. In the very first chapter Renan delivers himself of opinions which, were they to have come from almost any other writer of the century, would have been dismissed as the rankest prejudice. Semites, he begins

23. I have used the Prussian Academy edition of von Humboldt's *Gesammelte Schriften,* ed. Albert Leitzmann (Berlin: Behr, 1903-36), in this case vol. VII (1907), pt. 1.

24. The distinction had been made more insistently by Friedrich von Schlegel in his *Philosophie der Sprache und des Wortes* (1828-29), and the view rapidly gained currency. See the *Kritische Friedrich-Schlegel-Ausgabe,* ed. Ernest Behler (Munich: Verlag Ferdinand Schöningh, 1969), vol. X.

his long series of qualifications, are strangers to science and philosophy; in comparison with the Indo-European race, Semites "represente une combinaison inférieure de la nature humaine"; Semites have neither the high spiritualism of the Indians or the Germans, nor the sense of perfect measure and beauty willed by Greece to the neo-Latin nations, nor the delicate and profound sensibility of the Celtic peoples; Semites have a clear consciousness, but it is not a wide one, and they are incapable of a sense of multiplicity; the Semites never produced a mythology nor an epic literature; they are a fundamentally monotheistic people and hence fanatically intolerant; they do not have a creative imagination; Semites never produced sculpture or painting; the Semitic genius is incapable of either discipline or subordination; morally speaking, the Semite acknowledges duties only toward himself.

The climax of these descriptions comes when Renan avers that the Semites never produced a civilization as "we" understand that word: incapable of organizing empires, possessing no commerce, no public spirit, the Semitic peoples produced one sort of society only, that of the tent and of the tribe. And what is more, Semitic civilization is so limited as always to repeat itself, always to remain exactly the same.[25] Lastly,

> one sees that in all things the Semitic race appears to us to be an incomplete race by virtue of its simplicity. This race—if I dare use the analogy—is to the Indo-European family what a pencil sketch is to painting; it lacks the variety, that amplitude, that abundance of life which is the condition of perfectibility. Like those individuals who possess so little fecundity that, after a gracious childhood, they attain only the most mediocre virility, the Semitic nations experienced their fullest flowering in their first age and have never been able to achieve true maturity.[26]

We read similar structures, given more strident racialist expression, in the work of Gobineau, Renan's contemporary, a quasi Orientalist and scholar whom Renan cites in later editions of his Semitic philology. Gobineau does not coat the "truths" he expresses: the white race is superior; if there is any virtue to be seen among the brown or mixed races, it is because they have had white mixed in. In the *Essai sur l'inégalité des races humaines* Gobineau seems to treat the Semites

25. Ernest Renan, *Histoire générale et système comparé des langues semitiques*, 3d ed. (Paris: Michel Levy Freres, 1863), pp. 13–17.

26. *Ibid.*, p. 17 (the translation here, as in all the quotations from Renan, is mine). Renan's view is softened somewhat in his "Mahomet et les origines de l'islamisme," *La Revue des Deux Mondes*, Dec. 15, 1851.

with a little more respect than Renan did;[27] but that is because he sees whites and Semites closer together than Renan saw Semites and Indo-Europeans. What should be said plainly, however, is that both Renan and Gobineau, as well as later Orientalists, treat the Semites as perpetually determined by their simple origins. Linguistically such a treatment makes some slight sense, since Semitic is built around an omnipresent triliteral root and since after their early flourishing Semitic languages never underwent radical change or development. But from that to judge *the race* unvaryingly as a repetition of one simple fact amounts to an unconscionable intellectual failure.

It scarcely needs pointing out that what Renan and Gobineau say about the Semites is practically identical with what one finds in works by the modern Orientalists I discussed above. Indeed, the central distinction carried forward by generation after generation of Orientalists is that the Semites remained at the origin, whereas the West grew away and beyond it. If we add to this notion the very real sociopolitical dominance exerted by Europe over the Orient, we see that the distinction became institutionalized. It accommodates equally the scholarly enterprise of the learned investigator, the political and economic organization of the colonizer or multinational corporation, and the racial bias of the anthropologist. Semitic simplicity, by which both Renan and the twentieth-century Orientalist mean that it is possible to reduce the inconceivable variety of all (and especially Semitic) existence to a univocal set of features, is not only a canonical belief but also *a practice,* just as saying that blacks have a natural sense of rhythm is a belief and a practice: in other words, a myth. One treats the words as if they were true and converts one's own words into a method for giving reality one's own sovereign imprint. All instances of behavior are reduced to an endlessly recurrent feature, as when Henry Ford said of all history that it was bunk.

The Moroccan scholar Abdullah Laroui recently did a brilliant retrospective analysis of Gustave von Grunebaum's Orientalism using precisely the motif of reductive repetition in von Grunebaum's work as a practical tool of critical anti-Orientalist study. Laroui's case on the whole is impressively managed. He asks himself what it is that causes von Grunebaum's work, certainly among the most scholarly and detailed of that by contemporary Arabists, to remain reductive. Thus, Laroui says, "the adjectives that von Grunebaum affixes to the word Islam (medieval, classical, modern) are neutral or even

27. Comte de Gobineau, *Essai sur l'inégalité des races humaines* (Paris: Firmin-Didot, 1940), I, 225–365.

superfluous: there is no difference between classical Islam and medieval Islam or Islam plain and simple. . . . There is therefore [for von Grunebaum] only *one* Islam that changes within itself." [28] Modern Islam, according to von Grunebaum, has turned away from the West because it remains faithful to its original sense of itself; and yet Islam can only modernize itself by a self-reinterpretation from a Western point of view. Because of von Grunebaum's wide influence, his conclusions, which add up to a portrait of Islam as a culture incapable of innovation without the use of Western methods, have become almost a truism in Middle Eastern studies. [29]

Laroui's analysis shows how von Grunebaum employed A. L. Kroeber's culturalist theory to understand Islam, and how this tool necessarily entails a series of reductions and eliminations by which Islam is represented as a closed system of exclusions. Thus, each of the many diverse aspects of Islamic culture could be seen by von Grunebaum as a direct reflection of an unvarying matrix, a particular theory of God, that compelled them all into meaning and order. Development, history, tradition, reality in Islam are interchangeable. Laroui correctly maintains that history as a complex order of events, temporalities, and meanings cannot be reduced backward to such a notion of culture, in the same way that culture cannot be reduced to ideology, nor ideology to theology. Von Grunebaum has fallen prey to a particular feature of Islam, that there is to be found in it a highly articulated theory of religion and yet very few accounts of religious experience, a highly articulate political theory and few precise political documents, a theory of social structure and very few individualized actions, a theory of history and very few dated events, an articulated theory of economics and very few quantified series, and so on. [30] The net result, except for von Grunebaum's extraordinarily brilliant accounts of Islamic theories of articulation (poetry, grammar, and so on), is a historical vision of Islam entirely hobbled by a theory of the culture incapable of doing justice to, or examining, its existential reality in the experience of its adherents.

So deeply entrenched is the theory and practice of Semitic simplicity

28. "Pour une méthodologie des études islamiques: L'Islam au miroir de G. von Grunebaum," *Diogene*, no. 83 (July–Sept. 1973), p. 30.

29. David Gordon, for example, urges "maturity" on Arabs, Africans, and Asians. He argues that this can only be gained by learning from Western objectivity. See Gordon, *Self-Determination and History in the Third World* (Princeton: Princeton University Press, 1971).

30. Laroui, "Pour une méthodologie," p. 41.

that it operates with little defferentiation in well-known anti-Semitic European writings (*The Protocols of the Elders of Zion,* for example) as well as in such remarks as these by Chaim Weizmann to Arthur Balfour on May 30, 1918:

> The Arabs who are superficially clever and quick-witted, worship one thing, and one thing only—power and success. . . . The British authorities . . . knowing as they do the treacherous nature of the Arabs . . . have to watch carefully and constantly. . . . The fairer the English regime tries to be, the more arrogant the Arab becomes. . . . The present state of affairs would necessarily tend toward the creation of an Arab Palestine, if there were an Arab people in Palestine. It will not in fact produce that result because the fellah is at least four centuries behind the times, and the effendi . . . is dishonest, uneducated, greedy, and as unpatriotic as he is inefficient.[31]

The common denominator between Weizmann and the European anti-Semite is the Orientalist perspective, seeing Semites (or subdivisions thereof) as by nature lacking the desirable qualities of Occidentals. Yet the difference between Renan and Weizmann is that the latter had already gathered behind his rhetoric the solidity of institutions while the former had not as yet. Is there not in twentieth-century Orientalism that same unaging "gracious childhood"—heedlessly allied now with scholarship, now with a state and all its institutions— that Renan saw as the Semites' unchanging mode of being?

Yet with what greater harm has the twentieth-century version of the myth been maintained. It has produced a picture of the Arab as seen by an "advanced" quasi-occidental society. The Palestinian is either a stupid savage or a negligible quantity, morally and even existentially. According to Israeli law only a Jew has full civic rights and unqualified immigration privileges; Arabs are given lesser, more simple rights because they are less developed. Orientalism governs Israeli policy toward the Arab throughout. There are good Arabs (the ones who do as they are told) and bad Arabs (terrorists, who fit the picture the nineteenth-century anthropologists had of black savages in Africa for whom merciless punishment was paternal admonishment). Most of all, as the months before the October war testified, there were all those Arabs who, once defeated, could be expected to sit obediently behind an infallibly fortified line, manned by the smallest

31. Doreen Ingrams, *Palestine Papers, 1917-1922* (London: John Murray, 1972), pp. 31-32.

possible number of men, on the theory that Arabs have had to accept the myth of Israeli superiority and would never dare attack. One need only glance through the pages of Harkabi's magnum opus, that pathetically large collection of bias and racism dressed up as scholarship, to see how—as Robert Alter put it admiringly in *Commentary*[32]—"the Arab mind," depraved, anti-Semitic to the core, violent, unbalanced, could only produce rhetoric and little more. One myth supports and produces another. They answer each other, tending toward symmetries and patterns of the sort that as Orientals the Arabs themselves can be expected to produce, but as a man no Arab can afford: Israelis and Jews are superior, Watergate was a Zionist conspiracy, the CIA runs the Middle East.

As a set of beliefs and as a method of analysis, Orientalism cannot develop. Indeed, it is the doctrinal antithesis of development. Its central argument is the myth of the arrested development of the Semites. From this matrix other myths pour forward, each of them showing the Semite to be in opposition to a Westerner, and irremediably the victim of his own weaknesses. By a concatenation of events and circumstances known to most Arabs, the Semitic myth bifurcated in the Zionist movement. One Semite went the way of Orientalism and the other, the Arab, was forced the way of the Oriental. Each time "tent and tribe" are solicited, the myth is being employed; each time the concept of Arab national character is evoked, the myth is being employed. The hold these instruments have on the mind is increased by the institutions built around them. For every Orientalist, quite literally, there is a support system of staggering power, considering the ephemerality of the myths that Orientalism propagates. In order to write the kind of thing turned out by Middle East experts, one needs universities, institutes, teachers, other students, dozens of periodicals, an enormous clientele, armies, air forces, police. One should remember that Orientalism is as difficult a discourse to produce or maintain as that of clinical medicine, with its support system in the universities, the laboratories, the pharmaceutical companies, the societies, the state institutions. The myth is no mere chance effusion. It is a way of *being there: there* to be used when Orientals demand the justice and equality to which all men are entitled, *there* to beat back Orientals to a tent or an "endogamous family," *there* to drum out the chorus of Oriental depravity, rhetoric, vindictiveness, and underdevelopment. We must now ask what sort of will to power *over* Orientalism is necessary.

32. "Rhetoric and the Arab Mind," *Commentary*, XLVI, no. 4 (Oct. 1968), 61–65.

DEALING WITH THE MYTHS

It is no use opposing facts to myths, since, as Dwight Macdonald once showed, facts can be myths too. The price of the October war, with regard to the myths of the incompetent Arab, was not a simple fact disproving the old myths and proving that Arabs can be good fighters, can develop, etc. That is an ingenuous belief, since what really happens is that such "factual" challenges to the myths cause their break-up in order for a new, more adequate set to re-form.

Of the several problems seriously provoked by the war, the most pertinent to this analysis is that of devising a set of analytic instruments capable of responding first to the old and then to the re-formed myths. If we oppose "reality" to myths, then the burden of formulating reality falls very heavily upon us as demythifiers. In any case, there is no such thing as plain, or unadorned, or brute, or naïve reality. Every reality is a potential item of meaning; and since human perception is the act of making meaning, then *how* meaning is made—since it *is* made, never merely given—becomes the crucial question. Orientalism has been the chief producer of meaning, intellectually speaking, with regard at least to the relation between the Arabs and the rest of the world. If that set of myths is to be changed, as I believe it must, how and with what instruments can this be done? In response to this question, I shall argue for the need to develop a critical theory of Arab reality—a theory that substitutes self-consciousness for unconsciousness.

Theory can be abstract, but it is not abstraction *tout court*. As I understand it, *critical* theory is a way of producing reality and meaning, *not* as an engineer produces a blueprint, but as a fully conscious intelligence creatively perceives that combination of phenomena we call reality: historical, moral, effective, and self-definitional. Unfortunately, there is not a single institution in the Arab world today devoted exclusively either to the critical study of Arab contemporaneity or to the study of the West, the chief foreign participant, politically and economically, in modern Arab history. To be sure, there are numerous technical, social, and purely scientific institutes; there are institutes for the study of particular problems; there are groups for strategic, corporate, industrial, economic, and management research. But there is no institution devoted to the study of either foreign or local values and value-systems, nor to the critical theory of Arab or Western society, nor to the various processes by which historical actuality is produced.

All reading and writing is distortion, or at least de-formation. The difference between mythological reading and writing (Orientalism) and demythification (critical theory) is that the former pretends to have no theory, to be "scientific" factual reporting, whereas the latter openly admits its theoretical and even interested methods, for its premise is that society is process, and that the role of critical theory is to participate in that process, not to reify it into stable characteristics (like "tent and tribe," for example). Myths never go away of their own accord: they must be disassembled into the interests they serve but whose presence they always hide. Conversely, we must be able to show that a myth displaces something in addition to producing a particular meaning of its own. The immediate task, then, is to understand generally how meaning is produced—for it is a process taking place in a field of play—and *what* precisely it is that the myth has displaced which can then stand forth plainly.

In the case of the Orientalist myth, we can say that what it displaces is what it has reduced to the concept of "tent and tribe." Instead of seeing a whole web of Arab societies, cultures, realities, the myth volunteers one key to all mysteries and says, "This is all the Arab really is; do not be misled by his apparent modernity; it all comes down to tent and tribe. His temperament and character, now and always, are as follows." What enables us to deal with a myth such as this is not merely a gesturing at "humanism" or appeals to the rich traditions of the Islamic world. Rather, it is knowledge of how in fact Orientalism *works;* and the way we know that is by studying it in the context of other systems like it. Whereas mythological thought is *impertinent* (it pretends that certain statements, images, descriptions are natural when in fact they are made up; it pretends that words are not "only" words but the real thing), critical theory argues that all meaning and value-systems are man-made, have a provenance, and are cultural, and that nature is not a maker of sense but that men in society and history are. Moreover, it argues that all meaning has an intention, or what I have been calling a theory.

There is no meaning plain and simple; all meaning from the beginning is intended by who and whatever makes it.[33] Thus, if I say that "the Arabs must develop," I must also realize that I cannot intend very much when I say that unless I also specify for what they must develop, how they develop, and, indeed, what *develop* itself means. If I refuse to do that and content myself with repetitions

33. I have discussed this as a theoretical problem in *Beginnings: Intention and Method* (New York: Basic Books, 1975).

of *development*, then I stop the word from intending anything (and stopping it is an intention all its own, rather like the Orientalist myth). To stop the word is to deny that development is a process of a very specifiable sort, that it does take place in a multitude of possible ways, that it has a whole range of effects (all ascertainable) and a whole range of dialectical consequences (for example, if I develop a market economy, then the government must be of *this* sort).

All this is not very difficult. The truly important and difficult part is a method for describing the units of meaning and their relations with each other. The universality of intention needs first to be recognized; one cannot do that unselfconsciously, nor can that be left to chance. Thus everything making up contemporaneity must be envisaged as conveying—indeed, embodying—a definite man-made intention, or perspective, if you like. Clearly, the Orientalist who saw the immediate pre-October period and concluded that the Arabs were preparing for inaction saw only his own perspective, that of the observer to whom all Arabs are an endless confirmation of one or two terminal features like laziness or abstraction. If the perspective were not that of the mythologist, he might perhaps have read Naguib Mahfouz's 1973 novel, *Hub Taht il Mattar,* and recognized the kinds of processes taking place that only a novelist can *intend* and which perhaps may not have predicted a war but only confirmed a social actuality more dynamic than not.[34] That is, he would have realized that for any assessment to be worthy of the name, it would have to adumbrate the field in which the Arab lived, and that that field included a whole range of movement which was the opposite of retrograde Arab laziness or irrationality.

Since a people is at least as complex a thing as a literary text, we may say that to understand contemporaneity, we must at least be able to *read* it. Reading is decoding, or decipherment; even in one's own language what one reads is in fact a new foreign language being made, an idiolect.

The mental gymnastics imposed on any deciphering of a foreign language text, ancient or modern, is healthy training in the understanding of any *human context*, in that *understanding* characteristic of the humani-

---

34. It is the great virtue of some scholars to have attempted analyses based precisely upon those humanistic and literary elements that make up the more intimate, actual part of contemporary Arab culture. As instances, there are H. A. R. Gibb's studies, especially those collected in his *Studies on the Civilization of Islam* (London: Routledge & Kegan Paul, 1962); Jacques Berque's *Les Arabes d'hier à demain* (Paris: Seuil, 1960); and Albert Hourani's *Arabic Thought in the Liberal Age 1789-1932* (Oxford: Oxford University Press, 1962).

ties. This effort is of a particular kind, quite different from the procedure in mathematics in which one deduces consequences from a few, very simple axioms which have been isolated from the whole of reality. In any deciphering one is faced with a whole network of difficulties which present themselves in a lump at the same time: words, word-meanings, constructions, in themselves perhaps known to us, must be fitted together into that unique mosaic which alone makes sense—and, in addition (and this is again quite different from mathematics, which, once it has left the realm of outward reality, need not return to it), the particular outward situation described in the text may be unknown to us: the meaning of the text may become clear not by the *Sprachgefühl* for the particular language alone, but only by the additional application of our general experience which may tell us which word-meaning and which constructions might fit the outward situation described in the text.[35]

It seems to me apt to take this paragraph as a guide for decoding not only the verbal language of a society but also its people and objects; all of them are produced, but it is the sensitive attitude that sees them as *producing themselves* that principally delivers the decoder, or reader, from the tyranny of myths. Myths, after all, seem never to have been produced; still less can a mythological object like "the Arabs" appear to be more than a product of univocal traits and an undifferentiated sexual urge. If we take Arab contemporaneity as *being produced*, then everything in it has meaning, has intention, has theory whose sense and direction we can decode. But only if it is conceded that every meaning inhabits a context and does not take place in a vacuum can we maintain the dynamic perspective to keep myths at bay.

What I am advocating as a replacement for the mythical, reified discourse of Orientalism is the collaborative articulation of a theory for investigating (reading) the native forces giving Arab society (or societies) their specific identity (identities). No one person can do this alone. But the common attitude shared by critics must be that the tendency of myths is to reduce, stop, make everything monochromatic, whereas theory reveals the plurality of forces, their fields, their dialectic connections. And only by acknowledging the undisputable conviction that men *can* act consciously, intentionally, with a theoretical grasp of their world, will the work be done.[36]

35. Leo Spitzer, "Language—The Basis of Science, Philosophy and Poetry," in *Studies in Intellectual History* (Baltimore: Johns Hopkins University, History of Ideas Club, 1953), p. 82.

36. This is the thesis proposed by Georg Lukács in *History and Class Consciousness*, trans. Rodney Livingstone (London: Merlin Press, 1971), pp. 83-222.

In large measure, as I have been using the word *theory* I have also been implying *hypothesis*. For it is impossible for any person or persons to hope to grasp every particular of any given situation; this hope is the positivist pretense. When one has a healthy respect for the vast range of detail conveyed by a written text, how much more will his respect increase for the sheer wealth of detail expressed by a society? Yet the irrationalist attitude that says, "We can never know," is no answer either. Theory proposes a possible general framework for the tendencies that can be verified by the research I have been describing. As the results develop, the framework alters. But the very proposal of a theoretical framework is an act of will asserted against myths saying that "this, and only this, is Arab society."

The October war itself now seems like an act of theoretical will. To the extent that armies were ordered out of inaction, there must have been a general theoretical possibility that successful action might prove actual. The limited military gains of the war need not be the only gains: we can match the war's strictly material gains with an intellectual hostility to the myths (like the Bar Lev line) supposedly confining Arabs to "tent and tribe." The effort, although different in kind, must be no less great, and it must be far more successful. Two safeguards against mere theory-spinning are (1) an exhaustive attention at the beginning paid to determining the material for study, and (2) a concentration upon those activities in Arab society by which knowledge is transmitted, institutionalized, acted upon, preserved, reactivated, discarded.[37]

In the first place, too many recent studies passing themselves off as emanating from the social sciences avoid the problems presented by the absence in Islamic tradition of a developed reportorial or confessional or autobiographical literature. Thus, anyone seeking to study child-rearing practices, say, in northern Syria, must reckon that his informants (if he is not to rely exclusively upon what he can directly observe, which cannot be very much) can answer questions, but that they probably cannot formulate answers of the sort that would get at the essence of what in fact they do or think about child-rearing. Their answers are answers *for* the questions; they are made for those questions, which in turn necessarily impose the investigator's own training upon the material. This is a problem faced constantly by ethnographers. In the Arab context, it has been the case that the very muteness in the tradition vis-à-vis personal experience licenses the

37. For an elucidation, see Michel Foucault, "Response à une question," *Esprit*, no. 5 (May 1968), 850–74.

kind of impositions I associated with the Orientalist discourse. Therefore, critical theory must devote itself initially to this problem, and
to articulating a nuanced praxis for the definition of problems and
materials from within, or in some way out of, the cultural field itself.[38]

In the second place (and here I can only touch upon a truly vast
subject), every society has a systematically organized, although not
necessarily fully conscious, way of dealing with knowledge—of itself,
of the world, of the past, of the future and present. At certain moments
one can notice, for example, that certain figures and their teachings
from the past are reactivated, certain others discarded, certain others
altered in a particular way. The fame of a given poet or statesman
is a social reality which, in political discourse for instance, is drawn
upon and fashioned for a particular use. Similarly, in any culture
believing itself different from another (for example, Egypt as different
from England or from Syria) there is a tendency to make those
differences by absorbing certain kinds of knowledge and rejecting
certain others. How does this happen, and in what ways, in what
circumstances? By what peculiar concert of forces does this become
possible? Why is a certain type of expression considered more appropriate than another? The investigation would have to specify the place
from which answers are sought, the kind (not just the number) of
frequency and recurrence with which that knowledge turns up, and
so on. In other words, what needs examination is the value-system
by which something—say, a name or a slogan—appears correct and
another incorrect. Or even more interesting, how does a culture at
any given moment identify itself with sanity, and, by implication,
how does it formulate its notion of what is insane or irrational?[39]

These are some of the methods that can challenge the mythical
discourse that has been for so long a blight upon Arab self-knowledge
and self-making. The great lesson of the October war is that one
can take one's fate in one's own hands; this alone, as Vico and Marx
were among the first to realize, restores men to their history and
puts a distance between them and those myths about them that have
closed off their historical actuality. Every myth today speaks as if
what it says cannot be contradicted and as if there is nothing more
to be said. Yet once men know that no reality in history need be

38. I have discussed this in my "Al-tamanu' wal-tajanub wal-ta-'aruf," *Mawaqif*,
nos. 19-20 (Mar. 1972).

39. See Foucault, *Folie et deraison: Histoire de la folie à l'âge classique* (Paris:
Plon, 1961), and *Les Mots et les choses: Une archeologie des sciences humaines* (Paris:
Gallimard, 1966).

final—and this is not the same as saying pejoratively that Arabs cannot face reality—their consciousness is transformed from that of an object into that of the producing subject. The October war is but one among many perhaps less dramatic opportunities for changing Arab status from that of object to that of subject. A war finally determines nothing; at bottom it is only violence. What is most needed is the intellectual equivalent of the war, which is sustained antimythological, self-conscious thought.

Ayad Al-Qazzaz

IMAGES OF THE ARAB IN AMERICAN SOCIAL SCIENCE TEXTBOOKS

MANY STUDIES HAVE SOUGHT to investigate the sources of prejudice and stereotypes concerning ethnic and minority groups. It has been disclosed that the mass media of communication, including newspapers, novels, movies, radio, and television, are among the important factors involved in prejudice and negative stereotyping. To varying degrees, these media have both supported and reiterated negative stereotypes.[1]

Outside the sphere of mass media, social science and history textbooks have also been found to transmit distorted information concerning national, ethnic, and minority groups.[2] As far back as 1911, there was concern about the treatment of blacks in school textbooks.[3] Subsequent research revealed that expressions of bias permeated the textbook treatment of not only blacks but also American

---

A list of textbooks reviewed is to be found at the end of this paper. References to these works will be included within parentheses in the text. Each reference will give the appropriate code letter from the list and the page number of the material in question.

1. Gordon W. Allport, *The Nature of Prejudice* (Garden City, N.Y.: Doubleday, 1954), pp. 195–96.

2. Some social scientists argue that the transmission of antiminority literature in textbooks is related more to the American cultural tradition of prejudice than to any malicious intent on the part of textbook authors. See *ibid.*, p. 196; and George E. Simpson and J. Milton Yinger, *Racial and Cultural Minorities: An Analysis of Prejudice and Discrimination*, 4th ed. (New York: Harper & Row, 1972), chap. 5.

3. E. A. Johnson, *A School History of the Negro Race in America* (New York: Goldman, 1911).

Indians and Chinese. Bias was found also in accounts of American foreign relations and in material about Asia, Latin America, and even England.[4] In 1949 the American Council on Education published the results of a survey of over 300 textbooks which revealed that many of them perpetuated negative stereotypes.[5] Specifically, immigrants, Spanish Americans, Asiatics, and, to a larger degree, blacks received unfavorable treatment. Although some educators believe that there has been a considerable improvement in American textbooks over the years, a 1967 report by the National Education Association declares that "massive distortions continue in many textbooks."[6] More recently (1969), a controversy developed in California concerning school textbooks, and a special task force was established to evaluate new social science textbooks designed for use in lower (fourth to eighth) grades. The task force report condemned these textbooks on the grounds that they transmitted distorted information about minority group life which could result in a minority group child's rejection of his (her) ethnic identity.[7]

With reference to Middle East peoples, studies in this volume and elsewhere reveal that the portrayal of Arabs in the American daily newspapers and other media has been disparaging and stereotypical.[8] More research is needed in order to understand the social and institutional dynamics involved in the perpetuation of such images. In particular, there is a dearth of systematic research concerning the ways in which Arabs are portrayed in American social science textbooks. This research area is significant, partly because of the predomi-

4. See, for example, Bessie L. Pierce, *Civic Attitudes in American School Textbooks* (Chicago: University of Chicago Press, 1930); and Charles Altschul, *The American Revolution in Our School Textbooks* (New York: Doran, 1916).

5. *Intergroup Relations in Teaching Materials* (Washington, D.C.: American Council on Education, 1949).

6. National Education Association, "The Treatment of Minorities in Textbooks," *School and Society,* XCV (1967), 323.

7. See *Los Angeles Times,* Dec. 10, 1971.

8. See, among others, Michael W. Suleiman, "An Evaluation of Middle East News Coverage in Seven American Newsmagazines," *Middle East Forum,* XLI (Autumn 1965), 9–30; *idem,* "Mass Media and the June Conflict," in *The Arab-Israeli Confrontation of June 1967: An Arab Perspective,* ed. Ibrahim Abu-Lughod (Evanston, Ill.: Northwestern University Press, 1970), pp. 138–54; Edward Said, "The Arab Portrayed," in *ibid.,* pp. 1–9; Janice Terry, "A Content Analysis of American Newspapers," in *The Arab World: From Nationalism to Revolution,* ed. Abdeen Jabara and Janice Terry (Wilmette, Ill.: Medina University Press International, 1971), pp. 94–113; and Ahmad Baha el-Din, "World Media and the Arabs: An Arab Perspective," in *ibid.,* pp. 77–85.

nant use of textbooks at all school levels, often to the exclusion of supplementary reading materials, and partly because of the influence which these textbooks have on pupils during the early years of formal education. This paper attempts to make a modest contribution in this research area. Specifically, it seeks to investigate the images of the Arab as found in social science textbooks used in both elementary and junior high schools in California and elsewhere in the United States.

PROCEDURE

This study is a content analysis of thirty-six social science textbooks that were in use in elementary and junior high schools in California during the academic year 1974–75. Included among these textbooks are those published by the California State Department of Education and used almost exclusively within the state, as well as those published by private publishers and used throughout the United States.

Portions of the textbooks dealing with Arabs or Arab societies were examined with particular attention to (1) pictures and maps, (2) adjectives used to characterize the Arabs, (3) transmission of inaccurate, distorted, or false information, and (4) omission of qualifying statements or information that may give a positive image of the Arabs.

In order to enhance the findings from this analysis, interviews were held with about twenty elementary and junior high school teachers in the Sacramento area to determine teaching methods and supplementary materials used, as well as to obtain personal assessments of the textbook treatment of Arabs. Significantly, the respondents who had teaching experience outside of California believed that there was a similarity in orientation between the California social science textbooks and the textbooks they had used in other states. This belief was supported by the results of our own comparative analysis of the treatment of the Arab in the textbooks used exclusively in California and in those which were used also in other states.

FINDINGS

In examining the images of the Arab as portrayed in textbooks, we will focus on three major topics often discussed in the materials under investigation: nomadism, Islam, and the Arab-Israeli conflict.

Nomadism

The nomadic element of Arab society is emphasized more than any other in all the textbooks that discuss the Arab. Not a single one failed to mention the camel, the desert, and the Bedouin. Up to grade four, students encounter the Arab either as a Bedouin or as a peasant. The following examples will illustrate this point. A first-grade textbook contains a colorful picture of two camels, one standing and one sitting, along with tents and a few other animals (*F*, 31), while a supplementary third-year textbook has a picture of several Bedouins riding camels in the Sahara Desert (*T*, 1). In addition, a third-year textbook, in discussing clothing worn in different parts of the world, shows a guide riding a camel near Cairo (*S*, 101). The second-grade textbook published by the California Department of Education uses a large colored picture of a tent-dwelling family eating from a common dinner pot with their hands to show how families live in different environments. The people are depicted as nomads, typically dressed, with palm trees and the open desert as landscape (*G*, 87). And finally, a fourth-grade textbook has 300 words about the Arabs, along with nine pictures depicting in detail the various primitive aspects of nomadic life (*C*, 126).

In all textbooks nomadic Arabs, who constitute between 5 and 8 percent of the total Arab population, receive much more space than their numbers would warrant. For example, one fourth-grade textbook includes forty-four pages of material on the world's deserts (*M*, 188–62). Of this, thirty-three pages with thirty-four pictures detail the life, environment, and animals of the nomadic Arabs. The text uses the term *Arab* without the qualifier *nomadic*, thereby injecting in the reader's mind the impression that the majority of Arabs are nomads. This wrong impression is further buttressed by the authors' description of Egypt as the largest oasis on earth. Of the thirty-four relevant pictures presented in this book, seven are of camels. This same textbook includes only one paragraph on the discovery of oil and does not discuss the changes that this has brought about; only one modern picture of oil pumps is presented. It is interesting to note that the authors of this textbook allocate much less space to deserts in other parts of the world than they allocate to the Sahara and Arabian deserts.

Similarly, a fifth-grade textbook includes seven pages of material on the nomads, of which six deal with their primitive life and less than one, with the recent changes taking place among them (*X*, sec. on Arab nomads). Other aspects of Arab society are excluded. The question section in this textbook focuses heavily on primitive aspects.

Several textbooks tend to emphasize the negative characteristics of the nomad, such as raiding and plundering, and to overlook such qualities as honesty and hospitality. A supplementary sixth-grade textbook speaks of the nomads as follows: "Through all their long history, the Bedouins have been fighting men, battling each other for the best pastures and robbing travelers crossing the desert. Mounted on swift horses they would swoop out on the desert waste to attack a caravan or another tribe. On raids of this kind they would ride their camels and lead their horses until the enemy was in sight. Then leaving the camels in the charge of one or more herdsmen, the Bedouin raiders would mount their horses and attack" (*FF*, 133-34). Another supplementary textbook for grades five to eight describes the Bedouins as "nomads that live in the deserts of Arabia. Food is scarce here. These people have been known to rob others for food" (*II*, 39). In a similar vein, another text states: "When [the Bedouins] went out on a raid, they changed from camels to horses and swooped down on unsuspecting rivals shouting and shooting, and rode off with their enemies' horses, if possible" (*D*, 394). A seventh-grade textbook speaks of the nomads in the following terms: "The men were fearless warriors, and they liked nothing better than to ride their wonderfully swift Arabian horses into a fight where there was hope of plundering caravans crossing the desert between Egypt and the Persian Gulf, which for thousands of years were preyed upon by Arab bandits" (*K*, 286, 291).

Most textbooks and supplements fail to mention the changes and development taking place among the nomads. The authors of a third-year supplementary textbook discuss four kinds of desert: the American, the Sahara, the Gobi, and the Australian (*T*, 45-73). They refer to changes taking place in all deserts except the Sahara. For example, in discussing the Gobi Desert, they state: "The world around the Gobi Desert is changing. . . . Mongols see big factories, large cities are growing around the factories. Schools are being built in the new cities (*T*, 65). Likewise, they mention the changes taking place in the American deserts, from building houses with electricity, air conditioning, and running water, to using the desert as a place to build and test rockets (*T*, 51). No mention is made of changes in the Sahara, although notable progress has been brought about by the discovery of large reserves of oil in Libya and Algeria.

None of the textbooks attempts to show that nomadism as a way of life is rapidly disappearing, as thousands of Bedouins each year are sedentarized as a result of encouragement from Arab governments or because of new employment opportunities both in agriculture and industry. Many of yesterday's Bedouins are drillers or machinists employed by the oil companies in Kuwait, Saudi Arabia, Libya, Iraq, and the emirates. The process of settlement has been accelerated by the growth of more strongly centralized governments and the impact of Western technology, especially the advent of the automobile, the airplane, and the radio, which has ended the earlier isolation of many areas. In Egypt, for example, whereas in 1892 the number of nomads was estimated at 250,000, at the beginning of the twentieth century there were only 80,000–100,000 tribesmen, and today the estimate is less than 30,000.[9] In Iraq the number of nomads was estimated to be over 600,000 in 1938, while today they number less than 150,000.[10]

The textbooks seldom mention projects Arab governments are undertaking among the nomads in the fields of education, health, agriculture, and industry. For example, miles and miles along both sides of the desert highway from Cairo to Alexandria are now cultivated as a result of sedentarization projects. None of the books refers to the Arab Development Society, created by Musa al-Alami in the 1950s, which turned hundreds of square miles of desert land into a garden and provided opportunities for Palestinian youths. Yet when these textbooks discuss the Arab Bedouins in Israel, they often describe in detail Israel's efforts to settle them and to improve their conditions.[11]

None of the textbooks tells the reader that the camel is a vanishing species. And few of the books mention the new modes of transportation in the desert, such as the railway that crosses the Sinai desert, the line connecting northern Sudan with Egypt and the Red Sea, the railway connecting Syria and Iraq, and the Hijaz railway.

In contrast to the material on the Sahara and Arabian deserts, discussions of the deserts in Israel always emphasize the achievement of the Israelis in transforming the desert into an oasis. A third-grade textbook describes Israeli accomplishments as follows: "About thirty years ago, a new nation [Israel] was founded in the desert lands of Asia. . . . When they [Jews] arrived in Israel, they saw the dry, desolate land. Little rain fell. Few people lived in the desert. The early pioneers built a community in the desert. They planted crops. They built homes. Slowly the desert became green (Z, 164–66). The author of this textbook provides the reader two pictures—one of the

---

9. Gabriel Baer, *Population and Society in the Arab East,* trans. Hanna Szoke (New York: Praeger, 1964), p. 129.

10. Tareq Y. Ismael, *Government and Politics in the Middle East* (Homewood, Ill.: Dorsey Press, 1970), p. 23.

11. For example, one textbook notes that the Israeli government "has made land grants to the Arab nomads of the southern desert and encouraged them to take up farming. . . . Many are finding houses more comfortable"(R, 58–59).

desert which the Jews discovered upon their arrival in Palestine, and the other of the achievement of the Israelis in making the desert bloom.

Another third-grade textbook describes Israel's achievement: "The Negev was a desert for thousands of years. Once it was thought no crops could be raised on this hot dry land. The people of Israel settled on the Negev. They tamed the desert by hard work, water and science (A, 130). The authors of a fifth-grade textbook state: "Israel is a nation of people who through imaginative thinking, careful planning and hard work are creating fertile farms and vineyards from desert wasteland and swamps. . . . . Never has a people worked harder, against greater odds, to rebuild a land which had become lifeless and barren because of centuries of neglect. But the people of Israel are meeting the challenge with vision and vigor and with the help of modern science they are transforming a desolate, empty land into a bustling productive nation" (R, 6, 7). A sixth-grade textbook states: "When Jewish immigrants arrived in Palestine in the early 1900's they found a land of deserts. They came to Palestine with little money and few resources. Facing the hardship of trying to make a desert a farmland, the immigrants grouped together" (H, 244). And a seventh-grade textbook includes the following: "A canal, a tunnel and pipeline carry water to the Negev desert country in the south making it possible to farm thousands of additional acres of land. This is a good example of what can be done to make desert areas useful" (V, 328).

All of these textbooks perpetuate the Zionist myth that the land of Palestine was a desert when the Jewish settlers arrived there. The historical evidence overwhelmingly contradicts this claim. Richard Bevis, professor of English at the American University of Beirut, quotes many European travelers who visited Palestine in the seventeenth, eighteenth, and nineteenth centuries, in order to demonstrate that "substantial parts of Palestine have long been fertile and productive." [12] Mark Twain visited Palestine as a tourist in 1867. Near Dan, above Lake Tiberias, he found himself "in a green valley, five or six miles wide and fifteen long. The streams which are called the sources of the Jordan flow through it to Lake Hule. The lake is surrounded by a broad marsh grown with reeds. Between the marsh and the mountains which wall the valley, toward Dan, as much as half of the land is solid fertile and watered by the Jordan's sources." [13]

12. "Making the Desert Bloom," *Middle East Newsletter*, V, no. 2 (Feb.-Mar. 1971), 2-7.

13. *The Innocents Abroad* (1869), Signet ed., p. 345.

None of these textbooks informs the reader that since 1955 the irrigation projects in the Negev desert have been found to be uneconomical but have been continued for military and political reasons. An American expert observes that "it was a serious mistake to draw water all the way from the Jordan to the Negev because this left unirrigated equally large areas of just as good land near the source of water." [14]

The overemphasis on Arab desert life undoubtedly gives the impression that the majority of Arabs are desert people. This incorrect belief is, in fact, quite common among students. In 1972 a student of mine, at my request, asked 251 students in junior and senior high schools in Davis and Woodland the following question:

What do you think of when you hear of the following people? Please write words to describe your image of these people.
1. Arab, 2. Turk, 3. Israeli, 4. Persian.
The responses concerning Arabs were as follows:

Description	Number
desert people	140
striking physically	30
war-engaged	26
poor	13
bad guys	11
stoic	9
exotic riches	8
same as any other Middle Easterner	7
religious	7

Thus the majority of these junior and senior high school students associate the whole Arab world with nomadism and life in the desert. When the same students were asked for the source of their information about the Arab, 80 percent responded, "textbooks" and "mass media."

Another student of mine who was also an elementary school teacher asked her students in the spring of 1973 to sketch an Arab and an Israeli. The Arab was always portrayed as a Bedouin with wide robes, while the Israeli was always portrayed as a Westerner wearing Western clothes.

14. Alex Rubner, *The Economy of Israel* (London: Frank Cass, 1960), pp. 114–15.

Islam

Most textbooks reviewed in this study use the term *Islam* to describe the religion of the majority of the Arabs. Several textbooks note parenthetically that Islam is "often mistakenly called Mohammedanism." Only two textbooks surveyed in this study used the term *Mohammedanism,* one being a fifth-grade supplementary and the other a seventh-grade textbook.[15] A sixth-grade textbook and a seventh-grade textbook used both terms, *Islam* and *Mohammedanism,* interchangeably (*E; P*).

Most textbooks correctly, but briefly, explain the basic elements of Islam, including basic doctrine, the five elements of faith, and the five pillars. All of them give a short and oversimplified outline of Muhammad's life, his birth, childhood, marriage to a rich middle-aged widow, and his becoming a prophet. Several textbooks overemphasize the fact that he worked as a caravan driver. In almost all the textbooks surveyed, the reader encounters statements similar to this: "He traveled back and forth across the desert with his caravans." One textbook claims: "Once when Mohammed had gone alone into the desert to fast and pray, an angel came to him, he said, and ordered him to go forth to preach a new religion" (*Q,* 189). The authors of a seventh-grade textbook state that "as Mohammed traveled back and forth across the desert he thought much about religion" (*K,* 287). One textbook notes that "from time to time, Mohammed would withdraw from the city to quiet places in the desert" (*L,* 40).

Islamic contributions to world civilization are, on the whole, acknowledged in all textbooks. At times textbooks compare the crudeness of the crusaders with the high civilization of the Muslims. Most of the discussion, however, tends to be brief and oversimplified, possibly leaving the reader with the impression that it is not important. For instance, a seventh-grade textbook allocates less than 100 words to the Muslim contributions to world civilization (*B,* 88). Another seventh-grade textbook devotes only one paragraph to Islamic contributions (*W,* 152).

A few textbooks use words or adjectives which minimize the importance of Islamic contributions to world civilization. For example, one textbook notes that the "Islamic culture . . . was lacking creative genius for three centuries," and "the Arabs themselves were hardly

---

15. *Q, K.* The term *Mohammedanism* was coined by an Orientalist. It is both offensive and objectionable to the people who profess Islam because it suggests that Muhammad created the religion and that Muslims consider him as God.

more than rude conquerors or at best men of business and public affairs" (*GG*, 187–88). Another textbook attempts to minimize Muslim contributions to world civilization by accusing Muslims of burning the great library at Alexandria. "The Arab conquerors had destroyed some of what they found. When one conqueror seized Egypt, he burned the great library at Alexandria and so destroyed forever much priceless knowledge. Said he, 'If all these textbooks agree with the Koran, they are not needed and if they don't agree with the Koran, they are false and ought to be destroyed.' " [16]

Several textbooks tend to overemphasize the warlike character of Islam and thus give a distorted image of this faith. A seventh-grade supplementary textbook states that "the Mohammedans began to conquer other nations also, and force them all to accept the new religion" (*Q*, 190). A teacher's edition of a seventh-grade textbook reads: "The early Muslims spread their beliefs by the sword. Early Christians, on the other hand, had relied on the word" (*JJ*, 34). Similarly, another textbook states that "Mohammed's successors were known as Caliphs, and they accepted the Prophet's commands to spread the faith by the sword. Islam was a fighting religion which spread beyond the borders of Arabia" (*GG*, 185). "In the name of Allah," says one seventh-grade textbook "[Muslims] set out to conquer the world" (*P*, 167). A seventh-grade supplementary textbook describes the Muslim heaven as follows: "It is also filled mostly with Mohammedan warriors" (*E*, 222). According to a seventh-grade text, "Mohammed died in 632. By this time he had converted all the scattered Arab tribes to the new religion. It had been forced upon many of them by the sword" (*K*, 289).

Further examples of this tendency include: "The Moslems believed that they must teach all men what Mohammed had taught them. They were a war-like people" (*O*, 84). "Mohammed placed great emphasis on dying in battle for the faith. The Crescent became the symbol of the Moslem faith. It was the same shape as the Moslem sword" (*E*, 222). "The sword, said he, is the key of Heaven. He taught that if a man died in battle for Allah, all his sins would be forgiven. His fierce followers won battle after battle and before Mohammed's death (in A.D. 632) all the Arabs had been united into mighty Moham-

---

16. *Q*, 191. This passage, wittingly or not, perpetuates a fallacy that has long been discounted by thoughtful scholars of Islam. See, among others, Philip K. Hitti, *History of the Arabs from the Earliest Times to the Present*, 5th ed. (London: Macmillan, 1953); and Carl Brockelmann, *History of the Islamic Peoples* (New York: Capricorn, 1960).

medan nations" (*Q*, 190). "To spread the religion, Moslem leaders started many religious or holy wars" (*W*, 407). "The Muslims found it necessary to raid caravans to obtain supplies of food. Islam became a fighting religion, and Mohammed became a military and political leader as well as a religious prophet" (*J*, 209). "Mohammed urged his followers to spread their religion by the sword if necessary. 'The presence of one of you in the line of battle is better than all sorts of extra prayers'" (*CC*, 146).

Most textbooks fail to explain the Islamic policy of tolerance toward "people of the book," who were in fact protected through the ages by the Muslims. Nor do they mention that the Prophet himself and the gentlemen caliphs always advised their military leaders not to mutilate or kill children, old men, or women, not to cut palm trees or burn them, not to cut fruit trees that were bearing, and not to kill sheep, cattle, or camels except for needed food.

Furthermore, no distinction is made between Islam the religion, and Islam the state. Like other religions, Islam, is one of justice, equality, and high ideals. The Islam that conquered was not the religion but the state. The state, throughout the centuries, misused Islam and practiced many things that are not Islamic, both in form and content, in its name. It used Islam as a disguise for its own benefit.

Several textbooks report other miscellaneous inaccurate and/or misleading information about Islam. The following quotations concern women and slavery: "Slavery and the inferior state of women were accepted [in Islam]" (*GG*, 185). "Their holy book, the Koran, taught that women ought to be mere slaves to men. The slavery of men was also approved by the Koran" (*Q*, 191). A seventh-grade textbook shows a picture of a veiled woman with the caption: "The veiled woman is a symbol of Islamic culture" (*W*, 403). The authors in no way indicate that Islam did much to improve the position of both slaves and women in society.

One textbook speaks of the Muslim heaven as "a man's heaven, where women are mainly servants" (*CC*, 145). These authors mislead the reader and confuse the issue. According to Islam, a person is entitled to go to heaven if his or her deeds on earth are in conformity with the principles of Islam. Rewards and punishments are meted out not according to the sex of the individual but according to the degree of piousness and conformity to Islamic principles.

A supplementary textbook used in sixth through eighth grades describes the Muslim heaven: "To the Moslem, heaven is a sort of super Oasis, filled with wonderful things that are scarce in the desert"

(*E*, 222). Here we find an attempt to apply the desert image of the Muslim Arab even to heaven. The author takes as literal some of the descriptions of heaven found in the Koran which are symbolic of the heavenly state.

The reader will encounter some serious errors in the textbooks. A sixth-grade textbook, for example, states that "after the death of Mohammed his sayings were collected into a book called the Koran" (*O*, 88). Another sixth-grade text states that the "sacred book of Moslems, called the Koran, contains the writings and sayings of Mohammed" (*J*, 209). In both instances, the authors of the textbooks have confused the Koran, which according to the Muslims contains the word of God as revealed to his messenger Muhammad, with hadith, which contain statements attributed to the Prophet by his contemporary and later followers.[17] A sixth-grade textbook states, "One Persian Caliph changed the capital from Damascus in Syria to Baghdad on the Tigris" (*O*, 86). Here the author considers the Abbaside caliphs as Persians, while in fact they were Arab descendants of Abbas, the uncle of the Prophet.

Most textbooks do not blame the Arab Muslims for the Crusades, but rather blame the Turks, who conquered the Holy Land and made life difficult for the pilgrims. The Arabs are praised for their kind treatment of the pilgrims. A passage in a seventh-grade textbook reads: "Since the early days of the Moslem empire, Jerusalem had been in the hands of the Arabs. They had permitted Christian pilgrims to visit the city and its holy places. But in 1071 the Turks, another group of Moslems, drove the Arabs out of Jerusalem. They seized the shrines of the city and made it very difficult for pilgrims to visit them"(*JJ*, 167). Another seventh-grade textbook describes the Turks as barbarians who "took the Holy Land and Jerusalem. . . . The Turks killed many Christians, others were sold as slaves" (*P*, 283). The same textbook acknowledges the Arabs' kindness to pilgrims and describes Saladin as kind and a real gentleman who "allowed most of the Christians to go free after they paid ransoms" (*P*, 283, 287). In a similar vein: "While the Moslem Arabs ruled Palestine, they were friendly to the Christians and allowed them to visit most of the holy places there. About the year 1070, however, fierce Moslem Turks fought the Arabs and conquered much of their land. These Turks began to rob, torture, and even kill Christians in the holy land" (*B*, 166). "When the barbarian Turks got control of Palestine, they

---

17. Prophet Muhammad was only an intermediary for the reception and communication of revelation. His role was neither that of an author nor that of a compiler.

treated the pilgrims very cruelly, killing many and making slaves of others" (*Q*, 192). "The Arabs allowed European Christians to visit their sacred shrines in Palestine, but in 1071 a nomadic tribe, the Seljuk Turks, swept the Near East, taking Jerusalem. Christian travelers complained that the Turks were ruining the holy places and killing Christians" (*AA*, 54).

The Arab-Israeli Conflict

In the textbooks under investigation, all accounts concerning the Arab-Israeli conflict are either overtly or covertly pro-Israeli. None of these accounts can be considered even mildly pro-Arab. Also, Israel is given more space and discussed in much more detail than Arab countries. One sixth-grade textbook allocates two and one-half pages of text, along with nine good, modern pictures, to Israel, while Saudi Arabia and Iraq are given only two-thirds and one-quarter page, respectively (*I*, 123–30). Another text discusses eleven nations, two of which are Egypt and Israel. The authors allocate thirty-five pages to Egypt and almost twice as many, sixty-two, to Israel (*EE*).

Furthermore, teachers' editions or question sections at the ends of the chapters seem to stress pro-Israeli learning by suggesting that students write reports or do a project based on data obtained from the mass media of communication. At first glance it may appear that there is nothing objectionable about this exercise. However, available evidence indicates that the American mass media tend to favor Israel. Accordingly, these school exercises may unwittingly propagate pro-Israeli (and anti-Arab) feelings in schoolchildren.

In addition, most elementary and junior high school libraries contain more supplementary readings on Israel than on Arab countries. It is no secret that the authors of most of these supplementary readings are sympathetic to Israel. One junior high school in Sacramento has five books devoted exclusively to Israel, but only two on the Middle East in general, both of which include data on the Israelis as well as the Arabs. The readily available supplementary materials on Israel allow teachers to learn more about Israel. This situation also tends to encourage students to choose Israel rather than an Arab country as a subject for papers or projects: if a student wishes to choose an Arab country he or she must go to another library, an inconvenience that discourages not only twelve-year-olds, but college students and teachers as well.

Most textbooks overlook the legitimate rights of the Palestinian people, displaced from the land in which they had lived for thirteen centuries. Several textbooks substitute the word *Arab* for *Palestinian,* with the result that the reader will come to think of the conflict as between big Goliath and small David, Arab-Israeli, rather than as a Palestinian-Israeli conflict. For example: "The worst problem was caused by Arabs who fled from Israel during the fight" (*S,* 350). "When Israel was established, a half-million Arabs fled."[18] With reference to the conflict, a seventh-grade textbook states: "In 1948 the Arabs, aided by the Arab League, made war on Palestine" (*V,* 326). This textbook shows a picture of a woman and a young girl with the following caption: "This mother and child share the fate of 1-1/2 million Arab refugees made homeless by the war."[19] An eighth-grade textbook states, "Many Arabs who lived in western Palestine fled and became refugees" (*HH,* 761). In one form or another these textbooks add to the distorted picture given by Golda Meir and other Israeli leaders who claim that there are no Palestinians.

The textbooks under study are uniformly sympathetic toward the Jews. The typical account resembles the following: "Jews were living in Palestine for many years and, despite the Diaspora, dreamed of returning some day to the Promised Land, which they call Zion. The dream became reality in 1948, when Israel was established." These examples are from junior high school texts: "The Zionist wants to establish a homeland for Jews. Naturally they hoped to go back to their ancient home in Palestine" (*DD,* 758). "The new nation was Israel. . . . It was a homeland for Jews. These people had been driven away from their homeland hundreds of years ago" (*Z,* 164). "From then [A.D. 700] Jewish people dreamed of going back to their own land. But Palestine was firmly in the hands of Moslem rulers. The Jews could not return" (*S,* 349).

All textbooks refer to the November 19, 1947, resolution of the United Nations calling for the partition of Palestine into a Jewish and an Arab state. "The United Nations decided to divide Palestine in two. Half of it became a free country for Jewish people. The other became part of Jordan."[20] "On November 29, 1947, the General Assembly approved the partition of Palestine by a vote of 33 to 13,

18. *EE,* 237. Notice that the authors used the term *Arab,* not *Palestinian Arab.* Also notice that they underestimate the number of Palestinians who were forced from their land.

19. *V,* 253. Here the authors take for granted that Palestine is a Jewish land and the Arabs were making war on Palestine.

20. *S,* 350. Such practices as using the term *free* only for the Jewish country can bias children's attitudes against the Arabs and in favor of Israel.

with 13 nations not voting on the issue. Both the United States and the Soviet Union voted for partition" (*N*, 248). "The situation was now explosive, the U.N. intervened and recommended the division of Palestine into two separate Arab and Jewish states." [21] No textbook describes the November 29, 1947, resolution in full, including the clause calling for an international area around Jerusalem; nor does any inform the student that the United Nations had violated the principle of self-determination in passing such a resolution, or that the General Assembly had exceeded the scope of its jurisdiction as defined by the U.N. Charter. Furthermore, none of the textbooks discusses the fact that the General Assembly, on May 14, 1948, passed another resolution by a vote of 31 to 7, with 16 abstentions, which in effect suspended the effort to implement the partition resolution. The new resolution empowered "a mediator to examine the situation in its entirety and recommend such measures as he might deem advisable for the General Assembly to examine later on." [22]

Most if not all textbooks suggest that the Arabs were the aggressors in the conflict, having invaded the tiny state of Israel once it had declared its independence. Some textbooks claim that the Arabs intend to exterminate Israel. "On May 14, 1948, . . . the Jews proclaimed the state of Israel as a new and independent nation. The Arab states at once went to war with the new state" (*DD*, 759). "In 1948 the Arabs [meaning the Palestinians] aided by the Arab League [Egypt, Syria, Lebanon, Jordan, Iraq, Saudi Arabia, and Yemen] made war on Palestine" (*V*, 327). "Arab troops from a number of countries, including Egypt, Jordan, Syria and Iraq invaded Israel. The Jews were determined to keep their freedom. They drove the invader back" (*U*, 552). "The Arab nations of the Middle East and North Africa refused to recognize the new nation of Israel and were determined to destroy it. A war broke out in 1948 between Israel and the Arab nations" (*HH*, 761).

---

21. *BB*, 696. One fifth- to eighth-grade supplementary textbook claims that in 1947 "the U.N. divided Palestine into two states, Israel to the west, and Jordan to the east. Israel was to be a Jewish country and Jordan an Arab country" (*II*, 25). Here the author gives incorrect information concerning the size of British-mandated Palestine. East Jordan was not part of Palestine during the British mandate. Further, what the United Nations did on November 19, 1947, was to partition British-mandated Palestine into a Jewish state and an Arab state, with the area around Jerusalem to be an international zone. In other words, the United Nations did not create Jordan; Jordan came into being in 1923.

22. Fayez Sayegh, *The Arab-Israeli Conflict* (New York: Arab Information Center, 1964), p. 18.

The above are extremely misleading and distorted statements which can only bias students against the Arab. None of the textbooks cited above presents the Arab side of the story. None tells the student that the Zionists had occupied many villages, towns, and lands located in the "Arab portion of Palestine" long before May 15, 1948. The Zionist community in Palestine took matters into its own hands after the November 29 resolution and, resorting to force, attacked and occupied major cities and towns in Palestine before the withdrawal of the British forces on May 15, 1948, that is, before the formal establishment of the state of Israel. The former prime minister of Israel, Ben-Gurion, has written: "Until the British left, no Jewish settlement, however remote, was entered or seized by the Arabs, while the Haganah . . . captured many Arab positions and liberated Tiberias and Haifa, Jaffa and Safad . . . so, on the day of destiny that part of Palestine where the Haganah could operate was almost clear of Arabs."[23]

Several textbooks neglect to tell students why the Palestinians fled their land. The references to this exodus are brief and uninformative: "Today, however, there are few Arabs in Israel. Before the new nation was organized, there was war between the people of Israel and neighboring Arab lands, to which most of the Arabs in Israel fled" (D, 168). "[Thousands of] Arabs who had fled from Israel during the fight . . . had gone to neighboring Jordan."[24] "When Israel was established a half-million Arabs fled" (EE, 237). "Many of the Arabs who fled from Israel during the war were now homeless and rootless, living in poverty, inside Moslem borders." [25]

All textbooks fail to inform the student that Palestinians were driven out by a deliberate Zionist policy. All fail to discuss the Zionists extensive use of psychological warfare to create panic and fear among the Palestinians so that they would leave their homes. The single most devastating blow to the Palestinians was the massacre of some 250 old men, women, and children in the village of Deir Yassin. The Zionist terrorists mutilated corpses, transported survivors in open trucks through nearby Jerusalem to be spat upon, and called a press conference to announce that the deed was the work of a unit of Irgun,

23. David Ben-Gurion, *Rebirth and Destiny of Israel* (New York: Philosophical Library, 1954), pp. 530–31.

24. *S*, 350. Notice here the authors use the term *Arab* and not *Palestinian* for the inhabitants of Palestine.

25. *N*, 253. Here the authors did not use the term *Arab countries*, thereby confusing Muslim and Arab countries.

an underground terrorist organization. This and similar incidents created an atmosphere of panic, fear, and frustration that drove many Palestinians to search for safety in a neighboring country. Even before the formal establishment of Israel on May 15, 1948, over 300,000 Palestinians had fled Palestine to safety.[26]

Many textbooks omit facts that might damage Israel's image. For example, in discussing the assassination of U.N. mediator Count Bernadotte of Sweden with his French aide colonel on September 17, 1948, in Jerusalem, none of the textbooks surveyed in this study mentions that he was killed by the underground Stern Gang. A seventh-grade textbook simply states that "Count Bernadotte from Sweden was killed" (*U*, 552). Another reads: "The U.N. sent a mediation committee he⌐ded by Count Folke Bernadotte of Sweden to arrange an armistice. In September Bernadotte was assassinated in Jerusalem" (*DD*, 579). Also, none of the textbooks surveyed mentions that on July 22, 1946, a wing of the King David Hotel in which the government secretariat and part of the military headquarters were housed was blown up, causing the death of about 100 government officials, British, Arab, and Jewish.

Treatment of the 1956 war between the Egyptians and Israelis tends to be shallow and one-sided; in some texts it is not mentioned at all. "He [Nasser] is bitterly hostile to Israel, and his sharp clashes with Syria so alarmed Israel that late in 1956 Israel invaded Egypt. Great Britain and France, concerned for the safety of the Canal, also attacked Egypt" (*Y*, 704). "The second [war] came in 1956, as a result of President Nasser's having closed the Gulf of Aqaba" (*EE*, 237). "In 1956, British troops withdrew. Egypt seized the canal and closed it to Israel's shipping. Then Israel sent her army to take over the canal, and British and French forces landed to seize the canal area. They wanted to force Egypt to keep the canal open to ships of all nations" (*HH*, 761-62). None of the textbooks gives the Arab side of story, nor does any mention Israel's attack on a Gaza military post in February 1955 in which many Egyptian soldiers were killed, an event that led Egypt to revive interest in building a strong army.

Textbooks that discuss 1967 invariably blame the Arabs, particularly President Nasser of Egypt, for starting the war. "The Arabs determined to make an attack on Israel. . . . Egypt was the leader of the attack.

---

26. For a recent discussion of the nature and policies of Zionist settlement in Palestine, see Ibrahim Abu-Lughod and Baha Abu-Laban, eds., *Settler Regimes in Africa and the Arab World: The Illusion of Endurance* (Wilmette, Ill.: Medina University Press International, 1974).

. . . Israel was attacked once more from three sides by its Arab neighbors" (*N*, 253). "During the spring of 1967, Egypt interfered with an Israeli vessel moving from the Red Sea to the Gulf of Aqaba, Israel went to war immediately. . . . The third war was in 1967, and again the immediate cause was the closing of the Gulf of Aqaba."[27] "In June 1967, the UAR, still led by Nasser, blockaded Israel's outlet to the Red Sea and moved troops to Israel's border. Nasser called on all Arab states to crush Israel and reclaim it as Arab territory. But Israel pushed back the Arab armies" (*BB*, 735).

None of the textbooks speaks of Israel's aggressive behavior in the months preceding the 1967 June War, behavior which served to a large extent to increase tension and which led to the crisis that resulted in war. For example, on November 3, 1966, there had been a massive land strike against the Jordanian village of al-Samu in which a number of civilians and soldiers had been killed and a large part of the village leveled. Also, on April 7, 1967, an air strike against Syria had brought Israeli planes to within a few miles of Damascus. None of the textbooks mentions the inflammatory statements of the Israeli leaders against Syria in the month of April. The treatment of the 1967 war in the textbooks is indeed dismal and does not enable the student to appreciate the complexity of the matter or help him or her to make a sound judgment concerning the causes and the consequences of the war.

Finally, several textbooks blame the Arabs for the continuation of hostilities in the Middle East. One learns from a seventh-grade textbook that "the hostility of the Arab nations toward Israel also complicates matters in the Middle East" (*GG*, 721). Another textbook states: "The common hatred that the Arab feels for Israel constitutes what might be called a perpetual crisis" (*CC*, 689). None of the textbooks mentions Israeli hatred toward the Arab. Another textbook claims that Arab hostility toward Israel exists because Israel is a democratic country. "Israel's example of democracy creates a problem for some Arab countries. The rulers fear that their people, learning from examples set by the Jews, may demand a greater voice in selecting officials and in running the government. If this movement grows, dictatorial rule in several of the Arab nations may well be threatened" (*U*, 553). The reader is not informed of the persecution of the Arab minority

---

27. *EE*, 237. There is no evidence to support the allegation made here. Nasser stated that he would not allow ships with Israeli flags or ships carrying strategic cargo to pass through the Straits of Tiran. Israel did not send any ship to enter the straits before the 1967 June War.

in Israel and of the treatment of Palestinian Arabs as second-class citizens.

CONCLUSION

Students who use the elementary and junior high school social science textbooks reviewed in this study will likely develop a distorted idea of the Arab. A great deal of effort is needed to remedy this situation. To accomplish this, the following program is proposed: (1) New supplementary materials on the Arab, for elementary, junior high, and high school levels, should be made available to both teachers and students. (2) An attempt must be made to prevail upon publishers to remove biased, stereotyped, and distorted materials on the Arab. (3) Arab-Americans should approach boards of education in different states, demanding removal of biased textbooks from the approved lists. (4) Special symposia should be organized for elementary, junior high, and high school teachers where they can obtain accurate information about the Arab world.

TEXTBOOKS

A   Abramowitz, L. *The Earth, Region and People.* New York: Globe, 1971.
B   Ahlschwede, Ben F. *Exploring the Old World.* Sacramento: California State Department of Education, 1964.
C   Bacon, Phillip, *et al. Regions around the World.* Palo Alto, Calif.: Field Enterprises, Inc., 1972.
D   Barrows, Harlan H., *et al. Old World Lands,* Morristown, N.J.: Silver Burdett, 1961.
E   Bettersworth, John K., *et al. Your Old World Past.* Austin: Steck, 1961.
F   California State Series. *Concepts and Values.* First Grade. Sacramento: California State Department of Education, 1971.
G   _____. *The Social Science—Concepts and Values.* Second Grade. Sacramento: California State Department of Education, 1971.
H   _____. *The Social Science—Concepts and Values.* Sixth Grade. Sacramento: California State Department of Education, 1973.
I   Carls, Norman, *et al. Knowing Our Neighbors in the Eastern Hemisphere.* New York: Holt, Rinehart & Winston, 1968.
J   Cassidy, Vincent, *et al. Long Ago in the Old World.* Columbus, Ohio: Charles E. Merrill Books, 1964.
K   Clark, Thomas D., *et al. America's Old World Frontiers,* Sacramento: California State Department of Education, 1964.
L   Cooper, Kenneth S., *et al. The Changing Old World.* Sacramento: California State Department of Education, 1964.

M   Cutright, Prudence, *et al. Living in Our Country and Other Lands.* New York: Macmillan, 1969.

N   Davis, O. L., Jr., *et al. Learning about Countries and Societies.* New York: American Book Company, 1971.

O   Dawson, Grace S. *Our World.* Lexington, Mass.: Ginn, 1975.

P   Eibling, Harold H., *et al. Our Beginnings in the Old World.* Sacramento: California State Department of Education, 1964.

Q   Gardner, William. *The New World's Foundation in the Old.* Boston: Allyn & Bacon, 1964.

R   Gartler, Marion, *et al. Understanding Israel.* Sacramento: California State Department of Education, 1964.

S   Hunnicutt, C. W., *et al. The Great Adventure.* Syracuse: L. W. Singer, 1963.

T   King, Frederick M., *et al. Regions and Social Needs.* Sacramento: California State Department of Education, 1971.

U   Kolevzon, Edward R. *The Afro-Asian World.* Boston: Allyn & Bacon, 1969.

V   Kolevzon, Edward R., *et al. Our World and Its People.* Boston: Allyn & Bacon, 1968.

W   Linder, B. L. *Exploring Civilization: A Discovery Approach.* New York: Globe Book Co., 1971.

X   McCall, E. *Man and the Region of the World.* Chicago: Benefic Press, 1974.

Y   McCrocklin, James. *The Making of Today's World.* Boston: Allyn & Bacon, 1962.

Z   McKay, Susan Williams. *The Communities We Build.* Chicago: Follett, 1973.

AA Miller, Mary G. *Cultures in Transition.* Chicago: Follett, 1973.

BB Okun, Mitchell, *et al. The Challenge of America.* New York: Holt, Rinehart & Winston, 1973.

CC Platt, Nathaniel, *et al. Our World through the Ages.* Englewood Cliffs, N.J.: Prentice-Hall, 1967.

DD Rogers, Lester B. *Story of Nations.* New York: Holt, Rinehart & Winston, 1965.

EE Shorter, Bani, *et al. Eleven Nations.* Lexington, Mass.: Ginn, 1972.

FF Thralls, Zoe A. *The World around Us.* Sacramento: California State Department of Education, 1964.

GG Wallbank, T. Walter, *et al. Living World History.* Atlanta: Scott, Foresman, 1964.

HH Wood, Leonard C., *et al. America, Its People and Values.* New York: Harcourt Brace Jovanovich, 1975.

II Yates, Howard O. *How People Live in the Middle East.* Chicago: Benefic Press, 1970.

JJ Yohe, Ralph Sandlin. *Exploring Regions of the Eastern Hemisphere.* Chicago: Follett, 1971.

L. M. Kenny

THE MIDDLE EAST IN CANADIAN SOCIAL SCIENCE TEXTBOOKS

CONCERN ABOUT EXPRESSIONS of bias in textbooks dates back at least as far as 1889, when an international peace conference exhorted the world community to purge textbooks "of false ideas about the nature and causes of war."[1] During the first half of the twentieth century, many European countries, under the auspices of the Institute of Intellectual Cooperation (League of Nations), studied and criticized the nationalistic bias in history textbooks. In an attempt to guide the evaluation, revision, and writing of textbooks in the years following World War II, UNESCO proposed the following set of criteria: accuracy, fairness, balance, world-mindedness, and comprehensiveness.[2] Since 1950, several international conferences sponsored by UNESCO have been held to address major issues involved in the writing and revision of textbooks to eliminate distortions and all expressions of bias.[3]

A list of textbooks reviewed is to be found at the end of this paper. References to these works will be included within parentheses in the text. Each reference will give the appropriate code letter from the list and the page number of the material in question.

1. UNESCO, *Looking at the World through Textbooks* (Paris: UNESCO, 1946), quoted in Garnet McDiarmid and David Pratt, *Teaching Prejudice* (Toronto: Ontario Institute for Studies in Education, 1971), p. 1.

2. UNESCO, *A Handbook for the Improvement of Textbooks and Teaching Materials as Aids to International Understanding* (New York: Columbia University Press, 1949), pp. 78–81.

3. The first of these international conferences was held in Paris in 1956. This was followed by a conference in Tokyo in 1958, one in Wellington, New Zealand, in

Canada has lagged behind Europe and the United States in textbook research.[4] What studies there have been have centered around the treatment of the United States, of French and English Canadians in English- and French-language texts, of the Indians, and, to a lesser degree, of immigrant (or minority) groups. These studies have found that Canadian textbooks, like European ones, contain nationalistic bias, unfavorable treatment of ethnic groups other than one's own, and stereotyped beliefs concerning the Indians.[5] Of major importance in Canadian textbook criticism is McDiarmid and Pratt's recent survey of 143 English- and French-language texts authorized for social studies in Ontario.[6] The survey focused primarily on the treatment of Christians, Jews, Muslims, Negroes, Indians, and immigrants, with Christians being used as a control group. The results show that Christians and Jews were treated most favorably, whereas Negroes and Indians were treated least favorably.[7] The treatment of immigrants was slightly better than that of Muslims, but the "mean overall evaluation scores" for both groups were at the lower end of the continuum.[8]

The evaluative terms most frequently applied to Muslims were *infidels, fanatical, great, devout,* and *tolerant;* in contrast, the terms applied to Christians were *devoted, zealous, martyr, great,* and *famous;* and those applied to Jews were *great, faithful, just(ice), wise,* and *genius.*[9] In a technical appendix, the same authors examined the treatment of French-Canadians, Arabs, Negroes, and Indians in a textbook sample comprising sixty-nine texts authorized for use in grades five through twelve in the fall of 1968. On a scale ranging from

---

1960, and one in Goslar, West Germany, in 1962. See McDiarmid and Pratt, *Teaching Prejudice,* p. 9.

4. For a brief discussion of textbook research in Canada and elsewhere, see McDiarmid and Pratt, *Teaching Prejudice,* pp. 7–30.

5. See, for example, "The Canada-United States Committee on Education," *Canadian Education,* I (1945), 44–47; "A Study of National History Textbooks Used in the Schools of Canada and the United States," *Canadian Education,* II (1947), 3–92; Canada, *Report of the Royal Commission on Bilingualism and Biculturalism,* vol. II, *Education* (Ottawa: Queen's Printer, 1968); McDiarmid and Pratt, *Teaching Prejudice,* pp. 7–30.

6. McDiarmid and Pratt, *Teaching Prejudice,* pp. 7–30.

7. *Ibid.,* p. 44.

8. *Ibid.,* p. 42.

9. *Ibid.,* p. 41. The evaluative terms most often applied to the remainder of the groups were: *hardworking, enriched Canada, contribution, skillful,* and *problem* in relation to immigrants; *primitive, friendly, fierce, savage,* and *superstitious* in relation to Negroes; and *savage(s), friendly, fierce, hostile,* and *skillful* in relation to Indians.

−2 (unfavorable) to +2 (favorable), the "mean evaluative location scores" for the four groups were as follows: French-Canadians (+1.08), Arabs (−0.80), Negroes (−1.80), and Indians (−1.83).[10] The ten evaluative terms most often applied to Arabs were *great, cruel, feuding, kind, pagan, brilliant, dictator, fierce, friendly,* and *resentful;* in contrast, the terms most often applied to French-Canadians were *great, brave, courageous, skillful, heroic, determined, proud, devoted, famous,* and *daring.*[11]

The present study, focusing on the treatment of the Middle East in social science textbooks used in Ontario schools, will expand upon the relevant results of McDiarmid and Pratt's survey.[12]

RESEARCH PROCEDURE

This study was initiated in the fall of 1972 and is confined largely to the curricula guidelines set down by the Ontario Department of Education. Following examination of the guidelines, a total of seventy Canadian social science textbooks authorized for use in the Province of Ontario were reviewed. To determine the way in which the Middle East was treated, the technique of content analysis was applied to the relevant portions of these texts. Although the materials reviewed in this study were mainly those authorized for use in Ontario, information received from other provinces showed that the same textbooks were in use across English-speaking Canada.

In the Province of Ontario, matters relating to curricula and texts are left to local boards of education, schools, or individual teachers, within the confines of the Department of Education's guidelines. Therefore, to obtain information about relevant school programs as well as interpretations of the guidelines in relation to the Middle East, a survey of social science teachers in Canada was undertaken. A questionnaire was mailed in 1972 to approximately 1,400 subscribers to the *Canadian Journal of History and Social Science.* As stated in the covering letter, the aim of the study was to assess the place

10. *Ibid.,* p. 126.

11. *Ibid.,* p. 127. The ten evaluative terms most often applied to Negroes were *friendly, unfriendly, savage, faithful, kind, fierce, primitive, murder, violent,* and *backward;* and those applied to Indians were *savage, friendly, massacre, skillful, hostile, fierce, great, murder, unfriendly,* and *thief.*

12. This study grew out of an inquiry, initiated by the Middle East Studies Association in 1971-72, into "The Middle East Image in Secondary Schools." Earlier research was undertaken in collaboration with Prof. J. R. Blackburn of the University of Toronto.

which the history of the Middle East in the Islamic era occupied in Canadian secondary school curricula, and to evaluate the adequacy of the textbooks available for this purpose.

The questionnaire was divided into three sections. The first sought information about the respondent, about his (her) training, especially in the area of the Middle East, and about the type of school where he (she) taught. The second section was designed to yield information about the place of the Middle East in the history curriculum, pertinent topics discussed, the textbooks used and the extent of dependence on them, the impartiality of the texts, and the impressions of the teacher regarding Middle Eastern peoples. The last section attempted to elicit information about measures that might be taken to improve teacher training, teaching materials, and curricula with respect to the Middle East.

FINDINGS

The results of the study will be discussed in three parts. The first concerns the curricula guidelines and teachers' responses to the questionnaire; the second, the treatment of the Middle East in history textbooks; and the third, the treatment of the Middle East in geography textbooks.

The Curricula Guidelines and Teachers' Responses

The Ontario Department of Education curricula guidelines allow intermediate-level teachers to introduce other cultures of the world in the process of defining Canada's "multicultural" heritage. However, the Third World emerges as an area worthy of study for its own sake only at the senior level, especially in grade eleven.[13] At this level, under the broad subject "The Legacy of the Ancient and Medieval Worlds," some topics from Islamic Middle Eastern history are put forward. Examples of these include: "The Impact of Moslem Culture on Spain," "Contacts between the Middle East and Europe," "The Mongol Empire," and "The Medieval and Moslem Inheritance." The guidelines suggest that these ideas may be viewed in terms of "militant religion," "the transmission of knowledge," "finance and trade," and

13. Many of the teachers who returned the questionnaire (96 out of 126) indicated that Middle Eastern Islamic history enters the curriculum of their schools at grade eleven.

so forth. In grade thirteen the topic of "World Religions" also provides an opportunity for the study of the Islamic Middle East.

Turning to the teachers' responses, it should be noted first that a total of 126 questionnaires were returned, of which 113 were from Ontario. The remainder were from Quebec (10), Alberta (2), and Nova Scotia (1). Although the response rate was relatively low (about one out of ten), the replies from Ontario came from a sufficiently wide geographic distribution to suggest that they were representative.

Teachers' responses indicated that the scope and content of the Ontario history curriculum have undergone little change in recent years. The main areas studied, often practically the only ones, are still Canadian, American, and European (chiefly British and French) history. In grade eleven, however, other cultural areas are considered. At this level, the average estimate of the proportion of the history curriculum spent on the Third World was 12.3 percent.[14] Of this amount, China and Southeast Asia received the most attention (an average estimate of 41.8 percent), with the Middle East next (26.5 percent), and other areas following in this order: the Indian subcontinent (12.2 percent), sub-Saharan Africa (11.2 percent), and Latin America (8.2 percent). The data showed that almost without exception, active experimentation with new curricula took place in schools of larger metropolitan areas.

In response to a question concerning the materials available for classroom use by teachers and students, a good number of teachers indicated that they did not use specified textbooks at all, or that they employed them only sparingly, as back-up material, supplementing them with a wide range of such teaching aids as filmstrips, slides, documents, magazine and newspaper articles, records, and simulation games. The majority of teachers, however, indicated that they used textbooks, often relying heavily or exclusively on the information provide therein.

The reasons for dependence upon textbooks are not difficult to find. For overworked teachers and those inclined to take the path of least resistance, packaged materials offer a ready-made pabulum to give to their students. The teachers themselves, having little or no training or acquired expertise on the Middle East, do not feel qualified to go outside of the texts at hand. Furthermore, since the

---

14. The Ontario respondents (103) gave an average estimate of 11.8 percent, while those from Quebec (10) gave one slightly higher, 12.2 percent. The estimates of the amount of time spent on the Third World varied from 3 to 75 percent, although most clustered around the average.

range of the subject matter of history and geography is so vast both in time and space, embracing many cultural and linguistic areas over long periods of time, teachers cannot be expected to have firsthand knowledge of all they teach.

The following question was asked of the respondents: "Could you estimate for us how your textbooks treat each of the following topics, if they are covered?" The ten topics listed were Arabs, Turks, Iranians (Persians), Muslims, Jews, Egyptians, Israelis, Palestinians, Arab nationalism, and Zionism. For each of these topics three response categories were provided: "Pro-," "Anti-," and "Balanced." About one-third of the respondents did not give any opinion about textbooks, either because they did not use them or because the material in them was alleged to be insufficient to form a basis for judgment. Of those who answered the question, slightly more than half felt that on the average the textbooks treated the various groups in the Middle East in a balanced fashion. Nevertheless, 61 percent expressed the view that the textbooks tended to be pro-Jewish; 48 percent felt that they were pro-Israeli; and 40 percent felt that they were pro-Zionist. (In each of these instances, almost all of the other respondents expressed the view that the texts were balanced.) In contrast, while most of the respondents believed that Arabs, Turks, Egyptians, Palestinians, and Arab nationalism were fairly treated, sizable numbers expressed the view that textbooks were biased against them.[15]

In response to the question "What dominant characteristics do you associate with each of the following groups: Turks, Arabs, Iranians (Persians), Jews, Muslims, Christians, Egyptians, Israelis, Palestinians?" many teachers tended to mirror textbook biases uncovered by McDiarmid and Pratt, as well as this research. The dominant picture given of Turks was that of military and organizational ability which, according to some teachers, was exercised in a manner that was imperialistic, destructive, cruel, and ruthless to the point of genocide and corruption. As for Arabs, several teachers remarked on the connection between them and Islam and their contribution to Western civilization. The qualities most frequently associated with Arabs included wild, uncivilized, nomadic, backward, disorganized, and

---

15. About 30 percent of the respondents expressed the view that textbooks were biased against Arabs; 46 percent, against Turks; 27 percent, against Egyptians; 34 percent, against Palestinians; and 42 percent, against Arab nationalism. It might be noted that of all the textbooks reviewed in this study, a three-volume set in French by Savard and Dussault (M) was one of the most balanced in approach and accurate in information—even if noticeably Francocentric.

militant against Israel. Other teachers mentioned their exploitation at the hands of Western imperialism and their new-found oil wealth. The overwhelming reaction to "Palestinians" was one of pity for the refugees, a people who had been oppressed, persecuted, and manipulated. In addition, Palestinians were seen as frustrated and vengeful, as a result of which they had turned to guerrilla activities.

Respondents were asked to give their impressions of the three religious groups in the Middle East (Muslims, Christians, and Jews). The dominant trait attributed to Muslims was religious devotion, often tinged with fanaticism. Many respondents referred to the former brilliant Islamic civilization, contrasting it with its later decadence. Some respondents found Islam to be an "interesting" and "mysterious" religion. Turning to Christians in the Middle East, the responses suggest that there was some confusion between Eastern and Western Christendom. There were references to the lofty teachings of Christianity and also to its contributions to Western civilization. On the other hand, the picture given of Eastern Christians was one of rigid dogmatism, deceit, and hypocrisy—in short, of Byzantine deviousness. Finally, Jews were noted first as a religious, monotheistic group who, in spite of persecution and dispersion, have, by their toughness and courage, maintained their identity and given it national expression in Zionism. Jews were also said to be acquisitive, aggressive, arrogant, and at the center of conflict down through history.[16]

The Middle East in History Textbooks

Although it is at the senior level that aspects of Islamic civilization are treated for their own historical interest, textbooks at all curriculum levels mention the Middle East and events connected with its history. Almost all world history texts include a few pages on the Prophet Muhammad, the rise and dramatic spread of Islam, the central beliefs and rituals of the faith, external influences on its early development, and the cultural legacy of Islamic civilization.

The Rise and Expansion of Islam. Though often sympathetic, descriptions of early Islam are flawed by factual errors, questionable assertions, and significant omissions, all of which contribute to the perpetuation of fundamental misconceptions about the Muslim religion, culture, and civilization. The myth of a direct causal relationship between the large expanses of burning desert of Arabia and Islam

16. Israelis were described in very similar terms, but with added emphasis on their progressiveness, determination, and martial-mindedness.

still persists, stressing the debt of Islam to Arabian animism. It is asserted that Islam was born among the nomads of Arabia, who were "wholly illiterate," and for whom "caravan-raiding was a cherished pastime" (*F*, 321). To depict Arabia as completely illiterate is of course to contradict the fact of the recording of the Koranic revelation and to ignore the honored place the written word has occupied from the inception of Islam. And we are left to infer from the references to caravan-raiding that there were important commercial sedentary centers which were dependent upon the flourishing caravan trade. The same author attributes the development of Muslim culture and civilization to Greek and Roman learning, art, and law, omitting the important Judaic, Christian, and Persian influences, as well as the indigenous Arab contribution, although it is admitted that Muhammad "may have heard of Jewish or Christian ideas" (*F*, 320 f., 325).

When discussing Islamic beliefs and practices, the point is frequently made that Islam permitted polygamy and slavery (*H*, 286; *D*, 225). The explicit or implicit comparison is between Muslim and Judeo-Christian practices, neglecting of course to mention that Judaism allowed polygamy and that slavery was not outlawed by either Judaism or Christianity. Textbooks generally fail to mention the limitations that the Koran placed on polygamy, nor do they mention that the Koran improved the status of women in many ways. With regard to slavery, mention is made of the fact that slavery was much more tolerable in the Islamic East than in Christian America at a later date, that the slave was often an honored member of the family and society, and that the freeing of slaves was considered a highly meritorious act.

Among the many minor factual errors regarding early Islam, mention may be made of the confusion between the Black Stone and the Ka'bah (*F*, 321; *H*, 281); the assertion that the Ka'bah and Zem Zem are "objects of worship" (*H*, 283); the substitution of Mt. Ararat for 'Arafat (*H*, 284); and making Ramadan (instead of Dhu'l-Hijja) the month of pilgrimage (*H*, 286). Terms offensive to Muslims of today, such as *Mohommedan* and *Mohammedanism*, are still used (*F*, 322; *K*, 193). More serious is the use of pejorative language in recounting Islamic history at this and later stages—such expressions as "frenzied," "the wild warriors of Islam," and so forth (*H*, 286; *F*, 322).

The spread of Islam is generally said to have been accomplished by the sword; no distinction is made between the swift military conquests of the seventh and eighth centuries and the centuries-long process of conversion of subject populations to the Islamic faith, usually by persuasion or the force of circumstances. Attention is generally focused on the expansion westward across thinly populated North Africa and then northward through Spain into southern France, rather than northward and eastward into the populous and culturally rich domains of the Byzantines, Sassanian Persia, Central Asia, and India (*C*, 123; *H*, 285 f.; *F*, 324), although exceptions are to be found (*B*, 362-64). Historians of Islam will be surprised to learn that the capture of Alexandria "turned the desert tribesmen into a sea power," with their newly acquired naval forces supporting "the sweep across North Africa" (*F*, 324). The significance of the Battle of Tours in European history will doubtless continue to be overstated in Western textbooks, but surely they can be purged of such exaggerations as transforming the raiding party of the already overextended Muslim forces into the "Moslem host" which Charles Martel is credited with having defeated. As pointed out in one text (*P*, 287), it is Charles Martel's contemporary Leo III, the East Roman emperor, who deserves most of the credit for stemming the tide of expansionist Islam toward Christian Europe.

The Crusades and the Age of Discovery. Most school textbooks that touch upon the Islamic Middle East do so only in connection with two features of European history in the late Middle Ages—the Crusades and the Age of Discovery. There has been a vast improvement in the understanding of the mixed motives of the Crusades and their place in the long, drawn out conflict between Christendom and Islam, although instances of bias and ignorance persist. We are told, for instance, that "Moslem hearts did not melt," although "thousands of children perished or were sold into slavery in this mad enterprise," namely, the Children's Crusade (*F*, 426). The clear implication is that the Muslims were responsible for the death or slavery of these thousands of innocents, a baseless calumny. The Crusade, of course, came to an ignoble end in Europe with the death of many of the children in the hazardous march across the Alps and the sale of many of the survivors into slavery by Italian merchants. We are told, also, that Saladin "saved Mecca from a Christian attack" (*H*, 343-45). Such terms as *infidels* and *heathen* are still applied to the Muslim opponents of the crusaders (*C*, 149-51).

Most textbooks correctly attribute the age of maritme discovery to economic incentives rather than to religious zeal. Often, however they perpetuate the myth that the capture of Constantinople by the Ottoman Turks in 1453 brought the important spice trade with India and the Far East to a halt, and that this stimulated the discovery of new routes to the sources of supply (*B*, 218; *H*, 421). In truth, the bulk of the merchandise from the Orient reached Europe, not through the Black Sea region, but through the Mamluk ports of Egypt and Syria, from where its distribution to Europe was monopolized by the Italian commercial cities, chiefly Venice. It was to break the Venetian monopoly that the Portuguese set out to find a new sea route to India. The same sources, along with others (*D*, 220, 230; *F*, 434), place the incursion of the barbarian (but Muslim!) Turks into Europe after the fall of Constantinople, in 1453, instead of a century earlier.

The Legacy of Islamic Civilization. In reviewing textbook coverage of the cultural legacy of Islamic civilization, one is impressed as much by the poverty of the content as by the mediocrity of the treatment. Rarely is any serious effort made to discuss medieval Europe's debt to Islamic culture in such fields as medicine, philosophy, mathematics, astronomy, commerce, art, and architecture, to mention the most obvious. There are sparse references to Islamic Spain, where for seven centuries Muslim, Christian, and Jewish scholars worked together to develop such rich centers of learning as Cordova, Toledo, and Granada before universities were founded elsewhere in Europe. Mention of intellectual life in the Muslim heartlands is virtually nonexistent. Some authors are apparently reluctant to attribute anything original and creative to Islamic civilization; for example, one textbook states that "the so-called Arabic numerals and Algebra were derived from India" (*F*, 325). Although it is true that the "Arabic" numerals were borrowed from India, it is also well known that Muslim scholars invented algebra and made other contributions in the field of mathematics that enabled men from their own ranks to make brilliant advances in such sciences as astronomy and optics. This learning gradually reached Europe and contributed immeasurably to the Renaissance of the West.

The Modern Period: Colonialism versus Nationalism. Coming down to the more familiar territory of the modern period, one might have expected both a more knowledgeable and a more balanced treatment, but inherited prejudices and viewpoints are very difficult to eradicate. The most serious criticism of the coverage of the modern Middle East is its narrow, parochial, Western-oriented viewpoint, which appears very clearly in the treatment of European colonialism and regional nationalisms. The bias and lack of understanding of, or interest in, the viewpoint of the people most directly concerned are nowhere more clearly seen than in the approval given by some authors to the post-World War I "mandate" system—that great grab for territory, power bases, and control of resources and communications in the Middle East which was contrived by Britain and France to paper over their designs on the area. Thus Britain is said to have "accepted a mandate from the League of Nations to administer Palestine," and later to have "abandoned the thankless task of policing the country" (*J*, 435). Schoolchildren are still taught that the mandates were to provide "training for independence." If one of the "broad aims" of the World War I peace settlements was "to establish wherever possible liberal democratic states," why was this aim not applied in the Middle East, and to the Arab world in particular? The repressive French colonial rule in North Africa is described as "strict, efficient and good, for France was foremost in the assumption of the 'white man's burden,'" (*E*, 103; this text, I am glad to report, has been removed from the "authorized" list).

The inevitable result of the denial of national aspirations in the Middle East was the rise of strong and sometimes violent nationalistic movements, and the discrediting of the pseudo-democratic institutions that had been introduced. However, for our cool, impartial textbook writers, nationalism in the Middle East is a "fever" and is "self-destructive," and those who adopt this defense mechanism are branded as "reckless." This term is applied to Gamel Abdel Nasser for buying from the Eastern bloc, after being refused by the West, the arms needed to defend his country (*J*, 436). And for this action he is accused of harboring aggressive purposes (*G*, 387). The nationalists are described as "troublemakers" and "fiery," or as "rabid hater[s] of foreigners." To the incursion of foreign interests, it is reported, the unreasoning Middle Easterners have applied the unsavory term *imperialism*.

Such authors express astonishment at the "bitter hostility" of the peoples of the Middle East toward the West (*J*, 434). They do not explain that this antipathy is almost solely political in origin, a consequence of Western imperialism in its various forms. Nor do they emphasize that in spite of this, the peoples of the Middle East in general continue to be culturally oriented toward the West. It simply is not true, for instance, that "North Africans have an undying hatred of all things French" (*J*, 440). They may have hated French colonial domination, but their contact with the French culture is still strong.

The Middle East in Geography Textbooks

In the geography textbooks studied, the cultural area we refer to as the Islamic Middle East is often broken up along continental boundaries into two main sections: Southwest Asia and North Africa. This division violates the unifying geographic feature of the area—the vast arid expanse beginning with North Africa's great Sahara and continuing through the Arabian and Syrian deserts, across Central Asia, and nearly to the borders of China in an almost unbroken stretch. Some geography textbooks, however, treat southern Europe, North Africa, and the Near East as a unit (for example, A).

Overemphasis on Nomadism. One place where the geographic unity of the Islamic Middle East is recognized is in the geography and social science texts used in the lower grades, where the various kinds of climate are examined, the Middle East falling into the arid, desert category. Inhabitants of the Middle East are described as leading a nomadic type of existence. Although there are some very good descriptions of nomadic life under desert conditions, it is a travesty to picture the typical Arab of today as a Bedouin, dressed in Bedouin headgear and flowing robe, and accompanied by his ubiquitous camel. The desert nomad is a vanishing species—and his camel, too.[17] But still we read that Cairo is "a centre of river, rail and caravan routes" with "little motor traffic" (*I*, 343). (I wouldn't hazard a guess as to how many years it has been since a caravan laden with the silks and spices of the East has entered Cairo, and I'm sure the authors have never driven an automobile in the nightmare of Cairo's traffic.)

Another myth, related to the previous one, is that the Arabs are an ethnically pure species, the descendants of "various nomadic tribes that inhabited the Arabian and Sinai Peninsulas and the Syrian Desert" (*A*, 98). The fact that the 135,000,000 speakers of Arabic in North Africa and the Middle East are bound together linguistically and culturally does not mean that their forebears were wandering nomads in Arabia. Nor does the word *Arab* mean "a dweller in a moveable tent" (*L*, 204).

The textbook writers, in short, have not kept up with the demographic, social, and economic changes that have taken place in the Middle East. Roughly two-thirds of the population of the area (the vast majority of whom, needless to say, are sedentarized) still derive their income from agriculture. However, urbanization is proceeding apace, with all its attending problems; this subject is barely touched upon in most of the geography texts. The great urban centers such as Rabat, Algiers, Alexandria, Cairo (6,000,000 or more, not the 2,500,000 cited in some texts published as late as 1960–61), Beirut, Teheran, Ankara,

17. William Polk, the noted Middle Eastern scholar and traveler, recently related the frustrating delay he and his party suffered before setting out on a desert trip from Riyadh to Amman, owing to the difficulties the government had encountered in rounding up camel saddles for them. See William R. Polk and William J. Mares, *Passing Brave* (New York: Knopf, 1973), pp. 23–25, 41.

and Istanbul resemble their European counterparts much more than they do the local country village. Development is the watchword of the hour, and industrialization the accepted means to progress.

Treatment of Israel. Another area in which there is little understanding of or sympathy for Middle Eastern viewpoints is the Palestine problem. In general the proprietary rights of the indigenous Arab population, based on 1,300 years and more of continuous occupation, are glossed over, just as they were at the time of the Balfour Declaration. The antecedent and superior rights of the Israeli settler colonists, on the other hand, are taken for granted (*L*, 216).

In the geography textbooks Israel receives preferential treatment in the amount of space allocated to it and in the way it is described. The reasons for this are legion—historical, religious, and cultural. While no one can deny the accomplishments of the Zionists in industrial and agricultural development, this is no excuse to neglect the tremendous efforts being put forth in almost every other country of the Middle East, from Morocco to Afghanistan. The Israelis are not the only ones who have been "making the desert bloom." The Egyptians, for instance, have done the same for miles and miles along both sides of the desert highway from Cairo to Alexandria, now green with vineyards, citrus groves, and alfalfa fields.

CONCLUSION

We must not be satisfied with bemoaning the inadequacies and distortions in the image of the Middle East that is presented in our school systems, but should commit ourselves to improving the situation. Concerted action is needed in two main areas: the upgrading of teaching materials, and the enlightenment of the teachers—doubtless the more important consideration.

Teaching Materials on the Middle East

The Islamic Middle East presently receives in Canadian social science textbooks neither the quantity nor the quality of coverage it merits. We need better teaching materials, free from errors, stereotypes, and distortions, factually sound and up to date. There is an urgent need for well-researched textbooks and syllabi, with sound historical perspectives on the Middle East, which do justice to the nature and extent of the interaction between the Middle East and the West over the centuries. A teacher would search long and hard to find in present authorized texts enough material to take up such suggested topics as "The Impact of Moslem Culture on Spain," "The Medieval and Moslem Inheritance," or "The Urban Experience of Islamic Granada and Damascus." Above all, we need materials produced by writers who have a deep understanding of the Middle East and the West and who can portray both cultures fairly and dispassionately.

In their answers to the questionnaire, teachers were all but unanimous in welcoming the suggestion of a separate "unit of learning" on the Middle East and expressed the view that educational authorities would be receptive to its introduction. It was generally agreed that the unit should include a student's booklet, a teacher's manual, and an annotated bibliography, and be accompanied by audiovisual aids. The majority thought it should be used in the eleventh or twelfth grade and should last for six weeks or less. Other frequently made suggestions were that it should contain documents and source material on the history and the social and economic life of the region, that it should suggest discussion and research topics, that it should embrace a list of further source materials, such as slides and films, and also suggest the names of available speakers.

The inadequacies of the present materials should be exposed to publishers, departments of education, school boards, and the teachers themselves. Initial contacts made with all of these groups indicate that they are generally ready and willing to listen to those who know what they are talking about and can show them how to improve the situation.

If we can convince the right people of the need for a more adequate presentation of the Middle East in our schools, then we must take the next step of helping to produce better materials. It is up to those who claim to be experts to put their expertise to use and to find the right people to collaborate with and to choose the best methods and techniques in order to produce what will be acceptable and effective.[18]

Teacher Training on the Middle East

The goal of producing better-qualified teachers is more difficult than that of producing better teaching materials, since it depends in part on the reeducation of a whole society and the changing of

18. For a bibliography of works on the Islamic world, see E. Birnbaum *et al.*, *The Islamic Middle East: A Short Annotated Bibliography for High School Teachers and Librarians* (Toronto: University of Toronto, Department of Islamic Studies, 1975).

basic attitudes. Teachers, however, are key personnel in society, and so we must aim at them in particular.

A majority of the teachers responding to our questionnaire themselves expressed an interest in taking further university courses on the Islamic Middle East, preferably for credit (66 respondents), and an even higher number (101) were in favor of workshops on the area for secondary school teachers, though half of them were skeptical that their boards would reimburse them for their expenses. At the University of Toronto we have had one successful teachers' workshop on the Middle East and are pursuing the possibility of offering a special course on the Islamic Middle East for teachers. Such courses, along with those that might be offered in summer school, would provide longer exposure and greater coverage than brief workshops, though the latter have a place in offering a more concentrated quantum of knowledge in capsule form.

TEXTBOOKS

A   Clee, D., W. Hildebrand, and M. Wooley. *The Mediterranean, Its Lands and People.* Toronto: Holt, Rinehart & Winston, 1970.

B   Coulthard, Walter W., *et al. Patterns in Time.* Toronto: J. M. Dent, 1964.

C   Earl, D. W. L. *Roots of the Present.* Toronto: Sir Isaac Pitman, 1964.

D   Fishwick, D., *et al. The Foundations of the West.* Toronto: Clarke, Irwin, 1963.

E   Gwyne-Timothy, J., and D. A. Kearn. *Quest for Democracy: Revolution, Reaction and Conflict.* Toronto: McClelland & Stewart, 1970 (dropped from the latest authorized list).

F   Hardy, W. G., and J. R. W. Gwyne-Timothy. *Journey into the Past.* Toronto: McClelland & Stewart, 1965.

G   Lambert, R. S. *The Twentieth Century.* Canadian Heritage Series. Toronto: House of Grant, 1960.

H   Lavender, E., *et al. A Thousand Ages.* Toronto: McGraw Hill, 1962.

I   Lloyd, T., W. Russel, and M. Scarlett. *The Geographer's World.* Toronto: Ginn, 1968.

J   Peart, H. W., and John Shafter. *The Winds of Change.* Toronto: Ryerson, 1961.

K   Reid, Stewart, and E. McInnis. *Our Modern World.* Rev. ed. Toronto: J. M. Dent, 1963.

L   Ryckman, T. T., and H. E. Thompson. *Europe and Asia,* Aldine Geography, Book Four. Toronto: J. M. Dent, 1965.

M   Savard, P., and H. Dussault. *Histoire générale.* Montreal: Centre Educatif et Culturel, 1966–68. Vol. I, *L'Orient, la Grèce, Rome, le môyen age jusqu'en 1328;* vol. II, *De 1328 à 1815;* vol. III, *De 1815 à 1968.*

N   Spencer, Robert. *The West and a Wider World.* Toronto: Clarke, Irwin, 1969.

O   Swatridge, L. A., *et al. Selected Studies in Regional Geography.* Toronto: McGraw Hill, 1963.

P   Trueman, John. *The Enduring Past: Earliest Times to the Sixteenth Century.* Toronto: Ryerson, 1964.

Sharon McIrvin Abu-Laban

STEREOTYPES OF MIDDLE EAST PEOPLES: AN ANALYSIS OF CHURCH SCHOOL CURRICULA

SEVERAL writers have documented the difficulties in finding relatively objective North American analyses of Middle Eastern current events, life styles, religions and history.[1] For example, content analyses of school textbooks, American newspapers and United States government policies indicate that at both the formal and informal levels, pressure has been exerted to influence a predominantly one-sided approach to the Arab-Israeli conflict and negative stereotypy regarding the Arab people. To be sure, the Jewish people have been subjected to negative stereotyping by North Americans; however, in comparisons between Arabs and supporters of Israel, North American sentiment has been strongly in favor of Zionism and the state of Israel, with the result that the Arab people, as protagonists in this issue, have often been maligned and misunderstood. The consequences have ranged from the naive to the Machiavellian, the sophisticated to the coarse—a

A list of textbooks reviewed is to be found at the end of this paper. References to these works will be included within parentheses in the text. Each reference will give the appropriate code letter from the list and the page number of the material in question.

1. See, for example, H. S. Haddad, *Middle East History and the West* (Information Papers No. 9, December, 1973) (North Dartmouth, Mass.: Association of Arab-American University Graduates, 1973); and Edward W. Said's essay, "Orientalism and the October War: The Shattered Myths," in this volume.

multitude of American caricatures, attitudes and policy decisions directed against the Arab people.

This paper is concerned with one aspect of the structuring of thought and imagery in North America regarding Middle Eastern peoples. Specifically, this study focuses on aspects of the Protestant Church as an information control agency. Institutionalized Christianity is inalterably intertwined with the Middle East, partly because of Christianity's origins and partly because of its emphasis on biblical writings which are historically and culturally based in that region of the world. Denominational differences notwithstanding, Protestant churches are commonly united by interest in and production of information about the land of the Bible.

To the familiar maxim that "knowledge is power" should well be appended the more encompassing realization that, at both the formal and informal levels, that which is accepted as "knowledge" is defined and controlled by those in positions of power and authority. The church, as in the case of other societal institutions, may be looked upon as an agency of information control. In settings where the dissemination of information is formally organized, such as the public school or the church school, individuals and groups in positions of influence may exert considerable control over the teaching-learning process through an official curriculum. While the church school may have as its stated intent the provision of knowledge about Christianity and the mechanics of living the Christian life, there is also a "hidden curriculum," i.e., a body of implicit assumptions and informal messages which act to structure thought and action and, specific to our concern, may shape attitudes toward the world and its peoples. These informal learning messages are less easily deciphered. However, they are of major consideration in any attempt at an analytical understanding of the structuring of thought in such educational settings.

The tradition within the Protestant Church of separate educational programs for children suggests that large numbers of adult Americans have shared, to varying degrees, common exposure to the experience of Sunday school. Although church school programs claim far less time per week than the traditional school, the emphasis placed on the land and peoples of the Middle East is greater by far in the church school. Biblical stories, pictures and geography have provided and continue to provide successive generations of North American children with probably their most intensive and prolonged exposure to images of the Middle East. Such exposure, it might well be argued, can be particularly significant as it occurs in the impressionable years of childhood. Further, it occurs within a context of religious moralism.

The Protestant Church encompasses many denominations and a diversity of beliefs. However, a dimension of perhaps major significance to the issue at hand is the tendency among Protestant churches to polarize with regard to the presentation and interpretation of the results of biblical scholarship. One might expect that liberal Protestant denominations, less bound to rigid biblical interpretations, would be more objective in their portrayal of Middle Eastern peoples. For example, the conservative theological position, whose adherents are often called fundamentalists, regards the Bible as literally true. Associated with this position is the anticipated apocalyptic return of Jesus to earth. In this context, what is interpreted as the "re-birth" of the nation of Israel is seen as a partial fulfillment of biblical prophecy leading to the eventual "second coming of Christ." In contrast, liberal theologians view the Bible as written by divinely inspired men, influenced by their cultural and historical context. Accordingly, the liberal does not view the Bible, from cover to cover, as the word of God. Instead, he sees it as a basic source from which to draw "spiritual truths," with the result that justification for the existence of the modern state of Israel is not intertwined with sacred writings or prophecies. It is in the presentation and re-telling of biblical stories that there is a major focus on the Middle East. One might well expect that the differing orientations of the liberal and conservative denominations would be reflected in the way Middle Eastern peoples are portrayed.

Although the Bible may be regarded by some as inviolable, the hand of God writ large, no claim is made for the infallibility of Sunday school textbooks. They are the product of human thought and the human hand. Textbooks, which attempt to distinguish justice from injustice, goodness from evil, right from wrong, in the process of trying to create a well-trained Christian child, may also create a scenario of the Middle East complete with "just" and "unjust," "foreign" and "familiar," and "godly" and "ungodly" peoples. As a perhaps indirect by-product of their religious instruction, some church school programs may thereby be creating "black sheep" in the family of God.

The focus of this paper is on the treatment of Middle Eastern peoples in Protestant Sunday school materials. The information presented is derived from a content analysis of the pupil textbooks used by selected

Protestant denominations in their church school programs. The intent of the study is to examine the textbook messages, direct and indirect, about the peoples of the land of the Middle East.

TEXTBOOK SELECTION

The selection of specific church school textbooks for the purpose of content analysis was influenced by two factors: (1) extent of their audience or suspected influence as suggested by membership figures or the popularity of the particular publications; and (2) a concern that both the liberal and conservative religious orientations be represented. In addition to consulting statistics regarding church membership, ministers and church school Christian education directors were interviewed.[2] Four groups were finally selected: two major liberal denominations—the United Methodist Church and the United Church of Canada; and two major biblically conservative sources—the Southern Baptist Convention and the Gospel Light Press. Background descriptions for each group will follow.

The United Methodist Church

The United Methodist Church, formed by merger of the Methodist Church and the Evangelical United Brethren Church in 1968, is the largest liberal Protestant group in the United States. In 1971, the membership was listed at approximately 10,509,000.[3] Sunday school materials examined covered a one-year period (1973–74).

The United Church of Canada

The United Church of Canada is a liberal denomination and Canada's largest Protestant body. It emerged from a 1925 merger of Methodist,

2. Interestingly, determining and acquiring the appropriate materials was not as easy as I had expected. Some ministers and church school directors were suspicious about an outsider inquiring about their books. Some more evangelically inclined individuals demanded an explanation and justification of personal religious beliefs vis-a-vis their particular denomination (an unusual, but not necessarily unreasonable, demand for researcher-subject *quid pro quo*). Other church officials were very open, interested and helpful, giving no implication that their materials were closed to outsiders. I might add that the characteristic of suspicious arousal versus intellectual arousal did *not* follow liberal versus conservative religious divisions.

3. Membership figures are derived from: U.S. Bureau of the Census, *Statistical Abstract of the United States: 1973* (94th edition) (Washington, D.C.: U.S. Bureau of the Census, 1973).

Presbyterian and Congregational churches and has been said to be "as Canadian as the maple leaf and the beaver."[4] Approximately one-third of Canadian Protestants are affiliated with the United Church. The United Church's current core Sunday school curriculum made its initial appearance in the mid-1960's.[5] At that time, the new curriculum represented a major liberalization of church teachings regarding the Bible and sent a wide swath of shock through the Canadian public and pulpit.[6]

The Southern Baptist Convention

The massive Southern Baptist Convention, with a membership of 11,825,000 in 1971, is not only the largest conservative denomination but also the largest Protestant denomination in the United States. Their Sunday school materials are issued quarterly. The materials surveyed covered a one-year period (1973-74).

Gospel Light Press

Gospel Light Press is a very popular non-denominational conservative publishing house with headquarters in Glendale, California, and branch offices in seven major cities in the world. Their church school materials have a strong evangelical, fundamentalist orientation. As a free-lance press, Gospel Light particularly appeals to the many small conservative churches which cannot afford to publish their own books. For a fee, it will imprint the name of a specific church press. Additionally, as their materials are not changed quarterly, they can be re-used. The materials surveyed were for a one-year period (1973-74).

RESEARCH PROCEDURE

The method of content analysis involves a systematic and careful examination of the content of a particular form of message. In this case, the written stories in each pupil textbook were examined.

4. John Porter, *The Vertical Mosaic: An Analysis of Social Class and Power in Canada* (Toronto: University of Toronto Press, 1965), p. 519.

5. Up until recently the Anglican Church of Canada, the second largest Protestant body in the country, used the church school texts from the United Church program. The Anglicans began introducing a separate curriculum in the fall of 1974.

6. Amid the resulting furor, for example, at least two of the major English-language newspapers heralded the advent of the "new curriculum" with the somewhat spectacular headlines: "United Church also sinks Noah's Ark!"

Illustrations, which as would be expected were plentiful in these children's books, were not systematically examined. While frequencies were tabulated, the basic approach was one of qualitative content analysis. The main focus was on the pattern of ideas, the type of message given, and the presence or absence of some messages.

The materials were read initially as an aid to sensitizing the author to relevant categories of analysis. Upon careful re-reading, notations were made of all references to the following: Arabs; Jews; Judaism; Hebrew people; chosen people; promised land; the Easter story and crucifixion; Islam; the prophet Muhammad; ancient Israel; Palestine; modern Israel; the Crusades; contemporary Christians in the Middle East; and references to other contemporary non-Christian religions. After these citations were made, the selections were re-examined to determine the approach and pattern followed by each denominational group.

The resulting data are derived from the church school pupil textbooks of each of the four programs covering a one-year period for children ranging in age from approximately four through eleven, i.e., up to the end of elementary school. A total of seventy-one textbooks were examined. The focus of the analysis was thus on the younger age groups among whom Sunday school attendance is most common and for whom it may, if one subscribes to theories of primacy, provide an important grounding for later interpretations of the peoples of the Middle East.

The materials are directed at a captive audience within the church. Although one cannot predict how individual Sunday school teachers may use the materials, the fact that church school teachers are usually minimally trained (once-a-week volunteers), combined with the fact that the materials are official church textbooks, suggests that there would be heavy reliance on the prescribed curriculum.

It was initially hypothesized that the denominations less bound to rigid interpretations of the Bible (namely, the United Methodist Church and the United Church of Canada) would reflect a stronger tendency to portray Middle Eastern peoples in a balanced fashion than the biblical conservatives (i.e., the Southern Baptist Convention and the Gospel Light Press).

FINDINGS

The findings from this study will be presented under eight major headings: (1) Chosen People; (2) Promised Land; (3) The Crucifixion;

(4) Ancient and Modern Jewry; (5) Islam; (6) The Crusades; (7) Contemporary Arabs; and (8) Arab Christians in the Holy Land.

Chosen People

Throughout the Old Testament writings there is the recurring theme of the ancient Hebrews as God's "chosen people." Frank Epp has observed that "the universal theme of good land being promised to better people by superior gods has occurred frequently in history."[7] All four denominational presses repeat the notion of the uniqueness and speciality of the Jewish people. They differ, however, in the degree to which and in the manner in which this is emphasized. The conservative Gospel Light press does not refer to the idea of being "chosen" but refers to the Hebrews as "His [God's] people" (A,21; G,27). In contrast, the Southern Baptists and United Methodists both refer to the Jews as chosen people. To quote from these two sources:

Covenant—an agreement between persons; especially the agreement between God and his special chosen people. God agreed to take care of the Israelites as long as they worshipped and served him (QQ,33).

We [the Jews] are the chosen people of God. . . . Through Moses, God made a covenant with the people. Ever since that day we have been different from any other people because we have a covenant with God (SSS,7).

It is the United Church of Canada, however, which makes this idea almost a sub-theme running through their materials. There is frequent reference to the uniqueness of the Jews, Hebrews, or Israelites (the terms are used interchangeably). For example, in a text of 203 pages (BBB) (including pictures) there are seventeen references to the Hebrews as God's chosen people, as well as eight references to territorial claims of "promised land." In another United Church text (DDD,13-14) the statement is made ". . . Jesus Christ was born into God's specially trained Hebrew race."

There is, of course, an inherent problem in seeing Jews as the fathers of the faith in writings of the Old Testament and yet, at the same time, as those who reject the divinity of Jesus in the New Testament. This issue is not explored in the materials under study. However, the two liberal groups attempt to make a transition when

7. Frank H. Epp, *Whose Land Is Palestine?* (Grand Rapids: William B. Eerdmans, 1970), p. 41.

discussing Christianity. They assert that while in Old Testament times God's covenant was with the Jews, it is now with the Christian Church (CCC,197; RRR,37). This is a complex idea for children and is not reiterated as is the concept of "chosen people."

Promised Land

Territorial claims have, of course, been at the center of controversy in the Middle East. In view of this, it is interesting that all four Sunday school programs refer to the idea of a "promised land," i.e., one ordained by God for the Hebrew people, hence giving the sanction of the deity to land claims. For example, a United Church of Canada publication reads: "They were known as the people of Israel. This was their promised land and they believed themselves to be God's chosen people" (CCC,23). Referring to ancient conquests, a Gospel Light book claims: "No magic or soothsayer is strong enough to change God's plan. God wanted the Israelites to conquer the Promised Land" (Y,8). In a United Methodist publication we find, "The Hebrew people were going back to the land God had promised to Abraham" (LLL,16); and a Southern Baptist book states, "God's people were ready to cross the Jordan River and go into the Promised Land . . ." (LL,27).

Variations in the frequency of such references to land claims appear to be related to the degree to which Old Testament stories are examined and re-told. None of the church groups under study considers or clarifies the temporal limits (if any) of these claims. But the phrase "promised land" is repeated enough to be familiar to most young students exposed to these materials.

The Crucifixion

The death of Jesus and its symbolism are important components of the Christian faith. Jesus' death, however, in addition to being premeditated, occurred within the sensitive context of a general Jewish rejection of his teachings. At issue is the question of where responsibility for Jesus' death is placed. All four religious groups de-emphasize the harshest aspects of the crucifixion story for younger children. However, in the materials for older children more details are given, as well as attribution of blame, which appears to be a choice between representatives of the Roman government and representatives of the Jewish people of ancient Palestine. The United Methodists assert, "Jesus [was] killed by the Roman Government" (MMM,43). The other groups take different approaches.

It should be recognized that, even if writers elect to place responsibility for Jesus' death on Jewish leaders or Jewish crowds, as opposed to the Roman government or Roman soldiers, by avoiding the adjective *Jewish* they can also more successfully avoid giving the young reader a generalized impression of ethnic evil. They may, for example, refer to the priests as the Sanhedrin instead of Jewish priests or refer to Jesus' tormenters as jeering crowds instead of jeering Jews. The conservative Southern Baptist publications take this approach. Their materials carefully avoid connecting the adjective *Jewish* to participants in the events leading to Jesus' crucifixion. The information is there to make such connections, but it requires retention and integration of a chain of ideas covering several pages. We find, for example, the following:

> Then they took him before a council of very important men called the Sanhedrin. It was here that Caiaphas, the high priest, pronounced the death sentence upon Jesus (RR,6).
> By now, the mob led by the chief priests, was very angry. They took Jesus back to Pilate and demanded that he be put to death (RR,7).

In contrast to the above, the liberal United Church of Canada places responsibility more directly with the Jewish leaders and people. For example:

> At passover time it was customary to release one Jewish prisoner. Pilate offered Jesus, for he knew that jealousy and spite had caused Jesus to be condemned by the priests. But their influence with the Jews was far greater than Pilate's. "Crucify him!" the crowd shouted again and again (BBB,180).

The Gospel Light Press repeatedly uses the adjective *Jewish* in connection with attribution of blame for the crucifixion (e.g., S,17; R,2; V,35; Z,5 and so on). One text notes in addition:

> Did you know that the Jews wanted to put Jesus to death but it was against the law for the Sanhedrin to kill a man? Sometimes they stoned men to death when Pilate was out of town, even if it was against the law. . . . Perhaps they might have stoned Jesus if Pilate had not been in the city (Z,15).

The issue of "responsibility" for Jesus' death is, of course, not one of just idle historical interest. The epithet of 'Christ killer" has accompanied persecutions of Jews through the centuries. Independent of historical validity or invalidity, the directions taken by some interpretations of responsibility are often felt to reflect a potential for other problems. Glock and Stark, for example, note that "such a sinister linking of modern Jews with the 'crimes' attributed to their far-distant ancestors depends, in the first instance, upon believing that the ancient Jews actually were responsible for the death of Jesus."[8] Given that Zionists can not well argue that they (the ancient Jews) are not us (the modern Jews) and still support the validity of historic land claims, their alternative is to pressure for change of interpretation regarding the events leading to the crucifixion. The attribution of Jewish responsibility for the death of Jesus has, in fact, been successfully challenged by groups in the United States who have succeeded, for example, in forcing school textbook publishers to reverse their printed position and revise sections of their books in order to place responsibility for this event with the Romans.[9]

Ancient and Modern Jewry

The church school texts examined tend to portray the Jewish people as an unbroken historic entity extending from Old Testament times to the present. Little distinction is made between the ancient Hebrews and the modern state of Israel. Terms such as *Hebrew, Jew,* and *Israelite* tend to be used interchangeably. There sometimes appear to be intentional and at other times unintentional literary leaps from the residents of a pre-Christian era to the people of the 20th century. Children of ten or eleven years of age or younger are unlikely to be able to decipher the difference. For example:

If the Philistine war had been fought in our day, the newspaper would have run a banner headline: Israel Loses War (Gospel Light: BB,9).

Jews—The chosen people, to whom God gave the law at Mount Sinai, are called Hebrews in the early parts of the Old Testament, and later they are called Jews. In the New Testament the word "Israel" refers to these people (United Methodist: SSS,9).

It took a lot of courage for Abraham to choose to be different. But because Abraham chose to be different, God gave him a very special

8. Charles Y. Glock and Rodney Stark, *Christian Beliefs and Anti-Semitism* (New York: Harper and Row, 1966), p. 61.

9. For example, the Anti-Defamation League of B'nai B'rith pressured Ginn and Company publishers to "correct" a passage of a school text (*The Story of Man's Past* by Edith Ware) which had put responsibility for the crucifixion of Jesus on the Jews. See *The Jewish News*, New Jersey, February 14, 1974, p. 1.

responsibility. He was to be the father of a great nation. Today, in modern Israel, the descendants of Abraham honor him as the father of their nation (Southern Baptist: RR,31).

So Mahla's song helped the people of Israel to remember the words of God. The Israelites became a singing people and used music in their worship ever afterwards (United Church of Canada: AAA,25).

The existence of these linkages among both conservative and liberal presses has particular implications when one considers the possible stand of each group with respect to such issues as a promised land or the responsibility for the crucifixion of Jesus. For example, biblical references to Jews, Israelites, promised land, and Jerusalem have been used to validate beliefs in the prophetic "second coming of Christ," overlooking the variant meaning of these terms throughout the Bible. As Epp observes, "Zion, Jerusalem, and Israel . . . sometimes mean literal-historical places, but often they are used poetically and symbolically to communicate universal moral and spiritual truths." [10] These possible "universal truths" are muted, however, by their characterization in Sunday school texts as literal entities.

Linkages between Christianity and the whole historic spectrum of Judaism can also be made by emphasizing the Jewishness of early Christianity. The Jewish origins of the early Christians and God's love for Gentiles and Jews are stressed in the Southern Baptist materials. The two liberal denominations, in addition to emphasizing the Jewishness of the early Christians, also emphasize the Jewishness of Jesus. For example, Jesus is described as a Jew (000,43) who grew up with the help of his local rabbi (PPP,74), experienced a ceremony similar to today's Jewish Bar Mitzvah (CCC,40), was a rabbi (CCC,60), and had "Jewish parents" (CCC,39).

In contrast to the treatment of ancient and modern Jewry by the three groups discussed, the Gospel Light Press does not put Jewishness in a familiar or friendly light. Although they refer to Jews as believers in "the one true God" (R,40), their most frequent use of the adjective *Jewish* is in connection with descriptions of the malefactors of the crucifixion story.

However, for three of these church school programs, the "strangeness" of the distinctive clothing worn by ancient Jews in textbook illustrations is mitigated by an emphasis on commonalities. The common historical roots of modern Christianity and modern Judaism

10. Frank H. Epp, *Whose Land Is Palestine?* p. 241.

are emphasized to the young pupil. Judaism, in contrast to Islam (discussed below), is not generally treated as a remote faith practiced by an alien people.

Islam

Islam is commonly ignored in these church school texts, as one might suspect given their Christianizing intent. The two conservative publishers (Southern Baptist Convention and Gospel Light), which are more evangelical in orientation, omit any reference to either Islam or Muslims in their textbooks. Islam is mentioned by the two liberal groups but it is usually not only in alien but also in negative terms. In contrast to Judaism, which is a familiar religion with recognized links to Christianity, the common links between Christianity and Islam are overlooked and the differences are emphasized. For example, in one United Methodist book, definitions of a Jew and a Muslim provide interesting contrasts:

> Jew: a descendant of the Hebrew people of Old Testament times; a believer in the religion of the Jewish people (RRR,76).
> Muslim: a follower of Mohammed, who founded the religion called 'Islam'; a member of the Islamic faith. Muslims believe that Jesus was just one of God's many prophets and tht Mohammed was the last and greatest prophet (RRR,76).

In the definition above, the Muslim is erroneously portrayed as emphasizing Muhammad, while the linkage between Muslims and Christians of worshiping a common god is underplayed. The Muslim is further estranged by being described as believing that Jesus is *just* one of God's prophets; however, the Jewish view of Jesus, which is similarly at odds with the Christian view, is not mentioned in the United Methodist definition of a Jew. Another United Methodist text carrying a sympathetic story regarding the Arab refugees follows a similar pattern. The families are described as follows: "Most of them were not Christian. They worshiped Allah and followed the teachings of Mohammed" (QQQ,62). That the Muslim Allah and the Christian God are one and the same deity is not recognized.

Similarly the United Church of Canada refers to Muslims as "Mohammedans" who preached "of God whom they called Allah and of Mohammed who *claimed* to be his prophet" (DDD,52; italics added). It is interesting to contrast this statement with another in the same textbook where Buddha merits being referred to as "the great Indian teacher" (DDD,171).

The portrayal of Islam is possibly at some variance with the manifest intentions of the liberal United Methodist and United Church of Canada, both of which are more generally predisposed to religious tolerance. For example, on the back cover of one United Church of Canada text (DDD) is written ". . . between the Christian faith and other religions better and better relationships are growing. We should all be thankful to live in a day when people are learning to be more tolerant and open minded." Whatever their intent, however, textbook presentation in these two church school programs lends to the interpretation of the Islamic faith as not just different but also inferior.

The Crusades

The success of Islam during the years of conquest and its spread from China to Spain and the Balkans and the Christian Crusades to "re-capture" the Holy Land serve as historic reminders of the long running competition between the two faiths. The two liberal churches touch on this topic in their materials; the conservative churches ignore these issues completely.

In presenting a historical perspective on the development of Christianity, the United Church of Canada tends to describe the growth of the Muslim faith and the Christian Crusades from a one-sided view. For example:

> As Moslems grew in power, countless Christians were killed in conflict with them. Many lost heart, but some grew more determined to preach Jesus as Lord (DDD,52).

That *Muslims* were also killed in these battles is not suggested. The Crusades are summarized, regretfully, as "perhaps the one single movement that might have joined Christians of every land between A.D. 100 and A.D. 1300 . . . but the crusades were a miserable failure" (DDD,54).

United Methodist materials define *crusade* as "a 'holy war'; a fight against evil. Historically, one of the series of attempts by European Christians to take Palestine from the Muslims" (DDD,76). The Crusades are described as a reaction to Muslims' "fierce persecution of the Christians" (DDD,62). In evaluating the success of these early Christian missions, however, the United Methodists arrive at a somewhat different conclusion from that of the United Church of Canada. They note: "Note one non-Christian became a Christian while the *sword* was the church's weapon" (DDD,62). Discussion of historic events such as the Crusades or the Islamic conquest is probably difficult to achieve without opening up painful reminders of the consequences of religious warfare. However, there are major links between these two religions which could be further examined. As Baha el-Din has observed, there is a strong and positive tradition of cultural and historical ties which unite these two great faiths, one example being the important role played by Muslims in preserving elements of Western civilization during the Middle Ages.[11]

Contemporary Arabs

Modern Arabs are not discussed in the textbooks of either the United Church of Canada or the Southern Baptist Convention. Coverage given by the conservative Gospel Light Press is brief and negative, presenting the image of a nomadic adversary and territorial intruder. For example:

> If you were to visit Bible lands today you would see that many of the people in the Arab countries are nomads . . . (moving) from place to place to find food and water . . . (living) in tents made of goat skins and camel hair . . . (Y,35).
> The Israelites had no transportation that could compare with the speed of the Arabian camels. They were terrified of these nomads who swooped down upon their land. They destroyed their homes and food, then dashed away on their fast camels . . . today the descendants of the Midianites and Arabians continue to attack the cities of Israel trying to drive them out of the land (Y,52).

The emphasis on a nomadic, Bedouin image of the Arab is, of course, extremely misleading, given the small representation of nomadic peoples in the total Arab population.

The United Methodist Church is the only liberal group which has given attention to Arabs, indeed to Palestinians, in their official student texts. In one two-page article they sympathetically describe life in a refugee camp in Jordan, even noting: "All the families living together in the refugee village had much in common. They all held one hope—that someday they might return to their homes from which they had been forced to flee during the Arab-Israeli conflict" (QQQ, 62-63). In another text, the United Methodists devote four pages to

11. Ahmad Baha el-Din, "World Media and the Arabs: An Arab Perspective," in *The Arab World: From Nationalism to Revolution,* ed. Abdeen Jabara and Janice Terry (Wilmette, Ill.: Medina University Press International, 1971), pp. 77-85.

a discussion of the life of Kahlil, a Palestinian boy in Jordan. Descriptions are given of entertainment, food, school, employment and weddings. In addition there is a discussion of the Palestinian refugees. However, the movements of the Palestinians are made to sound voluntary, e.g.,

> I was born in Jerusalem and we lived there until 1967. But then war broke out in the Middle East and we decided to move to Jordan. . . . After the war, my father's travel business had to be closed. Now he is an antique dealer. . . . We like our home here, although we did not want to leave Jerusalem (SSS,77).

Also differential definitions of "immigration" and employment opportunites are not explained; hence we find the following statement:

> In 1948, when the nation of Israel was founded, many Arabs left Palestine and came to live in neighboring [countries]. . . . And many Jewish refugees from Arab countries fled from their homes to Israel. They were completely absorbed into the society, and, therefore, are not as well known as the Palestinian refugees (SSS,80)

However, the United Methodist Church stands as the only group in the study which has attempted to examine the problems of the contemporary Middle East in their official pupil texts and has, as well, sympathetically commented on problems of the Palestinians.

Arab Christians in the Holy Land

One might expect that Christian churches would wax enthusiastic about the presence of Christians in the land where their religion originated. In fact, only one Sunday school program has a discussion of Arab Christians. The United Methodist Church has a two-page article in one of its pupil texts on a Christian refugee family in Jordan which includes a description of their father teaching them about religion (QQQ,62–63). In contrast, while the United Church of Canada's publications refer to Christians in Korea, Japan, Hong Kong, India, South Africa and Brazil, there is no mention of contemporary Arab Christians. Similarly, Gospel Light and Southern Baptist textbooks, although less frequently mentioning missionary activities, neither discuss nor mention the existence of Arab Christians.

SUMMARY AND CONCLUSIONS

The Sunday school texts examined reveal some patterns that follow the liberal-conservative dimension and other patterns that criss-cross such distinctions. All four groups exhibit variants of the themes of a chosen people and a promised land. However, perhaps surprisingly, the liberal United Church of Canada repeats the chosen people theme most frequently. All of the groups except Gospel Light portray Judaism as a familiar, unalien, religion; but none of them makes distinctions of much note between ancient Jewry and modern Jewry. It is this absence of distinction which becomes potentially problematic for Jews when responsibility is laid regarding the crucifixion. Gospel Light publications carry the strongest indictment against the Jews. The Southern Baptist Convention alludes to Jewish responsibility. The United Methodists place responsibility with the Roman government. The two conservative Sunday school publications are consistent in overlooking the existence of Muslims and Arab Christians. Modern Arabs are referred to briefly and negatively by Gospel Light press. Of the two liberal denominations, the United Church of Canada ignores Arab Christians in the Holy Land, writes erroneously of Islam and negatively of the Muslim "role" in the Crusades. The United Methodist Church also gives an erroneous impression of Islam, emphasizes its differences from Christianity and writes negatively of early Muslims. However, the United Methodist Church is unique in having relatively sympathetic coverage of Arabs and Arab Christians.

The conservative church groups examined are closely tied to a narrow interpretation of the Bible as well as an evangelical orientation. While they might be amenable to suggestions for change regarding their presentation of the life style of contemporary Arabs, their general pattern of omitting discussion of religious and ethnic differences may remain. The liberal churches, given their inclinations toward rationality and non-literal biblical interpretations, are the ones with the highest potential for responsiveness to change. The United Methodist Church publishes new Sunday school materials quarterly. The United Church of Canada, which has maintained the same textbooks for over a decade, may conceivably eliminate stereotypes and inaccuracies when the existing curriculum materials are revised.

Considering the prospects of change, it seems important to note that there appears to be a shifting religious climate in North America in the 1970's in contrast to the decade of the 60's. Some analysts of Christian religion have pointed to a "neofundamentalism" trend in America.[12] Other observing a change in religious climate have referred to a "neopentecostal" movement finding its center in the charismata of the New Testament, i.e., the gifts from the Holy Spirit of "speaking in tongues," as well as personal witness, faith healing and prophecy. Kokosalakis observes that "there is evidence of an increase from within and from without the churches, of various pentecostal movements and a variety of magico-religious and superstitious phenomena such as astrology, belief in ghosts, spiritualism of various sorts, etc."[13]

The perhaps encapsulating statement that can be made about the changing religious climate is that there has been a movement from the rational to the emotional; from the "God is dead" theology and situational ethics philosophy of the 1960's to an emphasis on feeling, intuition and nonverbal communication. Within this characteristically non-intellectual movement, mainline liberal Protestant churches may find themselves labeled as cold and cerebral. The increasingly popular evangelical-pentecostal philosophies of the 1970's are piercing the very strongholds of liberal Protestantism.

The apparent trend away from rationalism sets a receptive stage for a return to the unquestioning acceptance of biblical writings. Although the evangelical-pentecostal approach need not encompass a fundamentalist interpretation of the Bible and biblical prophecy, there is evidence to suggest that some form of fundamentalism is in the offing. A case in point is the recent International Congress of World Evangelization held in Lausanne, Switzerland, in July of 1974. This ten-day conference attracted some 2,400 Protestant leaders from 150 countries. The conference presented a challenge to the established position of the theologically liberal World Council of Churches (formed in 1948), as it reflected on the current enthusiasm for the new religious emotionalism. A document entitled the "Lausanne Covenant" was signed by 1,900 representatives at the conference, affirming their belief not only in the earthly return of Jesus, but also in ". . . the divine inspiration, truthfulness and authority of both Old and New Testament Scriptures in their entirety. . . ."[14] That

12. Andrew Greeley, "Religion in a Secular Society," *Social Research*, 41 (Summer 1974), 226–40.

13. N. Kokosalakis, "The Contemporary Metamorphosis of Religion?" *The Human Context*, VI (1974), 243–49.

14. "A Challenge from Evangelicals," *Time Magazine*, August 5, 1974, pp. 46–47.

many of the leaders of these evangelical groups tied themselves to a fundamentalist interpretation of the Bible may have portent for the climate of opinion toward the Arab people and their resistance to the state of Israel.

Protestant Sunday schools continue to structure knowledge about the peoples of the Middle East. However, the potential willingness of these different denominations to revise their curricular materials in a direction away from literalist biblical orientations and toward broader acceptance of religious and ethnic diversity may be affected by the currently shifting religious climate. As many Sunday school textbooks now stand, they are creating, as an educational by-product, black sheep in the family of God. The results of this study suggest that the Arabs are the most excluded of the deity's descendants.

TEXTBOOKS

I. *Gospel Light Publications*

A   *My Bible Tells of God.* 4-Year-Olds. Glendale, Cal.: Gospel Light Publications, 1972.

B   *My Bible Tells of Jesus.* 4-Year-Olds. Glendale, Cal.: Gospel Light Publications, 1972.

C   *My Bible Tells of Pleasing God.* 4-Year-Olds. Glendale, Cal.: Gospel Light Publications, 1973.

D   *My Bible Tells of Jesus and His Friends.* 4-Year-Olds. Glendale, Cal.: Gospel Light Publications, 1973.

E   *I Learn of God's Plans.* 5-Year-Olds. Glendale, Cal.: Gospel Light Publications, 1973.

F   *I Learn of Jesus, God's Son.* 5-Year-Olds. Glendale, Cal.: Gospel Light Publications, 1973.

G   *I Learn about My Bible.* 5-Year-Olds. Glendale, Cal.: Gospel Light Publications, 1974.

H   *I Learn of Bible Friends.* 5-Year-Olds. Glendale, Cal.: Gospel Light Publications, 1974.

I   *First Bible Stories.* First Grade. Glendale, Cal.: The Sunday School House, Gospel Light Publications, 1965.

J   *Stories of Jacob's Family.* First Grade. Glendale, Cal.: Gospel Light Publications, 1966.

K   *First Stories of Jesus.* First Grade. Glendale, Cal.: Gospel Light Publications, 1965.

L   *Stories of Moses.* First Grade. Glendale, Cal.: Gospel Light Publications, 1966.

M   *Kings and Prophets.* Second Grade. Glendale, Cal.: Gospel Light Publications, 1964.

N   *Old Testament Stories.* Second Grade. Glendale, Cal.: Gospel Light Publications, 1963.

O   *Stories of David.* Second Grade. Glendale, Cal.: Gospel Light Publications, 1964.

P   *Words and Deeds of Jesus.* Second Grade. Glendale, Cal.: Gospel Light Publications, 1963.

Q   *Learning from God's Word.* Third Grade. Glendale, Cal.: Gospel Light Publications, 1972.

R   *The Adventures of Paul.* Third Grade. Glendale, Cal.: Gospel Light Publications, 1973.

S   *Jesus and His Disciple Peter.* Third Grade. Glendale, Cal.: Gospel Light Publications, 1972.

T   *Great Lessons Jesus Taught.* Third Grade. Glendale, Cal.: Gospel Light Publications, 1973.

U   *Adventures in the Wilderness.* Fourth Grade. Glendale, Cal.: Gospel Light Publications, 1974.

V   *Jesus, the Son of God.* Fourth Grade. Glendale, Cal.: Gospel Light Publications, 1968.

W   *Old Testament Heroes.* Fourth Grade. Glendale, Cal.: Gospel Light Publications, 1973.

X   *Stories of the Beginnings.* Fourth Grade. Glendale, Cal.: Gospel Light Publications, 1973.

Y   *Men of Courage.* Fifth Grade. Glendale, Cal.: Gospel Light Publications, 1968.

Z   *Lord of My Life.* Fifth Grade. Glendale, Cal.: Gospel Light Publications, 1968.

AA   *Adventures with New Leaders.* Fifth Grade. Glendale, Cal.: Gospel Light Publications, 1969.

BB   *One Nation under God.* Fifth Grade. Glendale, Cal.: Gospel Light Publications, 1969.

CC   Barrett, Ethel, *"The Strangest Thing Happened. . . .* Sixth Grade. Glendale, Cal.: Gospel Light Publications, 1969.

DD   Barrett, Ethel, *The Secret Sign.* Sixth Grade. Glendale, Cal.: Gospel Light Publications, 1970.

EE   Barrett, Ethel, *Which Way to Nineveh?* Sixth Grade. Glendale, Cal.: Gospel Light Publications, 1969.

II. Southern Baptist Convention

FF   *Growing.* January–March 1974, Kindergarten. Nashville: The Sunday School Board of the Southern Baptist Convention, 1973.

GG   *Growing.* April–June 1974, Kindergarten. Nashville: The Sunday School Board of the Southern Baptist Convention, 1974.

HH   *Growing.* July–September 1974, Kindergarten. Nashville: The Sunday School Board of the Southern Baptist Convention, 1974.

II   *Bible Learners.* January–March 1974, First & Second Grades. Nashville: The Sunday School Board of the Southern Baptist Convention, 1973.

JJ   *Bible Learners.* April–June 1974, First & Second Grades. Nashville: The Sunday School Board of the Southern Baptist Convention, 1974.

KK   *Bible Learners.* July–September 1974, First & Second Grades. Nashville: The Sunday School Board of the Southern Baptist Convention, 1974.

LL   *Bible Learners.* October–December 1974, First & Second Grades. Nashville: The Sunday School Board of the Southern Baptist Convention, 1974.

MM   *Bible Discoverers.* January–March 1974, Third & Fourth Grades. Nashville: The Sunday School Board of the Southern Baptist Convention, 1973.

NN   *Bible Discoverers.* April–June 1974, Third & Fourth Grades. Nashville: The Sunday School Board of the Southern Baptist Convention, 1974.

OO   *Bible Discoverers.* July–September 1974, Third & Fourth Grades. Nashville: The Sunday School Board of the Southern Baptist Convention, 1974.

PP   *Bible Discoverers.* July–September 1974, Third & Fourth Grades. Nashville: The Sunday School Board of the Southern Baptist Convention, 1974.

QQ   *Bible Searchers.* January–March 1974, Fifth & Sixth Grades. Nashville: The Sunday School Board of the Southern Baptist Convention, 1973.

RR   *Bible Searchers.* April–June 1974, Fifth & Sixth Grades. Nashville: The Sunday School Board of the Southern Baptist Convention, 1974.

SS   *Bible Searchers.* July–September 1974, Fifth & Sixth Grades. Nashville: The Sunday School Board of the Southern Baptist Convention, 1974.

TT   *Bible Searchers.* October–December 1974, Fifth & Sixth Grades. Nashville: The Sunday School Board of the Southern Baptist Convention, 1974.

III. United Church of Canada

UU   McLean, Robert K. N., *Time for Each Other.* Kindergarten 1. Toronto: The United Church Publishing House, 1964.

VV   McLean, Robert K. N., *Jesus and the Children.* Kindergarten 1. Toronto: The United Church Publishing House, 1964.

WW   Johnston, Nandy, *Praise Him, Praise Him.* Kindergarten 2. Toronto: The United Church Publishing House, 1965.

XX   Johnston, Nandy, *Friends Together.* Kindergarten 2. Toronto: The United Church Publishing House, 1965.

YY   McKim, Audrey, *God Is Always with Us.* Primary 1. Toronto: The United Church Publishing House, 1964.

ZZ   Hughes, Patricia M., *Fairest Lord Jesus.* Primary 2. Toronto: The United Church Publishing House, 1965.

AAA   Stewart, Charlotte L., *This Is My Church.* Primary 3. Toronto: The United Church Publishing House, 1966.

BBB   White, Peter Gordon, *The Mystery of the Rock.* Junior 1. Toronto: The United Church Publishing House, 1964.

CCC   Clarke, William F., *The Clue to the Mystery.* Junior 2. Toronto: The United Church Publishing House, 1965.

DDD   Clark, Isabel Squires, *The Mystery Continues.* Junior 3. Toronto: The United Church Publishing House, 1966.

IV. United Methodist Church

EEE   *We Learn from the Bible.* Kindergarten. Nashville: Graded Press, 1973.

FFF   *God's World—My World.* Kindergarten. Nashville: Graded Press, 1974.

GGG   *Working with God.* Kindergarten. Nashville: Graded Press, 1974.

HHH   *The People of God.* Kindergarten. Nashville: Graded Press, 1974.

III   *Persons Who Knew God—New Testament.* I-II Student. Nashville: Graded Press, 1973.

JJJ   *The Church—People of God.* I-II Student. Nashville: Graded Press, 1974.
KKK   *God's World/Our World.* I-II Student. Nashville: Graded Press, 1974.
LLL   *God Always Loves Us.* I-II Student. Nashville: Graded Press, 1974.
MMM   *Learning about Myself: A Child of God.* III-IV Student. Nashville: Graded Press, 1974.
NNN   *God, the Universe, and Me.* III-IV Student. Nashville: Graded Press, 1974.
OOO   *The God We Meet.* III-IV Student. Nashville: Graded Press, 1974.
PPP   *Love Is Here to Stay!* V-VI Student. Nashville: Graded Press, 1974.
QQQ   *In It Together.* V-VI Student. Nashville: Graded Press, 1974.
RRR   *Let It Happen!* V-VI Student. Nashville: Graded Press, 1974.
SSS   *The Law Is Fulfilled.* V-VI Student. Nashville: Graded Press, 1973.

Carlo Caldarola

FUNDAMENTALIST CHRISTIANITY: ISRAEL AND THE SECOND COMING

FOR OVER FIFTEEN HUNDRED YEARS Christian teaching had not entertained the possibility of the return of the Jews to Palestine, for the literal interpretation of the Bible had been generally rejected in favor of other interpretations adopted by the Fathers, especially the allegorical exegesis which had received the blessing of the Roman church. Accordingly, Old Testament passages referring to the return of the Jews to their homeland in the distant future and the primacy they would enjoy among the nations were believed to apply not to the Jews but to the Christian church and its faithful. Because the Jews had rejected and killed the Messiah, they had lost their privileged position and had been exiled. Therefore, the existence of the Jewish nation had come to an end forever. The prophecies on Jewish restoration were applied to "the true Israel," the Christian church, and to the Christian religion. For the Jews there was no hope of salvation except by embracing the Christian faith. These ideas became the source of anti-Semitism, which remained alive in the traditional churches, particularly in the Roman Catholic church, until recently.

With the Reformation, the Protestant exegesis replaced the symbolic and allegorical methods of biblical interpretation with a more "grammatical" and "literal" approach. The faithful were summoned to "return to the Bible" itself and to seek in it the simple, obvious meaning of the text. Since no limitation or restriction was imposed upon the reader, the door opened for innovations in important points of theology and for numerous new sects to organize around specific points of Christian belief.

This fundamentalist approach to the interpretation of the Bible, when applied to the prophecies concerning Israel, generated the idea of the necessity of the Jewish return to Zion for the fulfillment of the supreme goals of Christianity. This idea can be found clearly outlined by some British theologians of the seventeenth century, and it became quite popular in the subsequent religious movements that took place in England during the eighteenth and nineteenth centuries. The political events through the 1790s in Europe were particularly responsible for the revival of prophetic concern in England. The violent uprooting of European political and social institutions, the destruction of the papal power in France, the confiscation of church property, the establishment of a religion of reason, and the exile of the pope in 1798 were shocking events that induced many to believe that the end of the world was near. In that context it was felt that the restoration of Israel had to be realized and that it was the duty of the British government to do whatever was considered good and just according to God's will and intention. This popular belief eventually contributed to influencing the British government to take action for the resettlement of Jews in Palestine.[1]

By the middle of the nineteenth century, British millenarian theology had been imported into the United States and had become the most popular form of American millenarianism. It also contributed to the development of American fundamentalism. In about 1875, fundamentalism became a well-defined religious movement with its own structure and identity.[2] The movement became concerned with two firm doctrines: the personal, imminent return of Christ, and the literal interpretation of the Bible. Through periodicals, books, street preaching, and conferences, the millenarian message was announced as follows: The world is rushing toward judgment; nothing can save it from destruction, and attempts to ameliorate it are doomed to failure. Man's wickedness is beyond remedy; politics, philosophy, art, science, particularly the teaching of godless evolution, do nothing but amplify

1. See: Mayir Vreté, "The Restoration of the Jews in English Protestant Thought, 1790–1840," *Middle Eastern Studies*, VIII (Jan. 1972), 3–50 (to be followed by another article). See also Ernest R. Sandeen, *The Roots of Fundamentalism* (Chicago: University of Chicago Press, 1970).

2. For a historical analysis of the fundamentalist movement, see particularly Ernest R. Sandeen, *Toward a Historical Interpretation of the Origins of Fundamentalism* (Philadelphia: Fortress Press, 1968); Louis Gasper, *The Fundamentalist Movement* (The Hague: Mouton, 1963).

man's degeneration. Therefore, the wise Christian has to care about his salvation, for Christ will return to this world to rescue his church and will snatch it from the destruction which the world will soon suffer. Only after Christ's coming can the millennium be inaugurated in which Christ will finally establish his kingdom of peace and justice on earth.

This preaching proved appealing to immigrants, the unemployed, and spiritually troubled people. The leaders of the millenarian movement of this time were drawn primarily from the Episcopal, Presbyterian, Congregational, and Baptist denominations. By 1900, Episcopal and Congregational support had diminished considerably, and by the 1920s Presbyterian support decreased also, while nondenominational Bible groups boomed throughout the country so as to create a movement completely independent from the established churches. Today, the movement includes as its most militant expression a countless number of small evangelical groups (and their Bible schools) who exert a great influence in North America with their extensive radio and television programs, wide dissemination of religious literature, and missionary campaigns. Their teachings, despite marginal differences, converge on emphasizing the identity of religion and life and the intensity of spiritual experience, particularly the conversion experience through the baptism of the Holy Spirit. Ethical austerity is strongly inculcated, with rejection of liberal fashions, gambling, pastimes, and use of stimulants, and with emphasis upon the observance of the Lord's Day, tithing, daily duty, and ultimate loyalty to Christ. On the ideological level, absolute truth emerges from the literal reading of the Bible, which announces a message of salvation and the imminence of the Second Coming.

The events in the Middle East are of great significance to the fundamentalist believer. During the excitement of World War I, many millenarian conferences were held, particularly in 1918, when the British occupation of Palestine stirred hopes that prophecies relating to the return of the Jews to the Holy Land would soon be fulfilled. Since 1948, when Israel was restored as a nation, the excitement has been growing rapidly, reaching its highest peaks during the Middle East wars of 1967 and 1973.

Thus, fundamentalist statements about these two wars differ sharply from those made by the leaders of the mainline denominations. There is a growing tendency among church scholars to interpret the Bible in liberal and metaphorical ways. Also, ecumenical preoccupations suggest keeping an impartial and conciliatory tone between the two parties in the Middle East; such concerns are conveniently expressed in terms of general wishes for a just and peaceful solution to the controversies.[3] Alternatively, the evangelical groups, defending a strictly literal interpretation of the Bible, have been commenting on the Middle East events in prophetic language, explaining them in light of the vision of the approaching future as they see it outlined in the Bible, and therefore taking a definite pro-Israeli side. Church sermons, radio and television programs, and millions of books, pamphlets, and leaflets launched by evangelical groups in the past few years have given a vivid and dramatic picture of the eschatological time that is felt to be very near.[4]

The history of mankind, so the argument goes, revolves around the history of the Israeli people, for they have been "chosen" by God to fulfill the eternal design. In fact, there is no other nation in the world whose history has been written in advance. Since the prophecies concerning the fate of Israel have proven true so far, there is no reason why they should not find fulfillment in the future. The consistency shown in the past guarantees that God really means what he says and says what he means.

The following pages present a brief summary of the teachings of the most militant evangelical groups in this regard and give an idea of their missionary activity in the conversion of Jews to Christianity.

EVANGELICAL TEACHING ABOUT ISRAEL

Israel in the Prophecies of the Past

At the time when the Hebrews were en route from Egypt to possess the Promised Land of Palestine, Moses predicted that their nation would be punished by God twice for not believing Him and for

---

3. See, for example, Judith H. Banki, ed., *Christian Reactions to the Middle East Crisis* (New York: Jewish American Committee, 1967); *idem, Christian Responses to the Yom Kippur War: Implications for Christian-Jewish Relations* (New York: American Jewish Committee, 1974).

4. The literature in this regard abounds. Among the most important publications are: Wilbur M. Smith, *Israeli/Arab Conflict* (Glendale, Calif., 1967); Robert G. Lee, *If I Were a Jew* (Chicago: Moody Press, 1970); Hal Lindsey, *The Late Great Planet Earth* (Grand Rapids: Zondervan, 1970); J. Dwight Pentecost, *Prophecy for Today: The Middle East Crisis and the Future of the World* (Grand Rapids: Zondervan, 1961); Richard W. De Haan, *Israel and the Nations in Prophecy* (Grand Rapids: Zondervan, 1968); William L. Hull, *Israel: Key to Prophecy* (San Diego: Morris Cerullo World Evangelism, 1970); Emil A. Balliet and Morris Cerullo, *Who Will Win the War in the Middle-East? Israel, Egypt or Russia* (San Diego: Morris Cerullo World Evangelism, 1970); Herbert W. Armstrong, *The United States and British Commonwealth in Prophecy* (Pasadena, Calif.: Ambassador College Press, 1967). See also the monthly magazine issued by the Ambassador College, *The Plain Truth*.

rejecting His ways (Deut. 28:64-68). Isaiah added details to Moses' prediction by announcing the place of captivity, Babylon (Isa. 39:6), while Jeremiah foretold the length of captivity, seventy years (Jer. 25:11). Exactly as predicted, the Babylonians destroyed Jerusalem in 586 B.C. and carried the Hebrew slaves to Babylon for seventy years (2 Chron. 36:15-21). At the end of this period of enslavement, as predicted by Isaiah (Isa. 44:28; 45:4), the Persian King Cyrus released some of the prisoners (now called Jews), and they returned to Jerusalem and rebuilt the Temple (2 Chron. 36:22, 23).

In the same prophecy Moses also predicted the second stage of God's punishment. He said that because of its infidelity to God, Israel would be destroyed as a nation a second time and the survivors would be scattered throughout the world and would be continually persecuted. Many other prophets—Isaiah, Jeremiah, Ezekiel, and Amos, to name a few—predicted the exile of the Jews. Just before his arrest and crucifixion, Jesus announced that there would be great distress among the Jews, who "will fall by the edge of the sword, and will be led captive into all the nations" (Luke 21:22-24), and that this would occur in that same generation that crucified him (Matt. 23:36).

As predicted, the Romans destroyed Jerusalem and the Jewish nation in A.D. 70. For almost 2,000 years the Jews wandered the earth with no country of their own, in constant fear of persecution and death. The restoration of Israel after the world dispersion was also predicted, particularly by Ezekiel (Ezek. 36:8, 24-27; 37:11; 38:8). According to the prophecies, the restoration was to take place just one generation before the occurrence of the events culminating in the Second Coming of Christ (Matt. 24:32-34). A generation in the biblical context is something like forty years. Therefore, if this is a correct deduction, within forty years or so from the year 1948 the eschatological events will occur. It is a deep conviction of fundamentalists that we are living in the most significant period of prophetic history, in the times predicted by the prophets. The presence of the reborn nation of Israel, flourishing in prosperity, will impel a great enemy from the uttermost north of Palestine to launch an attack upon that nation which will call for the last world war and the Second Coming.

Israel in the Prophecies of the Future

The seven years preceding the Second Coming (called the countdown period) are marked by unique events, and the fundamentalists find in the Bible more prophecies for this period than for any other era. The period will be characterized by three major events: the emergence of a charismatic leader in Europe (Antichrist), the world destruction caused by the Third World War, and the Second Coming of Christ.

The Antichrist. The prophet Daniel predicted that a prince would come to power from the people who destroyed the city of Jerusalem and the second Temple (Dan. 9:27). And, since the Romans did this, it is logically expected that the coming prince would have to be someone out of the Roman culture. He is described as the leader of a ten-nation confederacy of European nations. Seven of them will recognize his authority willingly, and another three nations will be subdued by force (Dan. 7:24). For the fundamentalist, indications of this event can be found in the formation of the European Economic Community and the efforts of the Europeans to become united and independent from American influence. This leads one to think that the leadership of the West is going to shift from the United States to Europe. On the other hand, the present political crisis in the major European countries calls for a dictator who can give to those nations order, unity, and prosperity.

This new head of the revived Roman Empire is described as a man of such magnetism, such power, and such influence that for some time he will be the greatest dictator the world has ever known. He will be completely godless and diabolically evil. He is called the Antichrist in the Bible and is metaphorically pictured as a beast looking like a leopard, with feet like a bear, and a mouth like a lion (Rev. 13:1-2)—this meaning that his moves will be as rapid as those of a leopard, that he will be very strong and powerful, and that there will be an air about him which is self-assured and proud. He will take over at a time when people are so tired of war, so anxious for peace at any price, that they will willingly give their allegiance to a world dictator who promises them peace. He will make a "strong covenant" with the Israelis, guaranteeing their safety and protection. The Israelis then will rebuild the Temple of Jerusalem for the third time in history, an action that will be acknowledged with great hostility and fear by the Arabs.

Because of an ingenious settlement of the Middle East problem, the Antichrist will be respected by many nations in the world. He will bring about fantastic plans of economic prosperity, even to the underdeveloped countries. However, after three and a half years of remarkable progress, the Antichrist will proclaim himself God and will demand to be worshiped in the Temple of God in Jerusalem (2 Thess. 2:4; Matt. 2:4). He will also speak blasphemies against God and those who dwell in heaven (Rev. 13:6). Most people will follow him and love him, but the Christians will not obey him, and for this reason they will suffer persecution and will be executed en masse.

World War III. "At the time of the end, the king of the South [Egypt] shall attack him [Israel] . . . and the king of the North [Russia] shall rush upon him like a whirlwind, with chariots [mechanized army] and horsemen and with many ships" (Dan. 11:40). Israel will be the center of a concentrated attack by Egypt and Russia. The Red Army will invade Libya, Ethiopia, Egypt, and the countries of the Middle East, and will enter the "glorious land" of Israel, where it will establish its headquarters on Mount Moriah or in the Temple area, in Jerusalem (Dan. 11:45).

At this point the Orient (probably China) and the Western European countries under the Roman leader will mobilize their armies (Dan. 11:44). The Russians will be met by the European army and will be destroyed (Ezek. 38:18-22; 39:3-5).

A fearful event is predicted, for God says: "I will send on Magog [Russia] and upon those who dwell securely in the coastlands [various continents]" (Ezek. 39:6). From this, one can surmise that there would be a nuclear exchange between Russia and the Western countries. Finally, after this great battle, in which Russia will be defeated, the Israelites, joined by others, are pictured as burying the dead for a period of seven months (Ezek. 39:12-16).

After the destruction of Russia and its allies, the "Oriental [Chinese] army," it is predicted, will march to the Middle East in a challenge for world control, while the Western leaders will persuade all other nations of the world to destroy the last opposing force existing on earth (Rev. 16:13, 14, 16). The final battle will occur in a place which in Hebrew is called Armageddon, or the Mount of Megiddo, which literally means "to cut off, to slay." In biblical history countless bloody battles were fought in this area. In the Book of Joel this valley was called the "valley of Jehoshaphat." Today this valley's entrance has the port of Haifa at its western end.

The Oriental army is described as being 200 million strong and as wiping out a third of the earth's population (Rev. 9:15-18). The fight of Armageddon will be unprecedented—Isaiah speaks of a frightful carnage taking place south of the Dead Sea in ancient Edom (Isa. 63:1-4); the apostle John predicts that so many people will be slaughtered in the conflict that blood will stand to the horses' bridles for a total distance of 200 miles northward and southward of Jerusalem (Rev. 14:20). Jesus said that "there will be a great tribulation, such as had not occurred since the beginning of the world until now, nor ever shall," and that "unless those days had been cut short, no life would have been saved" (Matt. 24:21-22).

The Second Coming. As the battle of Armageddon reaches its climax, Jesus will return and save man from self-destruction.

His coming is described as sudden and startling. Perhaps the "sign of the Son of Man" will be a gigantic celestial image of Jesus flashed high in the sky for all to see. Christ described it as a quick lightning coming from the east and flashing to the west (Matt. 24:27). Everyone will see the Son of Man coming on the clouds of heaven with power and great glory (Matt. 24:30). Christ's feet will first touch the earth on the Mount of Olives (from where he departed), and the mountain will split in two with a great earthquake (Zech. 14). Daniel predicted (550 B.C.) that Christ will be given sovereignty and glory and kingly power so that all people and nations will serve him; that his dominion will be everlasting dominion, which shall not pass away; and that his kingdom shall not be destroyed (Dan. 7:13–14).

The Jews will be on the verge of annihilation; two-thirds of them will perish, but the remaining one-third will survive and convert to Christ. The fight of Armageddon will be stopped, and Christ will establish his kingdom of peace, which will last a thousand years. It is predicted that Jerusalem will be the spiritual center of the entire world and that all people of the earth will come annually to worship Jesus, who will rule there (Zech. 14:16–21; Isa. 2:3; Mic. 4:1–3). The remaining Jewish believers will be the spiritual leaders of the world and will teach all nations the ways of the Lord (Zech. 8:20–23; Isa. 66:23). The nonbelievers will be judged by Christ and be cast off the earth (Rev. 20:1–6; Matt. 25:41–46), and the surviving believers will repopulate the earth (Rev. 20:11–15; Matt. 25:31–40).

At the end of a thousand years Christ will completely change the old heaven and earth and create new ones (Rev. 21; Isa. 65:17; 2 Pet. 3:8–13). This will be the paradise in which only glorified persons without a sinful nature will be allowed to live forever.

Fundamentalists see in the present political and social world situation many convincing signs of the approaching end of the world. One of these is the gradual decline of the United States as a world superpower. Also, lack of moral principles in citizens and leaders is weakening law and order and is leading to anarchy. The military power of the United States has already been neutralized because no one has the courage to use it decisively. When the economy collapses, so will the military. As the United States loses power, Western Europe will be forced to unite and become the most important force in the Western world. The emergence of a United States of Europe is becoming a reality. Other important signs include the growing importance of the Middle East in world politics; the direct interest of the Russians in that area; the emergence of China as a world power;

the rapid spread of nuclear weapons; the increase of crime, poverty, and mental illness; the unusual interest in drugs, astrology, and witchcraft; and economic recession and moral corruption. All these are indicators of a mounting chaos that will lead to the emergence of the Antichrist.

MISSION TO THE JEWS

The nineteenth-century revival of British millenarianism called attention to the mission of the Jews as the Chosen People on earth and to the fulfillment of the biblical prophecies related to the restoration of Israel. In that context, the relation of the Christians to the Jews became understood differently in various Christian groups.

The Christadelphians boasted that they had received the divine privilege of sharing with the Jews God's promises of special protection, prosperity, and supremacy.[5] The British-Israelites, going even further, proclaimed that the Anglo-Saxon and Celtic people of Britain and its Commonwealth of Nations and the United States were literally the descendants of the ten lost tribes, and that they were the heirs of all promises.[6] There were also a number of movements composed of Jewish converts to Christianity and of Christian missionaries with the precise task of finding "Jews for Jesus." Thus, in 1813, Hebrew Christianity was born in England through the efforts of a group of converts calling themselves the Beni Abraham, or Sons of Abraham. This group was followed by a number of others variously known as the Episcopal Jew's Chapel Abrahamic Society (1835), the Hebrew Christian Union (1865), and the Hebrew Christian Prayer Union (1882).[7]

Today the most powerful missionary organization concerned with the conversion of Jews is the American Board of Missions to the

5. See Bryan R. Wilson, *Sects and Society: A Sociological Study of Three Religious Groups in Britain* (London: Heinemann, 1961), pp. 219–316.

6. See John Wilson, "British Israelism: The Ideological Restraints on Sect Organization," in *Patterns of Sectarianism*, ed. Bryan R. Wilson (London: Heinemann, 1967), pp. 345–76.

7. For a general historical outline of Jewish Christianity, see Hugh J. Schonfield, *The History of Jewish Christianity: From the First to the Twentieth Century* (London: Duckworth, 1936); B. Z. Sobel, *Hebrew Christianity: The Thirteenth Tribe* (New York: Wiley, 1974), pp. 127–74.

Jews (ABMJ). Founded in 1894 as the Williamsburg Mission to the Jews, it changed its name in 1924 to indicate the organization's broader scope. For a short while after its founding, the ABMJ was an adjunct of the Baptist Home Mission Society. At present it is an autonomous nondenominational organization.

The mission staff consists of about 100 people, half of whom are "Hebrew Christians" (as converted Jews are called), the other half being "Gentile Christians" who have felt the call for this kind of work. The usual missionary strategy is to organize a conference with the main theme "Prophecy and the Jew," to which at least one Hebrew Christian is invited to speak. An estimated 500 churches a year organize such conferences. The mission's annual budget is estimated to be over a million dollars.[8]

Despite the devotion and the zeal of the missionaries, the success of the mission in gaining converts is questionable; the total number of converts is said to range between 5,000 and 10,000 Jews in the past seventy years. Field studies reveal that Jewish converts frequently experience acute feelings of alienation from their families, friends, and communities, and at the same time are unable to adjust to the new Christian surroundings. Therefore many of them drift away from Christianity.[9]

Usually the mission encounters indifference or hostility from the Jews, who consider it a form of anti-Semitic expression attempting to replace Judaism with Christianity. A recent example of this unfavorable reaction to the mission can be found in connection with a national missionary campaign, Key '73, launched through the joint efforts of a number of evangelical groups. The campaign was aimed at contacting all non-Christian families living in North America by Christmas 1973. The announcement of this plan raised a great furor among rabbis, who feared that the ABMJ would "ride the coattails" of Key '73, causing further disruption of Christian-Jewish relations. Key '73 was defined as "an assault on the honor, dignity and truth of Judaism." Consequently, the American Jewish Committee (AJC) engaged in a crash program of "deepening" Jewish spiritual life to counter the

8. For literature related to the ABMJ, see particularly the movement's periodical, *The Chosen People*; Max Eisen, "Christian Mission to the Jews in North America and Great Britain," *Jewish Social Studies*, X (Jan. 1948), 31-66; Robert Blumstock, "Fundamentalism, Prejudice, and Mission to the Jews," *Canadian Review of Sociology and Anthropology*, V (Feb. 1968), 27-35; Sobel, *Hebrew Christianity*, pp. 127-74.

9. See, for example, Ira O. Glick, "The Hebrew Christians: A Marginal Religious Group," in *The Jews: Social Patterns of an American Group*, ed. Marshall Sklare (Glencoe, Ill.: Free Press, 1958), pp. 415-31; Sobel, *Hebrew Christianity*, pp. 225-94.

efforts of the evangelical campaign. Jewish scholars and rabbis visited college campuses and communities in order to emphasize the Jewish interpretation of the New Testament and to prevent Jewish believers from giving in to the pressures of Christian missionaries.[10]

The small group of Hebrew Christians (a few of whom live in Israel) who are deeply convinced of their faith consider themselves to be Christians and, at the same time, Jews. They consider Christianity the true fulfillment of Judaism. Zionist ideology is the key factor resolving the sharp paradox inherent in this position and well integrates the personality of the believer into the synthesis of two cultures. Because Zionism has the nature of a religio-political movement, it provides an opportunity for displaying solidarity with the political aspirations of the Jewish people and, at the same time, confers a higher religious motivation that, for the new believer, is best expressed within a Christian framework. Political Zionism is explained by the Hebrew Christians in terms of prophetic fulfillment, as only the beginning of the "crowning event" of the reign of Christ over Judah and the world. Thus, since the very first Zionist congress, in 1897, Hebrew Christians have consistently sought to prove that their Christian belief makes them the vanguard of Zionism. As one of them put it: "If any class of Jews are really prepared for Zionism, it is the Christian Jew, for he thoroughly believes in Zionism for Israel on Zion's sake according to the divine program and purposes of God for them. We Hebrew Christians are by the grace of God the advance guard in the movement."[11]

In practice, however, this strong self-image on the part of the believer is not equally recognized by the vast majority of Jews, and the Hebrew Christians remain a small marginal group even among their own people. It should be noted that no Hebrew Christian colony was ever successfully launched in Palestine.[12]

10. See "Jewish Furor over Key '73," *Christianity Today*, Dec. 22, 1972, pp. 37–38. On the Key '73 plan itself, see *ibid.*, Dec. 8, 1972, p. 48; Jan. 5, 1973, pp. 12–13.

11. "The Zionist Convention at Pittsburgh," *Hebrew Christian Alliance Quarterly*, II (Oct. 1918), p. 136, quoted in B. Z. Sobel, "The Tools of Legitimization: Zionism and the Hebrew Christian Movement," *Jewish Journal of Sociology*, X (Dec. 1968), 247. For a sociological analysis of the Hebrew Christian movement, see B. Z. Sobel, "Protestant Evangelists and the Formulation of a Jewish Racial Mystique: The Missionary Discovery of Sociology," *Journal for the Scientific Study of Religion*, V (Fall 1966), 343–56; *idem, Hebrew Christianity*, pp. 216–52. The last is the most comprehensive work on the subject.

12. Another marginal movement is the so-called Jewish Christian Community, whose members were not converted by missionaries as in the case of the Hebrew Christians. Their conversion to Christianity was mainly a response to physical and mental

CONCLUSION

The above presentation clearly indicates the role played by Christian fundamentalism in the support and reinforcement of Zionist ideology. Whether its message is preached to Westerners or to Jews, it gives a narrow and distorted picture of reality. Everything is explained from within a limited and limiting framework of a priori dogmatic belief and always in terms of a somewhat static core structure removed from historical reality. [13]

Clearly, the fundamentalist approach to the Bible lacks historical perspective. In the fundamentalist textbooks there is no distinction between the spiritual Israel of the Bible and the political Israel of today. They invariably talk about the "biblical prophecies," and these are applied literally to present events. Ancient Israel and Judah are continually equated with modern political Israel, and the latter is equated with Judaism and the Jews. The Arabs are only mentioned in passing as the "enemies" of the Israelis. In the Bible the Edomites represent the Arabs, and they are quoted as having said some harsh words against the Judahites (Ps. 83); this is taken to be proof of the unceasing hatred on the part of the Arabs for Israel down through the centuries. In the perspective presented by the fundamentalist exegesis, Israel and its actions represent the just and right hand of God, while the Arabs stand for the enemies of God, the children of Satan. Jews and Arabs are engaged in a fatal duel, the outcome

---

deprivation and stress under conditions of anti-Semitic persecution in the First World War. Most of the members were born in Germany, and many had relatives who were killed by the Nazis. Their belief system probably had therapeutic value in their troubled life experience; it supplied the answer to so much destruction, unhappiness, and hate. Their belief is strongly eschatological. For them the world war period which began in 1914 will end with the imminent Third World War, the Armageddon. Anti-Semitism will increase up to that day. The Arabs are "tools in the hands of Satan"; this explains their senseless hatred of Israel. But Christ will triumph in the end, and he will establish his kindgom on earth. The members call themselves Christian Zionists and reject assimilation with Gentile churches. They claim identity with the first Christians, who, they point out, were also Jews. They maintain that separation from Gentile Christians is necessary in order to carry out their mission, which is to act as a vanguard for the conversion of Israel. However, they do not engage in any organized missionary action because they believe that their task can be carried out by only a few when God inspires them to act. At present, the already small membership of the movement (a few hundred) is in sharp decline owing to changes in the particular conditions in Europe in which the movement arose. (See the movement's periodical, *Jerusalem.* For a sociological study of the movement, see Stephen Sharot, "A Jewish Christian Adventist Movement," *Jewish Journal of Sociology,* X [June 1968], 35–45.)

13. See William F. Stinespring, "Christian Fundamentalists and Zionism," *Middle East Perspectives* (July–Aug. 1968), pp. 3–4.

of which has been firmly decreed from eternity—the Jews will be exalted; the Arabs will be humiliated. Thus, Zionism is synonymous with enlightenment, progress, victory, while Arabism stands for obscurantism, backwardness, defeat.

For fundamentalists, the history of religions stopped at the New Testament time, when there were only Jews, Christians, and pagans. Islam, which arose after biblical times, is ignored. Similarly, other great religions (such as Hinduism, Buddhism, and Confucianism) which do not appear in the world of the Bible are also ignored. Indeed, biblical literalism separated from the spirit and the sociocultural context of the Bible is bound to bring confusion, prejudice, and conflict.

PART III: IMMIGRANT ARAB WORKERS

Dan Georgakas

BLACK AND ARAB AUTO WORKERS IN DETROIT

EARLY IN 1968, black workers began to form radical worker organizations in the automobile factories of Detroit, and shortly thereafter Arab workers began to form similar groups. These workers shared at least three major problems. (1) As members of nonwhite minorities, they were among the most exploited workers in the auto industry. They had the unhealthiest and most unsafe jobs in an industry in which one out of every ten workers is injured or made ill from on-the-job causes each year. (2) They were unable to look to their established union, the United Auto Workers (UAW), for support of grievances. (3) Most critically, they bore the brunt of production speed-ups and deteriorations in working conditions which were prevalent throughout the industry, especially in the Chrysler plants.

RACISM IN THE AUTO INDUSTRY

Racism has been a factor in the auto industry for decades. Henry Ford systematized its use as a control device. Beginning in the late 1920s, he made it a rule to employ blacks in his factory at every job level in the same proportion as there were blacks in the general population. Ford helped finance the all-black suburb of Inkster and always provided low-paying jobs for any unemployed residents. He also cultivated a select group of black clergy and professionals. Called a humanitarian for his action, Ford's motives were strictly business.

Research for this paper was carried out in conjunction with research for *Detroit: I Do Mind Dying*, by Dan Georgakas and Marvin Surkin (New York: St. Martin's, 1975).

His personal views on blacks, Jews, communists, and other "un-American" elements were expressed in the *Dearborn Independent,* a paper that he owned and personally financed for more than a decade at a loss of more than $5 million. Dearborn, the city that Ford built, the home of the mammoth River Rouge complex and the headquarters of the Ford empire, was not open to black residents.[1]

Except for Ford, which had a special policy of hiring large numbers of blacks as an antiunion ploy, none of the auto companies hired many black workers until the labor shortage of World War II. At that time, blacks, mainly fresh from the South, were hired by the tens of thousands. Many of their jobs were taken away during the recessions of the 1950s, but when automaking staged a comeback in the early 1960s, blacks were rehired.

In the 1960s the bulk of the black auto workers in Detroit proper were employed by Chrysler, because by this time Ford and General Motors had moved most of their operations out of the city. Blacks invariably got the worst and most dangerous jobs: those in the foundry, the body shop, and engine assembly; jobs requiring the greatest physical exertion and those that were the noisiest, dirtiest, and riskiest in the plant. In Dodge Main, a typical factory with many black workers, 99 percent of all general foremen were white, 95 percent of all foremen were white, 100 percent of superintendents were white, 90 percent of skilled tradesmen were white, and 90 percent of all skilled apprentices were white.[2] All the better jobs were overwhelmingly dominated by whites; and when whites did have difficult jobs there tended to be two workers assigned to a task that a black worker was expected to do alone. Sick slips signed by black doctors were refused as inadequate. As black revolutionary organizations, such as Dodge Revolutionary Union Movement (DRUM), have pointed out, the company deliberately cultivated and institutionalized racism so that white workers and black workers would face their workaday lives in racial conflict rather than in class solidarity.

Possibly the only group more exploited than blacks at Dodge Main were the recent Arab immigrants. In 1968 they numbered 500; by 1974, 2,000. These workers tended to be totally bewildered by American

1. Ironically, Dearborn came to have the highest concentration of Arabs in the Detroit area. For a study of this Arab community, see Barbara C. Aswad, "The Southeast Dearborn Arab Community Struggles for Survival against Urban Renewal," in *Arabic Speaking Communities in American Cities* (New York: Center for Migration Studies/AAUG, 1974), pp. 53–83.

2. Statistics are for 1968.

conditions and were fearful of losing their jobs or being deported. The bulk of them were men who lived alone and who sent most of their pay to relatives in the Middle East. A February 29, 1972, bulletin put out by SPARK, a radical caucus at Dodge Main, described the situation:

> Chrysler has a new version of an old trick up their sleeves. In the last year's time they have hired a good many Arab workers. This was done for one reason—Chrysler figures that Arab workers in this country are now in a position that makes it hard to fight back.
>
> They are new to the country so that many people are unsure what few rights they do have. There is always the possibility of being deported. People are trying hard to save as much money as possible in order to bring their family here. And until a person learns English he may not know what is happening around him—and he will find it hard to complain.
>
> Finally, Chrysler figures that no one else will try to help an Arab worker when Chrysler attacks him.
>
> So now Chrysler is attacking. Foremen tell Arab workers to do more work than their jobs call for. Eventually the "extra" work is "officially" added to the job. Other Arab workers are kept as floaters and continually put on the worst jobs, despite their seniority. Medical passes get put off. Reliefs are forgotten about. . . .
>
> It's the same kind of shit they have pulled for years with black people. At first, black people were given work only when Chrysler was trying to break a strike. Chrysler consciously set white workers against black workers—both fighting for the same job, during the desperate high unemployment of the Depression, when there was no union.
>
> Then when Chrysler did hire black workers regularly into the plant, it was only in the foundry (or the body shop a little later)—all the hot, heavy, dirty work around. No way to complain about one job, when all the others in the foundry were just about as bad. And if a black person did complain, he'd end up on the street, because of his "attitude."
>
> . . . Now today, Chrysler is trying the same thing again—bringing in still another group of workers. Chrysler hopes to make conditions worse for all of us by first attacking conditions for the Arab workers. And they count on turning us against each other so they can do this.

THE UAW AND WORKER GRIEVANCES

The Big Three, frightened by the radical spirit and mass actions of the late 1930s, made a deal with the UAW after the war. The union acceded to company demands and was rewarded with support in solving its own internal problems. One such support was that the company would deduct union dues directly from paychecks, freeing the union from the worker weapon of withholding dues if dissatisfied with union leadership. Company and union amiability went so far that during the General Motors strike of 1970, the company allowed the union to delay payment of $46 million into the health insurance program because of the enormous financial burden that it would place on the union. GM was paid 5 percent interest by the union after the strike was over. In effect, the company had floated the union a loan in the middle of the strike and was financing a work stoppage against itself. Such cooperation also found expression in three- and five-year contracts in which the mutual interests of company and union were insulated from annual crisis. The chief consequence of the long-term contracts was that there would be no work stoppages of any kind. An unauthorized (wildcat) strike could be punished by the courts as a breach of contract, thereby pitting the offending workers against the union as well as the company.

The only weapon left the worker was the grievance procedure. If a job was sped up or an extra procedure added, if safety equipment (such as goggles or gloves) was inadequate, or if a machine malfunctioned, the worker could not resolve it on the factory floor in direct confrontation with supervisors. He could only make out a complaint, file it with the union "rep," and wait for it to be processed. Meanwhile, the matter for contention remained in effect except in those cases where it was serious enough to trigger a general walkout by the workers. The grievance procedure became yet another device by which the company and the union eliminated worker participation in decision-making.

The company and the union had developed a convenient division of labor. The company looked after the machines and the union looked after the workers. American auto workers were told by the mass media that they had one of the highest standards of living in the world, but they were not told that they also had one of the world's most grueling standards of work.

The first line of defense against the racist policies described above should have been the union, but the union had lost touch with its mass base, especially the minorities. In 1969, at least 30 percent of the UAW membership was black, yet the twenty-six-person executive board had only two blacks, Nelson Jack Edwards and Marcellius Ivory. There were only seven positions held by blacks out of one hundred key staff positions. In that year, 14 percent of the union was female, but women had even fewer of these posts; and only one representative on the executive board, Olga Madar, was a woman. Once considered the cutting edge of militant industrial unionism, the UAW showed little interest in organizing the numerous nonunion feeder shops in the industry, in moving for unionization in the South, or in fighting for substantial gains such as forty hours pay for thirty hours work.

UAW President Walter Reuther, Vice President Leonard Woodcock, and Secretary-Treasurer Emile Mazey had once belonged to the Socialist party, but they had grown distant from dissident social movements and came to power within the UAW by purging the union of members and sympathizers of the Communist party. Reuther, who was president until his death in 1972, had once run for Congress as a Socialist and had worked in a Soviet auto plant, but he did not like the militants of the Student Non-Violent Coordinating Committee, the white radicals of the Students for a Democratic Society, or peace marchers who insulted the president of the United States. Rather than honest-to-goodness slugfists with the corporations, Reuther staged elaborate rituals in which neither side was badly hurt. He enjoyed having his photo taken embracing nonviolent activists, such as Martin Luther King and Cesar Chavez, but under his leadership the UAW did little to combat racism, anti-Semitism, or sexism either within its own ranks or wherever it had influence. William Serrin, a Pulitzer Prize winning reporter for the *Detroit Free Press* and author of a book entitled *The Company and the Union,* made the trenchant comment that the UAW was a right-of-center union with a left-of-center reputation. The UAW's reputation for being progressive on racism was based on the fact that however bad its own record, the UAW still compared favorably with the lily white and stridently racist unions that composed so much of the rest of the organized labor movement.

PRODUCTION SPEED-UPS

One of the strategies used by companies in order to maintain their profits is to increase the productivity of each worker. Public relations departments attribute rises in productivity to automation and managerial efficiency, but numerous scholars have established that higher productivity, as experienced in the past twenty years, is due primarily to speed-up: the extraction of more labor from each worker.

In the auto industry all operations are evaluated in terms of worker-hour and worker-minute costs. Time-study experts investigate each job to eliminate wasted motion and to invent new procedures for doubling up on work. One worker has explained the process: "They tell you, 'Put in ten screws,' and you do it. Then a couple of weeks later they say, 'Put in fifteen screws,' and next they say, 'Well, we don't need you no more. Give it to the next man.'" While management cannot bring back the "good old days" of Henry Ford, when workers were not allowed to talk during lunch, it has eliminated much nonwork time from the pay period: time for washing up, job preparation, and similar activities. Overtime became compulsory when the company discovered that it was cheaper, because of fringe benefits, to pay time-and-a-half for overtime than to increase the over-all work force by hiring additional workers.

On the issue of work speed-ups, as on so many others, the UAW cooperates with the company. Many UAW leaders go so far as to link all wage increases to increases in productivity. The capitalist dream may be realized in the not-too-distant future if contracts signed in 1973 are any indication of where UAW leadership is heading. In those contracts, the UAW agreed to only a 3 percent annual increase in wages in spite of double-digit inflation. This, in effect, was a negotiated pay cut. The contracts made some gains in the retirement area, but almost none on working conditions and other issues involving the active and younger work force. The contracts are due for renegotiation in 1976, at which time the companies may be in an even stronger bargaining position because the unions will be further weakened by high unemployment and economic suffering.

IMMIGRANT LABOR: A WORLD PHENOMENON

In the 1950s, European capital made massive use of cheap immigrant labor. Black Africans, Turks, Greeks, Arabs, Yugoslavs, southern Italians, and Spaniards found work in northern Europe at that time. They frequently were forced to live in separate compounds and were paid wages inferior to domestic labor. In French auto plants it was not uncommon to find workers of five or six nationalities, unable to speak the same language, on one assembly line. Similarly, in the early 1970s American capital began to import such labor for specific industries even though there was chronic unemployment in the United States. In the eastern United States, in addition to Puerto Ricans, who had been migrating for years, there were large influxes of South Americans and various Caribbean peoples, each with its own culture and language. On the West Coast, the cheap labor was primarily of Mexican and Asian ancestry. In Detroit the new labor pool was Arab.

Wilbur Haddock, a leader of the United Black Workers at the Ford plant in Mahwah, New Jersey, spoke to the author about the immigrant workers' role. The struggle between blacks and the company and between blacks and whites had been intensifying at Mahwah for years, culminating in several strikes. White and black American workers had finally begun to understand one another in the late 1960s At that time new workers were introduced to the scene. Black Haitians who spoke French appeared on the assembly line. They were followed by Dominicans who spoke Spanish and by West Indians who spoke English with a British accent. Tensions developed between American blacks and some of the West Indians because of cultural differences and because the Americans found the West Indians' accent "snobbish." Some of the new groups did not like each other or quarreled with the Puerto Ricans and Cubans. To the white workers from small towns in New York and New Jersey, the whole experience was perplexing. Organization of militant activities was definitely curtailed in the short run by the introduction of the various new immigrant workers.

The long-term effect of the newcomers, however, could be otherwise. In northern Italy, the migrants from the south have become the most radical of all the auto workers and now lead massive strikes. A few years back, in Germany, angry Turkish workers, incensed by systematic racism, tore up an entire assembly line. In Detroit, the Arab workers, with their particular interest in the Middle East, find communication with revolutionary worker groups more fruitful than communication with bread-and-butter trade-unionists. Ultimately the new workers, like the blacks before them, will have to organize on the job to protest the working conditions imposed by a not-very-robust capitalism which needs to exploit the workers more than ever in order to stave off economic disaster.

PROSPECTS FOR THE FUTURE

Like other immigrants, Arab workers are faced with problems in housing, medical treatment, educational institutions, and everyday life, in addition to problems in the work place.

In recent years the struggles in the Middle East have given special tone to Arab struggles in America. The State Department and other agencies of the central government have seen fit to institute special checks and procedures for Arab residents, tourists, and students, as well as for naturalized and native-born Americans of Arab ancestry. Legal and extralegal harassment has been directed against militant

Arab organizations. Though it is unlikely, it is not inconceivable that, under specific circumstances of United States military involvement in the Middle East, Arabs could be rounded up and put into concentration camps as was the case with Japanese Americans during World War II. It is more likely, however, that the government will use the sophisticated measures that it used against Greek Americans who, in the late 1940s, supported leftist guerrillas seeking to topple the Greek monarchy, which was being funded by American imperialists. They were harassed on their jobs and in their homes. Some were deported. Most of those put under pressure were involved in various American radical movements, especially dissident labor currents. Among the loudest in condemning them were the right-wing Greek-American merchants and church people.

What might transpire is, of course, conjecture, but certain lines of development seem well established. At the present time, the mass media, especially network television and mass circulation magazines, are softening their image of Arabs. There may well be a profitable fad of Arab cuisine, music, and clothing. Just as with the commercialization of black culture, this kind of "upbeat" in the mass media has a double edge. One of its major purposes is to draw a distinction between the reasonable "good niggers," who are interested only in culture, and the violent "bad niggers," who are political radicals. Such a distinction is of immense practical benefit to the rulers of America who like to present a nice liberal facade and at the same time use a heavy hand to deal with community, educational, and work problems.

The Arab auto worker, defined strictly as a production-line worker, will be asked to work harder and longer for lower real wages. Like most Third World workers, the Arabs, for the most part, will be locked in the lowest job categories with little hope of advancement in the near future. Their difficulties will be linked to political conflicts in the Middle East and to struggles involving other Arabs, such as those working in near slavery in the grape and lettuce fields of California. Productive alliances can be made on the shop floor with blacks. Both revolutionary and nationalistic blacks already view the Zionist state as one of the imperialist powers playing an exploitative role in Africa, and both groups support African guerrilla movements aimed at overthrowing colonists and native despots. They are not put off by Islam, dark skin, or the Arabic language. Other Third World workers, such as those from Puerto Rico and the Dominican Republic, can identify with the struggle for Palestine as they have had a similar experience trying to create an independent state opposed by the American government.

The position of the established white workers is also deteriorating, and Arabs need not assume that white workers cannot become allies. As Andrew Levison has shown in his article in the September 4, 1974, issue of the *New Yorker*, most American workers are in economic trouble. Thirty percent of all industrial workers make less than $7,000 a year, which is poverty level for urban families. Another 30 percent do only slightly better, earning between poverty level and what the government terms "intermediary income level." Levison has done an analysis of voting patterns which shows that when self-interest is clearly defined, white workers vote for socially progressive candidates and issues. Racism and political ideology aside, the issue of economic exploitation can unite all these workers. A harsh recession might trigger a massive, united worker movement directed against the companies, union leaders, and the government. Detroit, with 40 percent of its population directly involved in the manufacturing processes, with its tradition of radicalism, and with the nation's highest concentration of black workers, is certain to be part of any such movement.

Ismael Ahmed

ORGANIZING AN ARAB WORKERS' CAUCUS IN DETROIT

OF THE APPROXIMATELY 85,000 Arabs living in Michigan, nearly 15,000 are auto workers, most of them living in the Detroit metropolitan area—in many cases, within walking distance of work. Many of them live in South East Dearborn, only blocks away from the Ford Motor Company's River Rouge complex, one of the largest industrial complexes in the world. A second area of concentration is near Chrysler's Dodge Main Gear and Axle plant in Hamtramck, in the heart of what is otherwise a predominantly black community. A third is in the Six Mile-Woodward area of Detroit. Most of the Arab residents of South East Dearborn are of Yemeni, Palestinian, or Lebanese extraction; the Hamtramck community is predominantly Yemeni in make-up; and the Six Mile community is the home of many Iraqi auto workers.

Arab auto workers are faced with the language and cultural problems that immigrants adjusting to a new society generally meet. These include virtually nonexistent social services, urban renewal projects designed to break up their communities, substandard housing, and the constant threat of deportation. In addition, within the auto industry Arab workers are subjected to intense exploitation. Newly arrived workers, many of whom do not understand their role as employee and union member, are funneled into the dirtiest and hardest jobs in the plants and are constantly under attack by racist foremen, union bureaucrats, and even fellow workers. Workers in the Ford Rouge complex estimate that the largest concentration of Arab workers (about half) is in the foundry and stamping plant. This situation applies especially to Yemeni and Palestinian workers, many of whom immigrated during the 1960s or later.

One factor contributing to the building of an Arab workers' organization in Detroit has been this concentration of Arabs in the auto industry and, within it, in certain sections and on certain assembly lines. Three elements have been responsible for this concentration. (1) During the last several years there has emerged a practice of paying an influential foreman or company official as much as $500 for a special letter of introduction allowing one to be hired in preference to other workers. This practice has helped newly arrived Arab workers get jobs in one of the best-paying industries in the country without having to learn English. (2) With the growth of the black liberation movement in the late 1960s, there appeared revolutionary black plant organizations, for example, Eldon Gear and Axle Revolutionary Union Movement and Dodge Revolutionary Union Movement (DRUM). These organizations led two successful wildcat strikes that jolted the whole auto industry. From that time on, Chrysler began making a conscious effort to replace black workers with what officials considered to be more docile Arab workers. (3) Once Arab workers became concentrated in certain factories, they provided a friendly base from which other Arabs could search for jobs. Workers would let their friends know when plants were hiring, would help them arrange transportation, would translate forms and applications, and so on.

Arab nationalism has also played a significant role in the development of an Arab workers' organization in Detroit. Following the 1967 war and the 1968 battle of Karameh, in which Palestinian forces successfully battled the Israelis, a definite change could be noted among the residents of Detroit's Arab community. This was largely in response to the growing Palestinian Resistance Movement. At first there were teach-ins and small demonstrations on college and university campuses. Later these were held in the heart of the Arab communities. Arab organizations of all kinds grew significantly at this time.

THE OCTOBER WAR AND THE ARAB WORKERS' CAUCUS

When war broke out in the Middle East in early October 1973, Arab Americans and their organizations responded immediately. A demonstration was called in the heart of the Arab community in Detroit by a coalition of almost every Arab organization in the city. Nearly 2,000 people took part. Speakers linked the war to the corporate interests of the Big Three auto companies and talked about UAW holdings of Israel bonds. They called for an Arab workers' organization to protect the interests of Arabs at home and abroad. The demonstration was held at the Ford Rouge Plant Union Hall Local 600 to emphasize the protest against UAW bond holdings as much as against American involvement in the war. A petition by auto workers on this issue was drafted.

Existing Arab-American organizations were asked to send delegates to a citywide meeting of Arab auto workers. About seventy delegates representing nearly every auto plant in Detroit attended this meeting. It was decided to form an Arab workers' caucus, to proclaim a day of religious mourning for the fallen fighters in the war, and to organize a work stoppage and a demonstration against UAW President Leonard Woodcock, who was scheduled to receive a B'nai B'rith award at an Israeli fund-raising dinner. The Arab workers wanted to draw attention to the hypocrisy of a union leader who would force his constituency in effect to finance the murder of their brothers and sisters at home with their union dues.[1]

Organizing for the demonstration took place both in the plants and in the community. Nearly 70,000 leaflets, calling people in Arabic and in English to join the demonstration, were distributed. Arab radio stations and newspapers joined the efforts. Local religious leaders declared a day of mourning and wrote absence excuses for workers. On the day of the demonstration, Arab high school students went to the plant gates to inform workers who had not received the news. Nearly 2,000 Arab workers took the day off to demonstrate. The afternoon shift at the Dodge Main Gear and Axle plant was completely shut down. Other plants had line slowdowns. This was the first and most successful action of the caucus.

In Detroit, reaction to the shutdown was mixed. Workers at the Dodge Main plant received disciplinary notices; those at the Ford Truck plant received holiday pay. Nearly 500 warning slips were distributed to Arab workers. The news media played down the event, possibly hoping not to encourage further work stoppages. The UAW leadership denounced the caucus and labeled the demonstration "communist."

From this point on, Arab workers concentrated on building caucuses in their own plants. The first step in this process was to ascertain the number of Arab workers in each plant. Workers then checked

---

1. Money from Israel bonds is not used directly for the purchase of war goods, but it releases other money within the economy to be used for that purpose.

into UAW holdings of Israel bonds on a local level. After identifying those locals holding bonds, they united the membership to force the liquidation of these holdings. Nearly $48,000 worth of Israel bonds were liquidated, although the UAW International still holds $780,000 worth.

THE UAW CONSTITUTIONAL CONVENTION

Competing for positions as delegates to the UAW's Twenty-fourth Constitutional Convention, members of the Arab workers' caucus formulated a comprehensive program which not only embraced the Israel bonds issue but also called for greater union democracy, an end to racist practices, better work conditions, and special training and language programs for Arabs. Arab candidates did poorly: three delegates from Local 3 in Hamtramck won convention seats, and one delegate from the Ford Casting Center (through a compromise) was sent as an observer. The campaign had not given sufficient consideration to American workers, nor had it analyzed the feelings of most workers toward the convention itself. Most union members thought of the convention as no more than a vacation to California. "Full of booze and bullshit!" as one Dodge Truck worker put it. Former delegates had described the convention as heavily weighted in favor of the present International leadership, which controlled all the main committees of the convention. Most of the local leadership used their resources to ensure the election of *pro*-Woodcock representatives. Convention delegates were overwhelmingly union officials; there was very little rank-and-file participation.

In an attempt to learn from their mistakes, the caucus adopted a new strategy for the convention itself and stressed greater and more direct reliance on American workers and on opposition caucuses all over the country. As a first step, the Arab caucus joined the United National Caucus in calling for a demonstration at the convention. This was done at a news conference in Detroit. Five demands were made: initiate no more layoffs; fight discrimination; promote union democracy; stop runaway shops; and sell Israel bonds and break ties with Histadrut. Although half of the available time of this press conference was utilized by the representative of the Arab workers' caucus in carefully explaining the fifth demand, not one station or newspaper carried his remarks. Most papers printed only four demands, deleting the fifth.

Following this experience, the Arab workers' caucus began to publicize the demonstration in national trade-union and radical papers, urging all auto workers to support the demonstration and the demands. A member of the caucus was sent to California ten days prior to the convention to work with the Fremont Plant Brotherhood Caucus, which had also called for a demonstration at the convention. By this time a number of caucuses had come together around the same five demands. These groups included caucuses from all the major auto plants in California as well as UAW Alcoa workers and International Harvester workers. Arab and Iranian students joined forces to work for the demonstration. By the time of the convention, leaflets explaining each demand had been distributed at nearly every UAW plant in California. Caucuses in each plant had set up discussions with workers to explain the history of Israel, Histadrut, and the UAW bond holdings. Many of these discussions took place during the workers' lunch hours, on factory lawns, and across cafeteria tables. Many workers in different plants were impressed with the necessity of struggling against pro-Zionist tendencies in their union.

At the convention, resolutions were introduced calling on the UAW to divest itself of its Israel bonds, to support the right of the Palestinian people to control their own land and resources, and to oppose U.S. arms sales to Israel and U.S. intervention in the Middle East. No other resolutions were submitted to the convention on these questions. Yet on the second day of the convention, the Resolutions Committee, whose job it was to sum up the resolutions of the locals, published a resolution completely antithetical to the spirit and letter of the resolutions submitted by Locals 51 and 1364. This resolution not only reflected with satisfaction the official U.S. government policy on the Middle East, but also repeated popular myths about Israel as a bastion of democracy and attacked the Arab humanitarian support for Palestinian refugees. Furthermore, it promised to continue close ties and cooperation with Histadrut, in keeping with President Woodcock's call for such cooperation in his opening address. This Resolutions Committee was headed by Walter Dorash, the president of Local 600, who months earlier had promised Arab workers in his local that he would help get rid of Israel bonds.

Pro-caucus delegates lobbied the floor of the convention to fight for restoring the locals' resolutions. This would have taken a two-thirds vote, a feat that was virtually impossible. However, in the final analysis, all acts were in vain, for the Resolutions Committee's submission never reached the floor of the convention. That resolution was adopted without discussion. The convention had rubber-stamped not only the Middle East resolution but every resolution put forward by the

International Board, including fat pay raises and extensions of the terms of office of all the International executives.

FUTURE EFFORTS

Since the convention, the Arab workers' caucus has begun in-plant organizing in cooperation with other worker groups. It has come to rely more on rank-and-file auto workers than on union bureaucrats. As a result of this, a new, more militant attitude toward President Woodcock has developed. Arab workers continue fighting for the union and have actively participated in local and on-the-line struggles. In June 1974 Arab caucus members joined hands with other Dodge Truck strikers in a wildcat strike that closed the plant for four days, costing the company millions of dollars in lost production. The wildcat strike was continued despite police attacks, the firing of seventy-nine workers, and the arrest of thirty workers, and despite UAW leadership announcements urging the workers to go back to work. During the strike, caucus members printed signs in Arabic urging other Arabs to join the picket line. At the same time caucus members explained the Israel bonds issue, and how it relates to their immediate struggle, to their American comrades. This was done in a union meeting attended by nearly 600 strikers.

The work of the caucus has had some impact. There is now special training and English classes for Arab workers at Chrysler and Ford; and Ford has shown interest in the Arab Community Center for Economic and Social Services. The caucus has brought about the liquidation of a small part of the UAW's holdings of Israel bonds and has served notice on the International Executive Board that this issue will not die. Finally, and most importantly, there has been an integration of anti-imperialist ideas among rank-and-file workers, who are truly the heart of the union.

From the experience of organizing within the auto industry, the Arab workers' caucus appears to have learned to see itself as part of the general American workers' movement. It must now become integrated with that movement. It must continue to work among Arab workers, raising their demands and integrating them with the demands of the rest of the working class. Whether the caucus continues to exist and grow will depend on its ability to meet this challenge.

Mary Bisharat

YEMENI MIGRANT WORKERS IN CALIFORNIA

THE NUMBER OF STUDIES on Arab-American minorities is limited. Generally, existing studies have focused on migrants from those Arab countries on or near the eastern Mediterranean. Until recently, little attention has been given to immigrants from the Arabian Peninsula. Not only have these immigrants been ignored by social scientists, but their presence in the United States is generally unknown even to other Arab Americans.

It was only after reading about the violent death of Nagi Daifullah at the hands of a county sheriff in Lamont, California, in August 1973, that I became aware of the presence of Yemenis in the United States, particularly as a significant segment of the labor force in California agriculture. What I subsequently learned from interviews with these men and from my observations of their wretched living conditions sharpened my interest and focused my attention on the central importance of those conditions which typify their presence in California, namely, the conditions of exploitation.

CONDITIONS IN YEMEN

Yemenis have been roaming the world for a long time. It is estimated that one million, or about two-thirds the total number of, Yemeni males live outside Yemen. This has devastating consequences on the economic and social development of Yemen itself.

The opening of the Suez Canal in 1869 facilitated the western migration of Yemenis, and very shortly thereafter they began to arrive in America. They came through New York and made their way to other eastern cities, such as Buffalo and Detroit. Some went overland to California. Some Yemeni sailors jumped ship in San Francisco. Our oldest informant, a man of ninety years who has been in the United States since the early 1900s, said that his uncle had been here many years before that. Many of the early immigrants returned to Yemen; many died here.

The early Yemeni immigrants came chiefly from the British crown colony of Aden (since 1967, the People's Democratic Republic of Yemen). The primary reason for their emigration was the extreme poverty of the land, worsened by British imperialism. North Yemen contributed few, if any, immigrants to the early wave of migration because of the rigid policy of isolation imposed by Imam Yahya, a despot who ruled from 1902 until his assassination in 1948. His oppressive and backward rule virtually sealed his country off from the outside world in order to keep out any influences that might erode his power. Following his assassination, emigration from North Yemen began. It was not until the 1960s, however, that migrant workers were imported in large numbers from North Yemen.

It should be pointed out that there are great discrepancies between the figures provided by the U.S. Immigration and Naturalization Service (380 alien Yemenis registered in 1974) and those given by the TWA office in Los Angeles (100,000 immigrants over the past decade). Based on our field observations and on the statements of authoritative people with whom we spoke, there are no less than 2,500 Yemenis in Kern County alone.

A closer look at the severe poverty conditions that afflict both North and South Yemen is necessary, inasmuch as they constitute a primary factor in the massive emigration of the male population. The economy of a country is not only reflected in its gross national product and its balance of trade, but in the per capita income of its population as well. In 1973 in Yemen, the individual annual income was $94.00.[1] As in other underdeveloped countries, unemployment is endemic. Primitive industry employs less than 0.5 percent of the working population. Most of the population is engaged in agriculture, which, with a few lucrative exports, such as coffee and cotton, is on a subsistence level. The economies of North and South Yemen are heavily dependent on foreign aid from the United States, the Soviet Union, China, and other Arab countries. Consequences of the existing condi-

1. United Nations, *Statistical Yearbook,* 1974, p. 8.

tions of poverty are demonstrated by an average life expectancy of thirty-two years, an infant mortality rate of 160 per 1,000, and a 10 percent literacy rate. Average daily food intake is only 1,900 calories per person, and there is one doctor for every 30,000 persons.

From early times, Yemen has occupied a position on the periphery of Arab history. Consequently, its contact with the West was limited and its traditional social structure the least modified among the Arab nations. The weight of centuries of tradition has reinforced the basic family structure. In the Constitution of North Yemen, the revolutionary government explicitly placed value upon the family as the foundation of Yemeni society.[2] Among Yemenis in the United States, whether because of their isolation or in spite of it, group cohesion is very strong. They retain strong family ties and feel that they must succeed in order to return home to their waiting families.

THE GROWERS' ADVANTAGES

The Yemenis are late arrivals in a parade of minorities who have been brought into a relationship of exploitation by the California growers. What constitutes exploitation is the excessive profits of one party resulting from the underpaid labor of the other. While the conditions of the worker remained materially unchanged from 1972 to 1973, the net income of the growers of California increased by 62 percent in that year. In 1973, cash receipts from farming in California totaled over $7.2 billion, almost 13 percent of the total cash receipts from agriculture in the United States.

The degree of exploitation varies according to the power with which either party can manipulate the conditions of the relationship. The growers have a number of advantages that contribute to their power and enable them to maximize profits. Originally they had relied on American Indians because of their availability, but soon they found it possible and advantageous to import laborers from throughout the world: China, Japan, the Philippines, the Punjab, southern Europe, and Mexico.[3] In difficult times, such as the depression of the 1930s, even the poor whites accepted this exploitative relationship.

One advantage to the growers has been the immigration laws. Laws allowing for the importation of vast numbers of foreign laborers gave the growers a reserve labor force that stripped the local farmworker

2. For a detailed discussion, see Farouk Luqman, *Yemen 1970* (Aden, 1970).

3. *Sacramento Bee*, Sept. 17, 1972.

of his power to shape the relationship to his betterment. While through the quota system the immigration laws have prevented, and still do, vast numbers of people from entering the United States, these same laws have been manipulated to accommodate the needs of powerful business interests, among them the interests of the growers of California. The latest development in this exploitation is the reverse trend of taking American industries into the home countries of cheap labor and governments that give no protection to the worker. American-based agribusiness, however, must still largely rely on importation.

Another advantage to the growers is existing legislation. This remains the greatest single impediment to any change in the severe exploitation of the farmworker. On the state level, the growers have always enjoyed a solid backing from California's rural-based representatives. This advantage, though somewhat weakened by the recent reapportionment of representation, needs more analysis than can be attempted in this article.

On the national level, the growers have benefited from the Wagner Act of 1935, the National Labor Relations Act. Though this law authorizes and regulates collective bargaining between management and labor and protects new unionists from reprisals, it specifically excludes agricultural workers from its scope, leaving them at the mercy of the growers. Other legislative advantages contribute to the economic power of the growers; for example, generous government subsidies to growers amounted in 1973 to $105 million. There has been no legislation to restrict the growth of agribusiness; 6 percent of the growers in California own 75 percent of the farmland.[4]

THE WORKERS

The current profile of the Yemeni farm laborer is one of a young man in his twenties. His skin is deeply tanned, his frame is small, and he is slender, almost underweight. His clothing is drab but neat and fairly clean. He is shy, definitely wary, and hesitant to make any disclosure. He is Muslim, and though he does not observe the fast of Ramadan because of the arduous nature of his work, he prays five times a day in the field and attends the mosque whenever possible. He is married, but his wife and children have remained in Yemen. He speaks no English and makes no formal attempt to learn it. We were told that he can read and write Arabic. He is seclusive and

4. *California Crop and Livestock Reporting Service*, Sept. 30, 1974, p. 1.

associates with few people outside the circle of his fellow workers. He avoids any situation that might cause trouble, and to this end he polices his friends. Avoiding drinking, smoking, and public entertainment, he spends his leisure time with his fellow workers, talking and playing cards.

He sleeps in one of the bleak, company-owned, cinderblock houses that are aligned in long rows like barracks. Though the barrack areas are within verdant orchards and vineyards, there is little vegetation in and immediately around them. In the barracks he is provided with only a bed frame and a mattress. He must supply everything else. He takes his meals communally and adheres to the dietary proscriptions of Islam. An elected worker is charged with buying and cooking for the group, and the cost is shared. Food is prepared in large common pots; the portions are meted out sparingly in steel bowls and served at raw wooden tables in dining halls that reek of stale, hot, uncirculated air. At one orchard we visited, the food was prepared and served by the company at a price of three dollars a day, which was deducted from the worker's paycheck. The company obviously profited from this transaction. In general, substandard living conditions characterize the life of the Yemeni farm laborer. In 1974, 488 farm labor camps in California failed to meet the state's housing, safety, and sanitation standards.[5]

Each of the workers interviewed earned a nominal $2.30 an hour. Social security contributions are deducted from the worker's wages, but the worker will never draw the benefits because he is not allowed to retire in this country. Income tax deductions run as high as 20 percent. Other deductions made for workman's compensation and for busing from the barracks to the fields (three dollars per trip). Petty payroll chiseling, made possible by the worker's unfamiliarity with English, his lack of understanding of accounting procedures, and his general inability to challenge such practices, is also common.

The Yemeni worker's transportation to the United States is arranged within a credit system set up by TWA in Los Angeles. A relative or an interested friend pays a $100 deposit in California, and there is a cosigner in Yemen. The ticket, which costs $800, is paid for, with interest, in installments by the worker. Within hours of his arrival, still dressed in his somber suit and white shirt, looking apprehensive and bewildered, he finds himself in the hiring hall with a group of eleven others. Each group of twelve workers is represented by a spokesman who has already arranged to get social security numbers

5. *Sacramento Bee*, Mar. 20, 1974.

for them. Hired by the dozen, the Yemenis immediately go to work.

There is widespread neglect of the most elementary worker health and safety precautions. The risk of accident to migrant farm workers is high. Preventive health care for the newcomer is minimal. Illnesses and other emergencies are not provided for. There is no sick pay. Disability compensation is paid only for job-related accidents. Workers are not covered by unemployment insurance. Because of the high cost, workers use private medical care only in extreme cases. Although social welfare and other assistance programs are theoretically open to Yemeni migrant workers, for one reason or another they seldom qualify for these benefits.

The Yemenis suffer not only from the usual health problems of the rural poor—tuberculosis, venereal disease, and respiratory infections—but also from special problems endemic to the East, such as schistosomiasis. Existing institutions fail to meet their needs. Although the California State Department of Health is a large and copiously funded bureaucracy, the division concerned with farmworkers has a minuscule budget of $100,000. In addition, recent cuts have reduced its staff from twenty-eight to four. These four professionals are not even aware of the Yemenis, much less their special health problems. One bright spot in this otherwise bleak picture is a clinic in Lamont funded by the U.S. Department of Health, Education and Welfare and staffed by thirty professionals, including two doctors. It is trilingual (English, Spanish, and Arabic) and makes treatment available to the 1,000 or so Yemenis in that area.

Like other farm laborers, the Yemenis are paid only when they work. They work wherever and whenever work is available. One crew interviewed in July 1974 had worked willingly from sunup to sundown in over 100-degree heat for twelve consecutive days in order to earn whatever they could. They follow the harvest from the early asparagus to the later row crops, the stonefruits, and the grapes. After the harvests, the companies move them to base camps from which they are then employed in tasks of the fallow season. They prune the fruit trees and gird the grapevines and otherwise assist in the production of the season's crops. The remainder of the year they must seek their own shelter and provide for their general needs from their seasonal earnings.

The Yemeni worker usually sends $1,000 to $1,500 a year to his family, a sum that represents half of his annual income. The other half is consumed by the imperatives of his existence. Inflation and the increased costs of living have reduced the amount that he can send home.

Union Participation

Prior to the emergence of the United Farm Workers (UFW), no alternatives existed for the exploited Yemeni worker. Even after this organization began to grow, the Yemeni found himself in conflict. On the one hand, his consciousness of the power of unity and unionization must have been raised by the expectations of improving his lot. On the other hand, he could not afford to jeopardize his maximum earnings because of the importance of the dollar back home. His attempts, therefore, to support the UFW were at first tentative and indecisive. Though caught between a compelling financial need and the risk involved in joining the union, many joined. Mindful of the fact that the Yemenis were especially vulnerable to exploitation because they spoke neither English nor Spanish, the union made a determined effort to recruit them. (Their vulnerability to exploitation is exemplified by the preference of some ranchers to employ them because they are "easier to control.") Although the UFW is identified in the public's mind with Chicanos and the Catholic church, it is in fact a coalition of many ethnic groups.

Data on Yemeni union participation is relatively limited; it is known, however, that many Yemenis are active within the UFW. One Yemeni who was an extremely effective organizer worked for three years in the late 1960s among both Yemenis and Chicanos. A union spokesperson stated that the Yemenis showed a great deal of understanding and tolerance of other minorities, especially on the picket lines. As members of the UFW, Yemenis participated in every phase of activity from the grassroots union basic unit, "the ranch committee," to demonstrations in Los Angeles and Sacramento on behalf of a labor initiative on the state ballot in 1972.

The role played by Nagi Daifullah is an example of Yemeni activism. Cesar Chavez recently said, "[Nagi] often served as an interpreter at union functions, and gave himself fully to the grape strike and the assertion for farm worker justice."[6] An American Civil Liberties Union spokesperson said of Nagi, "He believed that the Filipinos, Chicanos and Yemenis had enough dignity to stand together." Becoming an activist was a gamble for Nagi, and he lost. Although it is difficult to estimate the impact of his death (and that of Juan de la Cruz) on his Yemeni coworkers, one might guess that it has increased their hesitancy to engage in active confrontation; but the very fact that he was made a martyr indicates their conviction in that direction.

Ideals, however, often must submit to the pragmatic. We find the

6. *El Malcriado*, Sept. 4, 1974, p. 2.

Yemenis, therefore, accepting work wherever they can get it. When the Teamsters challenged the jurisdiction of the UFW by signing collusive contracts with the growers, the Yemenis often worked for whichever union had the contracts. The intensity of need among the poor and the exploited discourages the cooperation essential to all of them. To the Yemeni, single-minded in his purpose, the risks of idealism are often too great to take.

The Yemenis are "a very proud people," said the Canadian-born wife of nearly forty years of an old-timer now retired in Lodi. "They were never lazy. They never forgot their families even though they were away for years." The pride of the Yemeni and his sense of duty and loyalty have sustained him in the past and have provided the goals that help him transcend the hardships of the present.

In recent years, the Yemeni's consciousness of Arab nationalism has increased considerably. In an interview with a ninety-year-old retired Yemeni farmworker this Arab pride was tellingly portrayed. A wise and witty commentator in both Arabic and English, he remarked: "Historians said the West would go up and the Arabs would go down. Well, it's true. The West went up to the moon and what did they find? They found dust. The Arabs, they went down, and what did they find? They found oil." He laughed triumphantly, and we joined him in relishing what seemed to be the irony of the century. Yet this gentleman was unmindful that his pride in the Arabs comes from a deep yearning for human dignity. The oil he bragged about, the wealth and the power it bestows on Saudi Arabia, is only next door to the Yemen he came from—one of the world's poorest countries.

The Yemenis are proud people and they continue to bear the indignities of exploitation and to experience the impotence brought about by intense deprivation. They can be proud of their tenacity and their endurance. But they need the help and support they are too proud to ask for.

Mahfoud Bennoune

MAGHRIBI WORKERS IN FRANCE

Emigration . . . is the voice of a people which has grown silent.

Heinrich Mann

SINCE THE AGE of mercantilism, the Western bourgeoisie has considered colonial expansion a necessary condition for sustained industrial growth and for the maintenance of capitalism. In accordance with this prescription, the entire Maghrib was conquered by France and transformed into a source for the extraction of raw materials and a market for manufactured products. The French expropriation of land from the Maghribi peasantry and the incorporation of the North African economy, which had been based in rural areas on agricultural activities and animal husbandry and in the cities on handicraft industries and trade, into that of the "metropolitan" capitalist market created a serious decline in the indigenous economic sector. The resulting erosion of the economic base of the Maghrib coincided with a tremendous increase in population. Impoverished peasants moved to the cities, where they joined the artisans in search of a way to eke out their livelihood. Because of the lack of opportunities in the cities, many of the pauperized masses were driven by hunger and want to cross the Mediterranean to Europe.

EARLY MIGRATION

The emigration of Maghribi workers to Western Europe can be traced back to 1871, when some unknown number of Algerian laborers first appeared in historical records in France and Belgium.[1] In 1905 several thousands of North Africans were reported at work in European coal mines, and in 1911 French authorities revealed that 3,000 North Africans were working in France. The next year, an official inquiry revealed the existence of 5,000 North African workers—among them, 1,500 miners.[2] Early immigration developed slowly owing to administrative restrictions imposed by the governor general of Algeria. In 1876, on the express demand of the *colons*, the governor general had promulgated a decree requiring a special travel permit for Algerians going to France. When this requirement was abolished in 1913, the movement of Algerian workers to France increased rapidly. On the eve of the First World War, 30,000 North Africans were working in France. Many of them were Moroccans employed in the metallurgical industries of Nantes and the mines of Pas de Calais.[3]

The First World War aggravated France's need for manpower. The mobilization of an immense number of the active population, mostly workers, for military service had resulted in a drastic decline in France's productive capacity. In order to keep the war industries running, French authorities turned to the "colonial reserve army" of pauperized masses. In Tunisia and Morocco, the French authorities used voluntary recruitment methods. In Algeria, however, forced recruitment brought about a "veritable mobilization, a civil requisition that was made possible by the sovereignty of France over the territory of the colony."[4] Once in France, this colonial manpower came under the direct jurisdiction of the Ministry of War, which was empowered to try workers before military tribunals in the event they refused to work. They were housed in special compounds where they were also obligated to take their meals. This operation of collective recruitment of colonial

1. Madeleine Trebous, *Migration and Development: The Case of Algeria* (Paris: Development Centre of the Organisation for Economic Co-operation and Development, 1970), pp. 56, 154; Jacques Augarde, "La Migration algérienne," *Hommes et Migrations*, no. 116 (1970), p. 23.

2. Tayeb Belloula, *Les Algériens en France* (Algiers: E.N.A., 1965), pp. 13-14.

3. Trebous, *Migration and Development*, pp. 56, 154.

4. Li Chao-King, *Les Travailleurs en France* (Paris: Presses universitaires de France, 1939), p. 29 (all translations into English are my own).

workers resulted in the introduction of 120,000 Algerians, 35,000 Moroccans, and 18,000 Tunisians into France.[5]

During the war of 1914–18, Algeria also provided 173,000 men for the French military service. By April 1917, 2.7 percent of the Algerian population had been in the French army in France.[6] Tunisia and Morocco also furnished thousands of men for the French war effort. After the armistice, many of the mobilized men were sent back home, but many others remained as laborers to rebuild the war-devastated zones. Since France found itself depopulated and economically paralyzed, the French government again resorted to North African colonial manpower to reconstruct its economy. Between 1920 and 1924, 120,000 Maghribi workers were called to France. In 1924 alone, 71,028 Algerian and 10,000 Moroccan workers were imported. This massive emigration from the Maghrib frightened the colonial entrepreneurs, who had until that time been imposing starvation wages on the workers of the lumpen proletariat. As usual, their pressures elicited a positive response from the colonial authorities. Thenceforth a work permit was required before emigrating. Although this restriction brought about a decrease in emigration, 71,000 Algerian workers arrived in France in 1929 alone. The 1929 economic crash slowed the tempo of this emigration, and many of the laborers already in Europe were forced to return to the Maghrib. The number of Algerian immigrant workers registered officially in the manpower office fell from 65,000 in 1932 to 32,000 in 1936.[7] The consequences of this economic crisis were felt strongly by those immigrant workers whose socioeconomic and legal status was, and still is, so precarious.

The Second World War provoked far-reaching changes in the nature, form, and magnitude of this trans-Mediterranean migration. Although the French minister of labor had requested, in January 1940, the dispatch of several thousand Algerian workers, the military debacle that resulted in the German occupation of France put a quick end to this request. With the ensuing disorganization of the French economy, 10,000 Maghribi workers were laid off and repatriated in the early spring of 1940. Later the German military authorities expelled an additional 16,000. During 1943 and 1944, the French colonial authorities prohibited all migration from Algeria. After the liberation

5. *Ibid.*

6. British Naval Intelligence, *Handbook Area Guide: Algeria* (1944), p. 45; Charles R. Ageron, *Les Algeriens musulmans et la France, 1871–1919* (Paris: Presses universitaires de France), II, 1157.

7. Belloula, *Les Algériens en France*, pp. 30–31.

of France, French management again turned to the North African labor force to reconstruct its ruined industries, communication networks, and housing.

As a result of the need of the French industrialists for manpower, the number of Algerians working in France increased by the tens of thousands each year, reaching approximately 400,000 by the mid-1950s.[8] The North African workers in Europe continued to be considered by the capitalist employers as a colonized labor force to be employed only "in occupations deserted by the European workers . . . or in the hardest, the dirtiest, and the most dangerous tasks." This situation has been interpreted as proof that "the 'native' status follows the Algerian worker, even when he crosses the Mediterranean Sea"; thus "the 'native' status is considered as being innate, deriving from the [ethnic] origin of the individual and attached to his person wherever he goes and whatever he does."[9] The Maghribi worker's wages were among the lowest in Europe, allowing the capitalists to extort from this colonized proletariat an exorbitant sum of surplus labor: superprofits.

MIGRATION AFTER INDEPENDENCE

Because of French demographic stagnation and simultaneous economic expansion in the 1960s, French management continued to depend on its neocolonial reserve army—at this time, to replace its shrinking local semiskilled and unskilled work force. As M. Massenet, the director of population in the Ministry of Labor, declared on television in 1968, "With an active French population of 40 percent, how could we ensure in France the standard of living of the population, ensure the retirement of the elderly, the charges of the students, ensure the social investments for children, without immigration?" Furthermore, the competition for jobs that results when many workers immigrate created a downward pressure on wages. Thus, the importation of a labor force to ensure the welfare of the French population continued to be a vital economic necessity.

The postcolonial states of the Maghrib have not yet resolved the basic problem created by colonialism, namely, economic underdevelopment aggravated by a population "explosion." In 1966, the Algerian

8. Augarde, "La Migration algérienne," p. 15.

9. Andrée Michel, *Les Travailleurs algériens en France* (Paris: C.N.R.S., 1956), p. 219. This quote is from a court ruling that deprived the Algerian workers of certain civil rights enjoyed by other European immigrant workers.

population exceeded 12 million, Morocco's population was close to 13 million, and Tunisia's was just under 5 million. The outflow of workers in search of employment in Western Europe not only followed its preindependence course but increased dramatically after 1962. The total number of North African laborers in France reached 1.1 million in 1973, including nearly 800,000 from Algeria.[10]

Since the primordial causes underlying this emigration are deeply rooted in the socioeconomic structures imposed by French colonialism, this phenomenon will not vanish until the circumstances which nourish the continuation of the dependent-dominant relationships and which tie the formerly colonized states to their "metropolis" are eradicated. However, the neocolonial relations between France and the states of the Maghrib have been maintained and consolidated in the postindependence period. In the decade between 1963 and 1972, only Algeria, as a result of its oil and natural gas exports, managed to establish a balance-of-payments surplus. France has maintained its position as the most important market for exports from the Maghrib and the primary source of its imports.[11]

This current state of affairs is conducive neither to economic development nor to political-economic independence. The North African countries continue primarily to export raw materials and labor power in order to import industrial equipment and manufactured consumer products. Only Algeria has made some real effort at industrialization. It has favored a capital intensive and laborsaving approach to "modernization," and this policy has had paradoxical results: external financial debts and technological dependence have been increasing, and, while Algeria has continued to export its unskilled and semiskilled manpower, it has been importing foreign technicians, engineers, doctors, and teachers. In a word, Algerian industrialization is not generating employment for the Algerian deruralized masses.

No North African state has yet carried out a thorough land reform in favor of the peasantry. In Tunisia and Morocco, the autochthonous landlords managed to buy a large number of hectares from the former *colons*. However, the new Tunisian ruling class failed at organizing cooperatives in the countryside, and the only state programs designed by the new Moroccan bureaucracy to improve agricultural production were for the benefit of only the comprador large landowners. "Socialist Algeria" did not undertake any serious land reform until 1971. The

---

10. Le Monde, *Dossiers et documents*, no. 4 (June 1973).

11. *The Middle East and North Africa, 1973-1974: A Survey and Directory* (London: Europa Publications, 1973), pp. 194, 520, 652, 653.

experience of self-management on colonial farms abandoned by the settlers was nipped in the bud by the postindependence petit bourgeois bureaucracy, which finally opted for state capitalism rather than develop, rectify, and perfect worker self-management. The new ruling classes in the Maghrib have thus far failed to resolve the basic problems facing their people: underdevelopment, neocolonial dependency, social inequality, obscurantism, despotism, and the enslavement of women.

Thus migration has been viewed by the French and North African governments as a safety valve for maintaining the prosperity of the metropolitan bourgeoisie and the stability of its satellite regimes in the Maghrib. Emigration from the former French colonies has played a role in freezing social struggle there. Political pressure stimulated by unemployment, which is in itself a consequence of economic neocolonialism, has been released by this emigration of pauperized masses. The shortage of indigenous manpower, which is a vulnerable economic weakness, has been astutely turned into a powerful political mechanism that permits the French ruling class to channel, through migration, the frustrations and energies of the immigrant workers in a way that reinforces its neocolonial relations with the Maghrib.

PROCEDURES FOR IMMIGRATION

In the past the procedures for introducing the immigrant workers into France differed slightly from one North African country to another. The bulk of Algerian immigrant workers entered France prior to 1962 as French citizens, and so the various agreements negotiated between the French and Algerian authorities regarding the "export" of labor power, wines, and petroleum to France guaranteed these workers a "special status." As for the Tunisian and Moroccan immigrant workers, they were exported as all other foreign workers are exported to France—on a work-contract basis binding them for a specified period of time (from six months to two years) to a French employer.

The postcolonial period in Algeria was initiated by the signing, in March 1962, of the Evian Agreement, which stipulated that "every Algerian carrying an identification card be free to circulate between France and Algeria." In order to "normalize" the migration of Algerian workers to France, a second Franco-Algerian accord was worked out in 1964. This agreement specified that the quarterly quota of immigrants would be determined on the basis of the availability of manpower in Algeria and the needs of the French labor market. Applicants for immigration were required to pass a medical examination in the "French medical mission." In 1968, some revisions were made to tighten administrative control over these immigrant workers. Algeria agreed to furnish 35,000 workers every year. (In 1971 this number was unilaterally reduced to 25,000 in retaliation for the nationalization of French oil interests.) The Algerian Board of Manpower was empowered to recruit immigrant workers. Once a worker is granted the "favor" of being accepted for immigration, he receives a permit authorizing him to enter France. When he arrives he has a nine-month period to find employment. If successful, he is automatically granted a five-year residence permit which is renewable.

The Moroccan and Tunisian immigrant workers are required to obtain work permits and medical clearance from the French National Board of Immigration. The majority of these workers immigrate clandestinely and are allowed to regularize their legal status once they find employment. In fact, the majority of immigrant workers in France follow this pattern of "spontaneous immigration"; in 1960, the proportion of such workers was 53 percent; in 1968, it was 86 percent.[12]

POSITION OF MAGHRIBI WORKERS IN FRANCE

Since the French authorities permit employers to hire immigrant workers only in industrial sectors where there is a French manpower deficit, these workers are automatically relegated to the dirtiest, most painful, and riskiest occupational positions. Immigrant workers, and especially the North Africans, are concentrated in certain basic industries: construction, metallurgy, chemical manufacturing, rubber and asbestos manufacturing, and, in general, industries with unhealthy working conditions. According to the 1968 French census, 35.6 percent of the foreign male workers were employed in building and public works, 13.5 percent in mechanical and electrical engineering, 9.2 percent in agriculture, fishing, and forestry, and 8.1 percent in commerce.[13] Of the women immigrant workers, 29 percent were employed in domestic services. The concentration of immigrant labor in the construction industry is noteworthy. The French working class

12. Bernard Granotier, *Les Travailleurs immigrés en France* (Paris: Maspero, 1970), p. 60.

13. I.N.S.E.E., *Recensement de 1968: Population de la France.* All figures are estimates; the 1968 French census underestimated the number of immigrant workers.

has abandoned this sector in which strenuous labor and geographic mobility are demanded of the worker in exchange for low wages and a low social status. Furthermore, this industry has a high rate of fatal accidents among workers.

Compared with other immigrant populations and with the French, the average rate of economic activity of the Maghribi population is high. In 1968, 52.5 percent of the total Algerian population living in France were economically active: 70.2 percent of the males and 4.8 percent of the females. Of this active population, 97.9 percent of the men and 94.9 percent of the women were wage laborers. The Algerian laboring masses, it was found, resided primarily in two regions: 43.7 percent in Paris and its environs and 18.1 percent in the Rhone-Alps area; the rest were scattered in eastern and northern France. Tunisian and Moroccan immigrants were similarly concentrated in the major industrial regions of France.[14]

Although the North African workers have become an indispensable labor force in the French economy, their socioeconomic status, even when compared with that of other immigrant nationalities, is low. Their subordinate position was strikingly demonstrated in a 1967 government survey on the status of industrial and commercial workers. The results of that survey indicated a functional stratification of immigrant laborers along nationality lines. Except for the Portuguese, all Europeans—Italians, Poles, Spaniards—enjoyed a higher socioeconomic position than North Africans; over 6 percent of the Europeans were nonmanual employees and a high proportion were skilled manual workers. The Portuguese, though very few of them were nonmanual workers, were represented by a fair portion of skilled workers. In contrast, semiskilled and unskilled workers constituted 87.2 percent of the Algerian, 81.4 percent of the Moroccan, and 70.3 percent of the Tunisian labor forces.[15] The qualitative differentiation in the occupational patterns of the various national groups of immigrant workers was matched by a quantitative differentiation in wages and social status.

This differential access to socioeconomic positions is determined by historical factors, underdevelopment of the Maghrib, and an official policy of the French government enabling employers to divide the alien workers from the French proletariat and the immigrant laborers

---

14. *Ibid.*

15. Data are from Enquête effectuée par le Ministre d'Etat Chargé des Affaires Sociales Auprès des Etablissements Industriels et Commerciaux de 10 Salariés et plus au 1er Juillet 1967.

among themselves. The hierarchy of national groups reflects the actual degree of hostility toward each of them expressed by the French population. Whereas the Italians are most favorably considered and the Spanish and Portuguese are more or less tolerated, there is very strong prejudice against North Africans, especially Algerians.[16] In a recent poll conducted by the Institut Français d'Opinion Publique, 62 percent of those questioned said that there were too many North Africans in France, while 27 percent thought there were too many Spaniards; at the time the number of southern European workers far exceeded the number of those from the Maghrib. Another recent poll of French workers found that 71 percent of the respondents thought there were too many North Africans while 50 percent thought there were too many Spaniards and Portuguese. The North Africans are rejected on the grounds that they are not only socially and economically "underdeveloped," but that they are also culturally too different, and consequently unassimilable. The "colonial fact" appears to override all others.

One thing that does distinguish the French proletariat from the immigrant workers is the fact that the immigrants are imported to work for a specified period of time. They are deliberately rotated in such a way that

> many of them remain only a few years, and are then replaced by others so that there are hardly any retired immigrants. Immigrants therefore have a higher than average rate of economic activity, and make contributions to health, unemployment and pension insurance far in excess of their demands on such schemes. Particularly high rates of activity are to be found among recently arrived groups.[17]

Deprived of their basic civil rights, the Arab workers, like all other foreign workers in Europe, are constantly threatened with deportation if they participate in the ongoing class struggle. While they are in France, they tend to slave in silence lest they be expelled. From the above, it becomes obvious that North African and other immigrant workers in France form the kernel of the productive process within the primary sectors of the French economy. The French bourgeoisie

16. Godula Kosack and Stephen Castles, "Immigrant Workers and Class Structure in France" (Paper presented before the British Sociological Association, Sept. 24, 1970), p. 4.

17. Stephen Castles and Godula Kosack, "Common Market Migrants," *New Left Review*, no. 73 (May–June 1972), p. 10.

would not have bothered to attract or to import these workers if it was not socially, politically, and economically profitable for them to do so.

SOCIAL AND ECONOMIC FACTORS

The migration of Maghribi workers to France is related to the worsening of working conditions in the principal productive sectors where these workers are employed. Since the French workers are either given supervisory positions or transferred to more remunerative occupations with a higher social status, the struggle for the improvement of working conditions in the sectors of production reserved for immigrant workers has ceased to preoccupy the French unions. Given the racist and chauvinistic aura permeating their new industrial establishments, the immigrant laborers, either ignorant of labor legislation or merely terrorized by the constant threat of deportation, often resign themselves to perform equal work with the French workers for lower wages. Deprived of basic civil rights and, in most cases, illiterate and lacking class or political consciousness, the immigrant workers cannot expose themselves to the wrath of their employers and the "law enforcement" agencies. Despite the fact that they are among the most productive elements within the French society—being engaged in primary activity generating productive branches on which numerous secondary sectors depend—these foreign laborers are the most exploited segment of the proletariat in Europe.

The French small-scale and archaic industries would not have been able to survive the tight competition imposed upon them by large industrial firms had it not been for this alien labor force. Through systematic discriminatory employment practices, financial fraud, starvation wages, and all sorts of manipulations, such as the constant shifts and rotations of immigrant workers, these petty entrepreneurs have been able to avoid paying or raising wages in accordance with seniority-rule requirements. As a result, the owners of these firms have managed to squeeze out enough surplus labor to compete with the highly concentrated and rationalized modern firms. The French large-scale enterprises have come to base their whole short-run and long-run industrial planning on this alien manpower whose forced obedience has allowed the French bourgeoisie to increase the rate of profits without even the risk of social unrest.

The importation of a predominantly male, alien labor force from Third World countries has not been accompanied by any serious attempt to create an adequate social infrastructure or to provide housing facilities, medical care, and other necessary services. These immigrants have not cost the host society a penny prior to their entry into its labor market. When an immigrant laborer arrives in France from the Maghrib, the costs of his rearing and basic education have already been paid by the exporting society. According to the French demographer Alfred Sauvy, "The total cost to the country of a young man to the age of eighteen, that is, to the level of a simple qualification, amounts to nine or ten years of work."[18] Thus, one of the major benefits of immigration for the receiving country is the fact that all the basic social costs until working age have been assumed by the countries of origin.

As soon as immigrant laborers start working in France, they are compelled to pay full social security fees, even though they receive only partial benefits in return. It has been calculated that an immigrant worker leaves behind him, when he returns to his native country, as much as 20 percent of his wages in social security.[19] All North African immigrant workers whose dependents are left in the Maghrib receive only 60 percent or less of their family allowance. "Many lose even the benefit of this allowance either because of sheer ignorance or because they are deterred by tedious administrative difficulties."[20]

The profits derived from the utilization of the Maghribi laborers are enormous. In 1966, a French civil servant, Yves Chaigneau, calculated the amount of the Algerian workers' annual contribution to French economic production. He arrived at an estimate of between 2.2 and 3.5 billion old francs. Subtracting the wages paid to these workers, and the social benefits and aid given at that time to Algeria by France, he was able to determine that the balance of profits made by the French capitalists amounted to no less than 1.5 billion old francs per year.[21]

HOUSING CONDITIONS

Despite the fact that many of the Maghribi workers are employed in building and construction trades, their own housing is wretched.

18. Quoted in Juliette Minces, *Les Travailleurs étrangers en France* (Paris: Seuil, 1973), p. 38.

19. Charles Caporale, *Revue de l'Action Sociale*, June 1965.

20. Minces, *Les Travailleurs étrangers en France*, p. 39.

21. Cited in Granotier, *Les Travailleurs immigrés en France*, p. 238.

What is available to them falls into three categories: *bidonvilles*, or shanty towns; *hôtels meublés*, or furnished hostels; and *foyers sauvages*, or slum boardinghouses.[22]

Bidonvilles are "islets on the periphery of the industrial centers, more or less extending over open spots, on which barracks of old wood, metal, or cars have been constructed." These dwellings lack heat, running water, and electricity, and are overcrowded and noisy. Many of the Maghribi workers who brought their families with them to France in the late 1950s and 1960s lived in bidonvilles. After 1968, the French government decided, without making any preparations, to rehouse these bidonville dwellers and to suppress the bidonvilles. During the campaign that followed, there were numerous instances of police brutality directed against the roofless population of these slums. Some of those evicted came together in smaller groupings in "vertical microbidonvilles" in the industrial working-class suburbs. However, according to recent official statistics, almost 20 percent of the Maghribi workers in France continue to live in bidonvilles, accounting for about 42 percent of the bidonville population (the other residents are mainly immigrants from southern Europe).[23]

A Tunisian immigrant worker speaks of the situation in bidonvilles: "What we are leading here is not a life. Even the rats come to eat us. I swear to you that one time A. was bitten by a rat on his foot while he was asleep. But what do you want? When every one of us remembers his situation before, . . . he sleeps on his woes and bears everything." A second worker adds: "There is no difference between us and the animals. And I swear to you that even the animals live better than we. From time to time, when I look at the dogs around, . . . I get disgusted with life."[24] In the words of a young Algerian woman:

> My most horrible experience was that of the *bidonville* where I have lived about nine years. I was seventeen upon my arrival in France. The location of the *bidonville* was so close to the Seine that many children were drowned. Others had awful accidents. I have witnessed a six-month-old baby half-eaten by rats. His nose, chin, and the ends of his fingers

---

22. "Le Logement des migrants," *Droit et Liberté*, 1973. The present section on housing draws heavily from this study.

23. Granotier, *Les Travailleurs immigrés en France*, p. 97.

24. Quoted in Tidjani Ben Sassi, "Les Travailleurs tunisiens dans la region parisienne," *Hommes et Migrations*, no. 109 (1968), pp. 94-95.

had been eaten off. He died in the hospital. I shall never forget this. Another one was burned to death. The barrack where he was asleep caught fire while his mother was talking with her next-door neighbor. When she saw the flames, she rushed home to save her child; but out of fright he had hidden himself in a drawer where no one thought to look. During this time, I had run to the manager of the *centre de transit* [center reserved for immigrants] opposite to the *bidonville* to call the firemen. I explained to him that a child was about to burn alive, would he please let me phone. But he couldn't stand the people of the *bidonville*, and therefore he refused to call the fire department.[25]

The French administrative bureaucracy has established certain requirements which further burden the residents of bidonvilles. For example, several times a year immigrant workers are required to furnish a certificate of residence from a landlord in order to qualify for the benefits of social security, etc. Because bidonvilles are not officially recognized as residential quarters, workers living in them must purchase these certificates on the black market for an exorbitant price.

Hôtels meublés are unhygienic rundown buildings located in slum quarters in the suburbs of large industrial areas. According to the 1962 census, there were 12,280 buildings of this kind in Paris alone. The conditions in these slum lodgings are more or less similar to those in bidonvilles. The buildings are decayed, unhygienic, and overcrowded.[26] The *hôtels meublés* are operated by "merchants of sleep," who are merciless in taxing the immigrant workers. Each room in the hostel is crammed with as many as five beds. Quite often each bed is rented to three different workers, each of whom is obliged to pay the rental price for the entire room. The workers are expected to arrange their shifts in such a way as to make it possible for each to have access to the bed for at least six hours in twenty-four. Ben Sassi, in his study of Tunisian workers in Paris, found that the average number of workers living in each room of these hostels was between seven and eight, but that sometimes twenty or more workers would be rented "a living space of fifteen square meters, without any ventilation except through the door, which is most often closed." In some of the hostels, the salon of the café is used at night as a dormitory. "The owner lays down mattresses on the floor in midwinter

---

25. Quoted in Catherine Valabrègue, *L'Homme déraciné* (Paris: Mercure de France, 1973), p. 38.

26. "Le Logement des migrants," p. 38.

as soon as the café closes. But he never forgets, of course, to collect fifty francs per month from every worker."[27]

Foyers sauvages are old buildings rented to immigrant workers by individuals specializing in this booming business. The environment is characterized by "insalubrity, racism, and exploitation." A militaristic discipline restricts the privacy of the tenants—for example, women are not allowed to enter the rooms. These lodgings constitute a ghetto within which the immigrant laborers live under hellish conditions. Recently in Sochaux, 216 Algerian workers were living in such a slum lodging. Each floor had 36 persons and one toilet, and each room was inhabited by an average of 20 to 22 persons. Since there was no kitchen, tenants had to cook their food in their rooms. The landlord provided neither beds nor blankets. Each occupant had to pay forty-five francs per month. In Bordeaux, 80 Maghribi workers were living in an unheated *foyer sauvage* with twenty-four rooms and two toilets. The building had no running water. The rent was eighty francs per month per person.

Many other forms of lodgings for immigrant workers exhibit the same features as those described. In the course of my field research in Alsace and Lorraine—in Thionville, Metz, St. Louis, Mulhouse, and Strasbourg—I found housing for Maghribi workers to be vastly inadequate. In St. Louis, a boardinghouse built during the Franco-Algerian war by the Service de l'Action Sociale en Faveur des Migrants with funds left by Algerian workers in social security as a result of differential payment of family allowances had been turned over in the early 1960s to a *pied-noir* to manage as a real estate enterprise. Given the shortage of housing and the systematic refusal of local residents to rent even their attics to the North African workers, this "merchant of sleep" was able to extort 780 francs per month for a single room crammed with five or six people. Ben Sassi's description of the housing conditions of the Tunisian immigrant workers is representative of those of the Maghribi population in France.

> We have found that the quasi totality of the Tunisian workers in Paris and its regions are living in "boxes of sardines," to use their own expression, which are characterized by decay, humidity, and filth. In a word, there is no hygiene, no comfort, and consequently there is no social life. In examining these slums, I asked myself how is it possible to conserve a passable health in such lodgings after 59 hours of work per week.[28]

27. "Les Travailleurs tunisiens," pp. 88–89.
28. *Ibid.*, p. 90.

HEALTH AND EDUCATION OF THE IMMIGRANT POPULATION

French doctors have indicated that the immigrant laborers in France and their families constitute "a group with a high risk"[29] for the contraction of both somatic and extrasomatic diseases as a result of lamentably deficient living and working conditions. A team of French doctors who studied the immigrant population attributed its "pathology" to two types of disease: diseases of acquisition and those of adaptation.[30]

Diseases of acquisition are physical illnesses contracted after the immigrants' arrival in France. (Since all immigrant workers must pass a medical examination either before they leave their country of origin or before they regularize their legal situation in France, one can dismiss the claims made by French racists that the immigrants carry with them these diseases from their native countries.) One of the most lethal of such diseases, attacking a large proportion of the immigrant workers and their families in general, and the North and sub-Saharan Africans in particular, is tuberculosis. The Maghribi population in France often contracts pulmonary tuberculosis, which spreads rapidly within the immigrant communities. A study conducted during the 1968–70 period revealed that of the patients who entered the sanatoriums, 51 percent were North African. The immigrant workers affected by tuberculosis belonged to the lowest strata of the proletariat.[31] Tuberculosis was described by the team of French doctors as a

disease of transplantation which is caused by a multiplicity of factors: malnutrition, undernourishment, overworking, diverse psychological shocks, overcrowding, confinement, lack of hygiene, frailty, and over-contamination. It is the result of all these causally interwoven factors. The immigrant workers, who are introduced into France in good health, usually contract this disease after having stayed six to eighteen months.[32]

Other diseases listed among the major causes for the hospitalization of Maghribi workers are digestive troubles, such as colitis, cholecystitis, gastroduodenal ulcers, etc. These are also contracted in France as

29. Comité médical et médico-social d'aide aux migrants, "La Santé des migrants," *Droit et Liberté*, 1972. The present section on health conditions draws heavily from this study.

30. *Ibid.*, pp. 22–24.

31. *Ibid.*, p. 93.

32. *Ibid.*, pp. 94–95.

a direct consequence of the subhuman working and living conditions imposed upon Maghribi workers.

The diseases of adaptation, called by some psychiatrists the pathology of transplantation, exhibit acute polymorphous reactional psychoses. Many newly arrived immigrants suffer multivarious neurotic reactions, recurrent depression, "sinistroses," and a multitude of other syndromes. These immigrant workers receive no organized assistance when they enter the French labor market. The initial impact of "culture shock," which is generated by the sudden environmental changes, the difficulties in linguistic communication, the stress involved in job hunting, and the absence of adequate accommodations, is followed by repeated encounters with racism and hostility. All of this is likely to trigger severe "psychological shocks," undermining the psychic balance of the newly transplanted proletarian. According to Dr. Somia, most of the diseases affecting the Maghribi immigrant workers are socially engendered.

> Of 727 files of North Africans who had been examined in the psychiatric centers of the Parisian region, it was demonstrated that 90 percent of the cases were related to the labor market. Therefore, when there is unemployment or work difficulty, psychiatric symptoms appear, aggravated in this anxious man who has the responsibility of a family that is not nearby to comfort him.[33]

The health of the children of immigrant workers is even worse than that of the adults. These children account for 40 percent of all infant hospitalizations in France, though the entire immigrant population constitutes only 6.5 percent of the total population of the country. In the Paris region, an investigation of the social backgrounds of these infants showed that in 45 percent of the cases the family lived in a single room in a hostel; in 20 percent, a bidonville; in 20 percent a *centre de transit;* and in 15 percent, worn-out lodgings. These children were constantly exposed to all sorts of germs and harmful animals such as rats, which carry parasites and microbes.[34]

This state of affairs also militates against the normal education of these children. An inquiry conducted in six major French cities revealed that only 20 percent of the children of immigrant workers succeeded either in obtaining the certificate of primary education

33. "La Santé des Algériens en France," in *Colloque sur la migration algérienne en France,* Association France-Algérie, Oct. 1966, p. 142.
34. "Le Logement des migrants," p. 76.

or in entering the sixth grade. Twenty percent failed completely (that is, when they stopped going to school, they could not read or write); 60 percent failed partially. Furthermore, 75 percent of the children lagged one to three years behind their age level. In addition to these terrible disadvantages, the French authorities instituted an annual quota system in professional schools—for example, only 10 percent of the students in the training centers may be from the alien population. Finally, upon graduation, those who do manage to obtain diplomas are hired by French employers as only semiskilled workers. This systematic discriminatory policy is designed to maintain a source of cheap manpower for the French ruling class.

The racist hostility in the schools in which the alien child is not only educated but acculturated undermines his intellectual development. Many recent studies on the education of young children have demonstrated that the level of intellectual development of any individual depends to a great extent on the sociobiological environment during his first years of acculturation. Poverty and malnutrition, when combined, generate a cumulative effect on the intellectual development of a child reared in a family that is relegated to the lowest socioeconomic levels of a stratified society. "Once more we find," wrote Catherine Valabreque, "that the difficulties of the child [in school] originate in racism. Provided that he has an accent, he will be mocked and scorned by his French classmates. 'Do not ask me if I am an Arab,' said a small boy. 'It makes me think of "dirty Arab." I am a Moroccan.'" A French mother is reported to have said to her child, "If I see you speaking to a Muslim, I shall kill you."[35] This hostility is certain to psychologically inhibit the child, who, in becoming anxious when confronted with permanent insecurity, has only two courses to follow: to resort to overt aggressive behavior as a sign of defiance, or to withdraw in order to avoid conflict. Neither of these alternatives is conducive to success in school.

WORKER MILITANCY

On January 19, 1971, in a factory in Lyon, a Maghribi worker was smashed to pieces by the chain of a worn-out machine in the workshop. This defective engine should have been removed for reasons of safety long before the accident occurred. The chain of the machine

35. Valabrègue, L'Homme déraciné, p. 160.

was so weakened that it had broken. On the specific order of the management, in order to conceal its responsibility in this fatal accident, the chain was hidden and replaced by a new one. The workers were told that any one of them who dared to give the investigators a different version of the accident than that of the management would be fired. However, when the police came to investigate, one worker defied the management and not only gave the true cause of his companion's death but showed the investigators where the hidden chain was. In protest against the working conditions, the Maghribi workers struck for six hours. A second strike was organized on February 9, 1972, which lasted twenty-two days. This strike shook the whole working-class movement and French management. Thenceforth, the immigrant workers began "to fight for their rights—striking for better wages and working conditions, protesting scandalous rent for rotten quarters." [36]

In 1973 the militancy of the immigrant workers increased.

One of the most dramatic expressions of this new militancy was the long and effective strike started in the spring of 1973 by some 370 assembly line workers . . . [mostly Algerians] at the Renault automobile plant outside Paris. The main demand was "equal pay for equal work." The workers were protesting not only ruthless working conditions, but also the fact that they were getting paid substantially less than the French workers doing similar tasks.[37]

What started as a spontaneous wildcat strike was immediately joined by 12,000 semiskilled workers, 9,000 of whom were immigrants, and resulted in a partial victory for the Renault workers.

But its real significance lay in the fact that it showed the immigrants finally emerging from their long political passivity and isolation. This new activism has also been demonstrated in struggles in many slum tenements. . . . Immigrant workers have organized rent strikes, refusing to pay the exorbitant rents demanded for tiny unheated, overcrowded rooms, or else banding together to fight arbitrary evictions. Many of these actions have been successful in at least extracting small concessions or thwarting outrageous cases of discrimination.[38]

36. Quoted in Schofield Coryell, "Europe's Immigrant Workers: New Grapes of Wrath," *Ramparts*, Mar. 1974, pp. 16-20.

37. Coryell, "Europe's Immigrant Workers."

38. *Ibid.*

A neofascist movement called the Ordre Nouveau mounted vicious racist campaigns in opposition to the ongoing struggle for survival organized by the Maghribi immigrant workers and others. The Ordre Nouveau is an "organization whose leaders boast of their support for the Nazis during World War II."[39] A French antifascist youth organization, the Ligue Communiste, mounted a counterdemonstration against the racist hysterics of the Ordre Nouveau which resulted in the dissolution of the Ligue Communiste by the French government and the imprisonment of its leader, Alain Krivine. Despite the law against racist propaganda, newspapers such as *Minute* continue to denounce

the waves of syphilis-bearing, rape-prone undesirables. On June 23—just two days after the Ordre Nouveau rally—shots were fired from speeding cars into several Algerian cafes in the Paris suburbs. On July 3, in Vitry, . . . three racists murdered a Portuguese worker, then attacked an Algerian. In the southern resort city of Nice, on August 2, two Algerian workers were badly wounded in a fight with the owner of the building in which they lived. Racial violence erupted in the city of Toulon, where the municipal council declared a "state of emergency" on August 10.[40]

The widespread animosity against the immigrant workers degenerated into further acts of violence and murder after August 25, 1973, when a mentally disturbed Algerian laborer, whose brain had been damaged in a fight with some French fascists, killed a bus driver in Marseille. The French reactionary press, in search of any excuse to launch a hysterical campaign against the Algerian workers in particular (because of their noticeable role in the struggle for the improvement of working and living conditions) and the Third World immigrant workers in general, seized upon this event. The major southern French newspaper, *Le Meridional*, led the anti-Algerian crusade: "We have had enough of Algerian thieves, Algerian thugs, Algerian braggarts, Algerian trouble-makers, Algerian syphilitics, Algerian rapists, Algerian pimps, Algerian lunatics, Algerian killers." A committee for the defense of Marseille was established by the local members of the Ordre Nouveau to instigate criminal acts against the North African laborers and to denounce the "brown threat." "The Algerian [who killed the bus driver] was nearly lynched and the local press used the tragedy to whip up anti-Algerian fury throughout

39. *Ibid.*
40. *Ibid.*

the region, where many former *colons* live and memories of the Algerian war are vivid."[41] This isolated crime provided the French fascist groups with a pretext to move into action. Between August 26 and September 29, 1973, twelve Algerian workers were assassinated across France. On December 14, a bomb was put in the room in the Algerian consulate in Marseille where the workers wait while their identification cards and various other papers are processed by the consular clerks. The bomb killed 4 people and wounded 100. As a direct result of this incident, the Algerian government decided to cut off the annual flow of 25,000 workers to France. (Other instances of fascist-organized mass murder had taken place earlier; for example, in 1971, when Algeria nationalized French oil interests, 21 immigrant workers in France were killed. The French police have as yet made no arrests in connection with any of these crimes.)

The North African workers responded to the 1973 racist hysteria with protective reactions. In the fall of 1973 and thereafter, the Movement of Arab Workers, a Pan-Maghribi clandestine organization, organized many strikes and massive street demonstrations in the industrial centers of France. One demonstration to protest the assasinations

> was highlighted by a meeting of thousands of Arab workers in front of the Paris mosque, following a massive walkout of immigrants from the construction sites and factories of the Paris area. For the first time, production was halted at the Citroen plant when Arab workers there, joined by other immigrants, put down their tools and marched out *en masse*. Cafes and restaurants in Arab neighborhoods were closed for the day.[42]

The growing racist hostility toward Arab immigrant workers in France has forced many of them to envisage a return home if employment there is made available. An Algerian worker, the father of five, who has been working in eastern France since 1962, wrote a letter to the personnel director of one of the Algerian state industrial organizations on September 3, 1973, requesting a job as an aid-mechanic. This letter reveals both the eagerness of immigrant workers to return home and their psychological stress in France. "We are fortifying the hand that is oppressing us," this worker concluded. But the director replied two months later, turning down the request

41. *Ibid.*
42. *Ibid.*

on the grounds that "in order to be reintegrated into our factory you must possess the following qualifications: a certificate of primary education and a certificate of professional training in general mechanics."

The courageous struggle of the Maghribi workers in France for the purpose of defending their interests must be extended to North Africa, where the major cause of their exploitation lies. In the final analysis, it is the North African societies that must be changed along revolutionary lines, whereby the collectivization not only of the means of production but also of labor itself will be carried out. The remnants of colonial structures must be destroyed and be replaced by genuinely egalitarian socioeconomic structures that will guarantee a popular participatory democracy as well as channel, in a very consequential way, the energies of the masses for the construction of just societies in the Maghrib.

PART IV: THE QUESTION OF PALESTINE

James A. McClure

THE ARABS: AN AMERICAN AWAKENING

THE TOPIC of my remarks represents both a pleasant and a difficult task to me. I am pleased that such major strides have been taken in the long trip that Americans have begun toward an understanding of the Arab peoples and their lands, but I am also personally aware of the many roadblocks and dangers that still lie ahead.

Increasing numbers of Americans are beginning to question the oversimplified, usually inaccurate, Arab picture which they have been shown for most of their lives. And this, actually, is a main characteristic of an awakening—a questioning of old ideas and a search for better ones. We can all be thankful that this questioning has begun, but we surely should not assume that people looking for the right answers will automatically find them. In issues involving Arabs, it is more likely that—left alone—questioning Americans will not find accuracy and completeness.

I would like to give you just one example of the problems that face those of us who work to correct the inaccurate and sometimes totally false statements made regarding Arabs. This particular example involves two of the most politically explosive issues in the United States today: inflation and oil prices. In most of the American press, these issues are combined as if they were one. They are not. And the continued belief by most Americans that they are constitutes a major obstacle to the dual search for domestic economic well-being and for peace in the Middle East.

Some in the American government might feel that it is politically "smart" to blame inflation on Arab oil prices. But they run a double risk: first, the risk of building dangerous animosity toward the oil-producers, both Arab and non-Arab; and, second, the risk that the populace, when it finds that it has been deceived, and that inflation does not go away when oil prices go down, will be outraged. It is foolish and self-defeating to mislead the American people into thinking that the United States can solve its economic problems simply by lowering the price it pays for oil. There is no doubt, of course, that the higher oil prices of the past year are a matter of major concern, involving questions of capital flow, balance of payments, and capital accumulation—questions that can determine the future stability of the international economic community—but they must not be allowed to distract attention from the true causes of inflation.

Now, to substantiate my position that inflation and oil prices are separate issues, I could quote from various economic experts in the Arab world; but to avoid any possible criticism involving the use of non-U.S. statistical data—always a risky undertaking—I will use another source: the United States government. These data, I believe, additionally disclose one of the obstacles that we must overcome in furthering the American awakening—namely, the typical bureaucratic syndrome that if you can find someone to blame for your problems—and it is easier to blame them than to solve the problem—then do it.

The data that I use are from both the U.S. Department of Commerce and the President's Energy Committee. They show, simply, that the increase in imported oil prices—not just Arab oil, but all imported oil, including oil imported from Canada—could account for no more than an additional 1 percent increase in the consumer price index. In other words, while the cost of living actually increased in the United States during the first six months of 1974 at an annual rate of 12.4 percent, if imported oil prices had not increased over their pre-October 1973 figure, then the annual rate of inflation would still have been over 11 percent—more accurately, 11.5 percent.

So the administration's efforts to blame inflation on the Arabs are nonsense. However, and it is unfortunate, the American press has not yet discovered this fact and reported it to the people. Of course the only mention that I have made of my analysis before tonight was on the floor of the Senate. But it is becoming well known in Washington that about the only people who consistently read the *Congressional Record* are in the Arab and Israeli embassies.

In another area of the American awakening, though, there is encouraging progress. This involves the moral and legal questions concerning the rights of the Palestinian people. I believe that there is reason to be both surprised and pleased at the relatively rapid changes in the American understanding of the Palestinian question. It is sometimes hard to remember that only a year ago even the word *Palestinian* was not used accurately by most Americans. For those who have spent a lifetime researching the Palestinian cause and carefully documenting their findings, this is probably a shocking and discouraging fact. But it is still a fact.

Before October 1973, the majority of Americans thought of Palestinians as either refugees or terrorists—if they thought of them at all. Many Americans, I know, thought that the Palestinians really no longer existed as a people. But think of the awakening that has occurred. As just one example, recently, alongside a picture in the *Washington Post* of an injured Israeli there was a picture of an injured Palestinian. This may seem only simple truth. But earlier there were no pictures of bombed Palestinian homes or injured Palestinian children.[1] Now no one can claim that the Palestinians are all terrorists or that they do not exist. It may shock some that it could have ever been otherwise, but it was. The American people are now more likely to support efforts to see that such pictures will not be seen again—but because such tragedies will have stopped, and not because of indifference or bias.

I believe that the question of justice for the Palestinian people must now move into a new, definitive stage. Now that the American people are learning about the basis for the Palestinian demands for justice, the word *justice* has to be defined. But this definition cannot come from the Americans, or the Europeans, or the Russians, or even the other Arabs. It must come from the Palestinian people—but there are limits.

When I traveled in the Middle East last year, I learned much about the Arab people and their culture. In Saudi Arabia, I learned one particular Arab proverb which, I believe, is fitting here this evening: Your friend is one who tells you the truth, not one who tells you what you wish to hear. I have quoted this proverb when questioned by those who disagree with my statements concerning the Middle East—those who accuse me of being anti-Israeli. I have told them that the political leaders promising Israel total and absolute support—

1. Similarly, recently Milton Viorst, a writer for the *Washington Star*, presented one of the more stirring descriptions of the Palestinian quest for justice. What he said could have been written and would have been just as accurate a year ago, or two years ago, or a quarter of a century ago. But it wasn't. See Viorst. "Israeli Intransigence," *Washington Star*, Oct. 14, 1974.

regardless of Israel's actions—are telling them what they wish to hear, but not the truth. I believe that my position concerning the Middle East is best not only for the United States but also for Israel and for the Arab nations. I will continue to speak as a friend.

The Palestinian people must decide if their demand for justice will be met by the creation of a new state of Palestine—if that is the name that they would choose to call their new homeland. I know that for some this would not be sufficient. There are those who will settle for nothing less than the destruction of the state of Israel. And we must remember that to the American people, destruction of Israel is synonymous with the killing of every man, woman, and child in Israel. This the American people will not accept. Those who believe that creation of a new Palestinian state is the first step to the total destruction of Israel must share the blame for the continued exile of the Palestinians.

I am aware of the arguments which say that creation of a new state would not represent total justice for the Palestinians. But this is something that the Palestinian people themselves will have to decide. Do they want to begin now defining and structuring a new state within the boundaries possible, or do they wish to continue to demand that the new state include lands within the pre-1967 boundaries of Israel? Their decision is being awaited by many in the United States.

I do know that even the creation of a new state—based on the West Bank and Gaza—is not a certainty. It is well known that there is strong opposition to such a move. But I also know that regardless of the odds against it, creation of a new state of Palestine has a greater opportunity for success than does any proposal affecting pre-1967 Israel. But, as I said, the decision of what represents justice for Palestinians will have to be made by Palestinians. I can only present what I believe to be the best opportunity for justice and peace in the Middle East. My cautious optimism toward a new state, though, was considerably bolstered by Jordan's affirmative vote in the United Nations action regarding recognition of the Palestinians. I will await with great interest, however, as will many other members of the United States Congress, the decision of the Palestinians with regard to the creation of a new state or alternative solutions.

Another area of American awakening centers about Jerusalem. Few Americans have understood the religious significance that El-Quds el-Sherif holds for Muslim Arabs. Jerusalem has always, of course, held a special place for Christians. And most Americans are aware of the significance of the Wailing Wall and other sites to Jews. But it has come as a surprise to many of my countrymen to find that

Muslims also consider Jerusalem a holy city. This lack of religious knowledge has had severe political ramifications. It is only within recent months that many Americans have taken seriously King Faisal's concern for the mosques and other holy sites in that part of the city occupied by Israel since 1967. But it is a concern that will have to be recognized if a true peace is to be found in the Middle East.

I have been fortunate in receiving a copy of *The Noble Sanctuary,* which includes beautiful photographs of the Muslim sites in Jerusalem and provides a useful brief history of the city.[2] It is this type of work that could help in the further awakening of the American people to the true Arab concern with this holy city. I hope further efforts such as this will become more widely available. I'd like to ,see a copy of this book, and others like it, in every school and university library. It would be both a religious and a historical reference for the new American generations. I believe that once the true religious significance of Jerusalem is recognized, serious efforts can begin to resolve the conflict and to guarantee protection of the holy sites for each faith.

The complexity of the Middle East conflict stems from the interrelationship of economics, geopolitics, military confrontation, and religious and cultural differences. Any solution neglecting one of these will provide only a short breathing space—if even that—before the neglected area will once again erupt. In the months ahead, while we search for the answers to each of these critical, complex problems, there is one temptation that each side must avoid—ending the frustration of seemingly endless conferences and meetings with a so-called quick military solution. If this temptation proves too much, then the United States will find itself reluctantly being pushed to make the decisions that should be made by the nations and peoples directly involved. At this time, I do not think that anyone knows for certain what the United States would do. And I think it is best if we never find out. The Arabs might find that the United States is willing to go to far greater lengths on behalf of Israel than they had expected. On the other hand, the Israelis might find that the United States is not willing to go as far as they had expected. It would be a gamble that neither side should consider taking. And it would be a gamble where the only possible winner would be the Soviet Union.

It is indeed unfortunate—even tragic—that the American news media have failed to inform the people of the basic antipathy that exists

2. Alistair Duncan, *The Noble Sanctuary* (London: Longmans, 1972).

between the Arab nations and the communist regimes. This split is caused to some extent by the same substantiated fears that any nation can be expected to have of Soviet expansionist goals. The grim lessons of Hungary and Czechoslovakia serve as reminders that nations which once fall under the military control of the Russians do not always have a good chance of regaining self-government. But even deeper than this is the unbridgeable gulf between communism and Islam. They cannot exist together, anymore than communism and Christianity can coexist, within the same society. I have no doubt that the religious persecution that is officially sanctioned within the Soviet Union would be quickly extended to any Arab country that came under direct military control.

It is essential, however, that the American people understand the nature of these basic conflicts. When they do, they will begin to wonder why Arabs turn to the Soviet Union for both economic and military aid—aid that ultimately results in a dangerous Soviet presence in their countries.

This, of course, is the result of an imbalanced American foreign policy—a policy that hurts not only the United States and the Arab nations, but Israel as well. But this has to be made known to the people. Only then will the Congress—responding to the demands of the electorate—begin a serious reevaluation of present American policies.

Those in America who support the present Middle East policies of the United States have, I believe, already begun to realize that Israel's only hope for the future is to make peace with its Arab neighbors. Two recent reports should sober the most ardent advocate of unlimited military assistance to Israel. I refer to the probable loss of the Azores as an intermediate landing base for air transports to Israel, and to the inability of the United States Army to quickly make up the losses in main battle tanks sent to Israel since October 1973. As a United States senator, these reports would be disturbing to me even if Israel were not concerned. They are matters affecting the national security of my country. But I would think that they would create genuine consternation in any Israeli military commander who was counting on the United States to make up any future combat losses.

It is ironic that those in the U.S. Congress who most loudly proclaim their support for Israel are among those who also oppose the necessary funding for a strong military defense force. They are also the political leaders who have opposed the development of domestic energy sources, calling instead for unlimited importation of crude and refined petroleum. It is also ironic that I have been one of those in the Congress who has urged a strong military defense and increased production of domestic oil, natural gas, coal, and nuclear energy supplies. I suppose if that were the test, it would make me a pro-Israeli Congressman.

But such misconceptions have abounded within the American population. It has been only within the past year that large numbers of people have begun to question the stock, and usually contradictory, statements that were fed them by the national press. They are beginning to wonder how someone can be pro-Arab oil and anti-Arab. Or, how can a senator urge sending M-60 tanks and F-4 jets to Israel, and at the same time oppose sending them to the United States Army and Air Force? The answers to these questions are part of the American awakening. But, as I said earlier, the answers will not come forth automatically—as they should. They will have to be dragged out into the open.

In all the areas of concern in this quest for truth and accuracy, the field of Arab history stands out as one that has been unduly neglected. To understand a people, it is necessary to know its history. Improvements in American education concerning the Middle East are critically needed. I have great confidence in the inherent intelligence and fairness of the American people. Their slumber over the past decades regarding the Arab people is a result of many factors, some still present and others—such as the war in Vietnam—now faded from the forefront. I can understand the disappointment and hard feelings that have resulted from misrepresentation, particularly within the news media. But I believe that the American awakening is a reality. And such an awakening can only be beneficial—not just for the Arabs, the Israelis, and America's European allies—but primarily for the American people.

Fayez A. Sayegh

PROSPECTS OF THE PALESTINIAN CAUSE IN THE DIPLOMATIC ARENA

WHEN, IN JULY 1974, I proposed "Prospects of the Palestinian Cause in the Diplomatic Arena" as the theme of my address this evening, I was confident that it would be a timely subject. Little did I reckon, however, with the possibility that it might be *too* timely! Yet this is precisely the situation. At this very moment, perhaps, the foreign ministers of the Arab states are winding up their meeting in Rabat, in preparation for the Seventh Arab Summit Conference, which will convene tomorrow. And in less than two weeks the General Assembly of the United Nations will embark on its historic debate on "the question of Palestine." These regional and international discussions cannot fail to have a significant impact on the prospects of the Palestinian cause in the diplomatic arena for at least the immediate future.

Before I speak about the future, I would like to devote a few minutes to a discussion of the recent past, which provides the background against which the present status and future prospects of the Palestinian cause must be viewed. I shall focus in particular upon two trends in international thinking which are of direct relevance to our subject.

First, in the year that has elapsed since the October war, the Palestinian problem has thrust itself into the foreground of discussions about the situation in the Middle East instead of remaining—as it had for many years—in the background.

You will recall that shortly after the 1967 June War, when the international community endeavored to formulate the terms of a comprehensive and final settlement of the Arab-Israeli conflict, it produced U.N. Security Council resolution 242, which was adopted unanimously on November 22, 1967, and which has since become the basic framework within which international diplomacy has sought to achieve a lasting settlement in the Middle East. But resolution 242 did not deal in any way with the problem of Palestine: the name of Palestine was not even mentioned in that document; and the only allusion to any aspect of the problem—namely, "a just settlement of the refugee problem"—appeared in a subparagraph of a subordinate paragraph of the resolution and refrained from specifying the identity of the refugees and from defining the terms under which a "just settlement" of their problem might be achieved. That, then, was the way in which the international community viewed the Arab-Israeli conflict seven short years ago. But the Palestine problem, which was so unceremoniously swept under the carpet in the aftermath of the 1967 war, has now been rediscovered by the international community. Less than a month ago, the General Assembly of the United Nations decided to inscribe "The Question of Palestine" on the agenda of its current session—not as an adjunct to the item "The Situation in the Middle East," but as a separate item in its own right; and not as a companion to the item "The Report of the Commissioner General of the United Nations Relief and Works Agency for Palestine Refugees in the Near East," which deals with the administration of international relief to the refugees, but as a comprehensive political item dealing with all aspects of the fate of Palestine and the Palestinian people. When the decision to add this new item to the crowded agenda of the session was taken, only the representative of Israel was heard to murmur a perfunctory reservation.

Let us cite another indication of the change in the awareness of the problem. In 1969, Israeli prime ministers Eshkol and Meir—in February and June, respectively—made public statements denying the existence of the Palestinians. But three weeks ago, when he made his statement before the General Assembly during the general debate, the foreign minister of Israel found himself capable of pronouncing the theretofore unmentionable word *Palestinians*. If I remember rightly, he uttered that word twenty-two times in the course of his not-too-lengthy statement. In other words, Israel is now ready to admit what five years ago two successive Israeli leaders insisted on publicly and vehemently denying: namely, that Palestinians do exist and that there is indeed a Palestinian problem. There is little doubt that this change in the position of Israel reflects an awareness—reluctant and painful, indeed, but nevertheless real—of the overwhelming reality of the Palestinian movement and an equally reluctant and painful awareness of the well-nigh universal recognition of the existence and the national rights of the Palestinian people.

The second important development of the past year has been the growing recognition of the Palestine Liberation Organization as the legitimate representative of the Palestinian people, and its growing acceptance by and in the international community.

During the past thirteen months, formal recognition of the Palestine Liberation Organization as the legitimate representative of the Palestinian people was expressed by the Fourth Conference of the Heads of State or Government of Non-aligned Countries, the Second Islamic Summit Conference, and the Twenty-third Session of the Council of Ministers of the Organization of African Unity. The second and third of these conferences went so far as to affirm that the PLO is the sole legitimate representative of the Palestinian people. Moreover, on November 9, 1973, representatives of seventy-one member-states of the United Nations, including about a dozen whose governments did not participate in any of the three conferences I mentioned, signed an official United Nations document (A/SPC. 164) in which the PLO was described as "the legitimate representative of the Arab people of Palestine, the principal party to the Palestine question."

Furthermore, since February 1974, representatives of the PLO have attended, as observers, the following five international conferences: the Diplomatic Conference on the Reaffirmation and Development of International Humanitarian Law Applicable in Armed Conflicts; the Third Conference on the Law of the Sea; the World Population Conference; the Assembly of the International Civil Aviation Organization; and the General Conference of UNESCO; and they are due to attend the World Food Conference in November 1974.

The most dramatic recognition of the PLO came eleven days ago, when the General Assembly of the United Nations adopted resolution 3210 (XXIX), which describes the PLO as "the representative of the Palestinian people." As you know, while only 3 countries joined Israel in opposing this resolution, no less than 105 countries voted in favor. Permit me to pause for a moment to comment on some of the elements of this important decision.

First, the resolution affirms in its preamble that "the Palestinian people is the principal party to the question of Palestine." The people whose existence the Security Council totally ignored in 1967 and two Israeli premiers categorically denied in 1969 has now been recognized by the world community as the "principal party" to the question of Palestine.

Second, the resolution affirms, in its operative paragraph, that the PLO is "the representative of the Palestinian people." I should emphasize that whereas the decisions to permit representatives of the PLO to attend the international conferences I mentioned earlier were all made on the basis of the recognition of the PLO by the League of Arab States, the recent resolution of the General Assembly authorizes the PLO to participate in the deliberations of that principal organ of the United Nations in its own right and on its own merits, as the representative of the Palestinian people, and not on the strength of anyone else's testimony.

Third, the use in the resolution of the word *invites* is important. The General Assembly did not accede to a request by the PLO: the Assembly itself took the initiative in inviting the PLO.

Fourth, the resolution specifies that the participation of the PLO shall be "in plenary meetings" of the General Assembly. Other organizations have been permitted in the past to address meetings of committees of the Assembly; but there is no precedent of anyone who is not a representative of a state addressing, and participating in the deliberations of, the General Assembly in plenary meetings. It has been said by some that the appearance of the pope before the Assembly was such a precedent; but it should be remembered, to the contrary, that the pope is not only the head of the Catholic church but also the head of the Vatican state.

Having said all this, however, let me hasten to inject two words of caution. First, the true credentials of the Palestine Liberation Organization as the sole legitimate representative of the Palestinian people are not granted by international bodies—however lofty their stature, however numerous their membership, however overwhelming their vote. The true credentials of the PLO are bestowed upon it by the Palestinian people itself. Only minutes before the General Assembly proceeded to vote on resolution 3210 (XXIX), I reminded it—and I was the last speaker before the vote—that more important than the recognition of the PLO by the states and organizations mentioned by the preceding speakers was the fact that the PLO was recognized by "every popular organization of Palestinians in existence." "It is the Palestinian people itself that has acknowledged and recognized the Palestine Liberation Organization as its legitimate representative," I stated then, and I now reiterate. International recognition is derivative: the original recognition comes from the Palestinian people itself.

And it follows that the PLO will cease to be the legitimate representative of the Palestinian people—even if the entire world continues to insist that it is so—if it permits the umbilical cord connecting it to the Palestinian masses to be severed; if it pursues, in its diplomacy, courses incompatible with the aspirations of the Palestinian people; or if it begins to strive for political objectives that militate against, or obstruct, the restoration of its people's inalienable national and human rights.

Second, let me also caution against some exaggerated interpretations of General Assembly resolution 3210 (XXIX). Important as this resolution is as a milestone in the diplomatic struggle of the Palestinian people, it neither grants the PLO the status of permanent observer at the United Nations nor deals substantively with the question of the national rights of the people of Palestine. Both of these questions have yet to be discussed and acted upon.

To a greater or lesser extent, the prospects of the Palestinian cause in the diplomatic arena are likely to be affected—in the near future, at any rate—by the positions and policies of four parties: the Soviet Union and the United States (the two cochairmen of the Geneva Conference, if and when it reconvenes), Israel, and the Arab states. The decisive factor, however, remains the struggle and diplomacy of the Palestinian people itself. Before discussing the recent trends in Palestinian diplomacy, we must look at the changes, if any, that have taken place in the attitudes of those parties since the October war.

Perhaps the most constant policy has been that of the Soviet Union. As a Palestinian and an Arab, I cannot but speak with gratitude about the support of the Soviet Union. The U.S.S.R. has steadfastly opposed Israeli aggression and the resultant Israeli expansion; it has consistently called for Israeli withdrawal from all Arab territories occupied in 1967 and for recognition of Palestinian national rights. But we should not lose sight of the fact that this Soviet position is by no means identical with ours. What the Soviet Union opposes—and in that opposition it identifies itself with one of our aspirations—is the expansion of Israel; but the Soviet Union neither opposes the existence of Israel as an exclusionist, racist, usurper regime nor endorses our opposition to Zionism. In defending the existence, but opposing the policies and the territorial expansion, of Israel, while also championing the idea of setting up a Palestinian state where the Palestinian people can exercise self-determination in a part of Palestine, the Soviet Union maintains in 1974 the same basic policy it adopted as early as 1947, when it supported the partition of Palestine. One practical aspect of recent Soviet policy, however, is ominous: the facilitation of mass emigration of Soviet Jews to Israel and to the Arab territories occupied by Israel since 1967. The advent of some 100,000 new Jewish immigrants from the Soviet Union in the past few years—augmenting the manpower available for Israeli colonization, occupation, expansion, and economic development—can hardly be viewed as consistent with the objective of putting an end to Israeli occupation of Arab lands seized in 1967 and making room for a Palestinian state in a part of Palestine.

The change in America's Middle Eastern diplomacy since the October war and the Arab oil embargo has been more apparent than real. It has been a change in style, not in substance. Even as such, it relates to America's attitude to the interstate, Arab-Israeli conflict, and not to America's attitude to the Palestine problem.

With regard to the interstate, Arab-Israeli conflict, the United States now appears to be prepared to consider the demands of the Arab states concerned, for the restoration of their occupied territories, as having some validity—provided that such restoration be effected within the context of unequivocal acknowledgment by the Arab states concerned of Israel's alleged right to exist as an independent "Jewish" state. However, the territorial implications of America's support *in principle* of those Arab demands are still undefined; and its preparedness *in practice* to adopt policies, including allocation of military and economic aid, conducive to the satisfaction of those demands has yet to be demonstrated.

As for the Palestine problem, the United States has not given any indication that it recognizes any of the following principles: that the Arab-Israeli conflict is a derivative conflict resulting from the Palestine problem itself, and that therefore there can be no durable—let alone just—settlement of the Arab-Israeli conflict without effecting a just solution to the original problem of Palestine; that the Palestinians constitute a people, with a national identity and national rights of its own; that the basic human rights of Palestinians as individuals—including the right to return to their homes and property—are inalienable rights, and that therefore the exercise of these rights must not be contingent upon the assurance that it will have no adverse effect upon the exclusivist, racist "Jewishness" of Israel; and that the Palestine Liberation Organization is the representative of the Palestinian people. With regard to the rights and aspirations of the Palestinian people, then, America's policy remains one of implacable hostility.

As far as Israeli diplomacy is concerned, it is clear by now that the early intimations of some sobering effects of the October war have given way to resuscitated intransigence on the part of the public as well as the government of Israel.

At a time when the Arab states most directly concerned have been giving up the famous "nos" of the Khartoum summit conference one after the other, Israel has been busily putting together an impressive string of "nos" of its own. Israeli policy now rests on the following six negatives, which are enunciated by Israeli decision-makers as absolute principles: (1) no return to the demarcation lines of June 4, 1967, *under any circumstances, including full-fledged peace;* (2) no *partial* withdrawal from the territory of any Arab state except in return for politico-juridical and other concessions by that state which are tantamount to its effective withdrawal from the Arab-Israeli confrontation and its de facto cession of the remainder of its occupied territory to Israel; (3) no recognition of the Palestinians as a people with a national identity and national rights of its own; (4) no separate Palestinian state on any part of Palestine; (5) no recognition that Palestinians, as individuals, have a right to return to their homes in territories under Israeli control; and (6) no dialogue with the Palestine Liberation Organization under any circumstances or in any form—except "on the battlefield."

I have suggested thus far that since the October war, Soviet Middle Eastern policy has remained substantially unchanged; that United States diplomacy, which has endeavored to appear somewhat more flexible and less totally partisan with respect to the Arab-Israeli conflict, has remained implacably hostile to the national rights and aspirations of the Palestinian people; and that Israel has come to articulate its intransigent policies—regarding withdrawal from the territories of the Arab states as well as the restoration of the national rights of the Palestinian people—with even greater boldness than it had done between 1967 and 1973. I now submit that it is only in the diplomacy of the fourth party—the Arab states most directly concerned—that there has been fundamental and far-reaching change since the October war.

Soon after the disastrous 1967 June War, which transformed Israel from a state occupying the greater part of Palestine into a state occupying all of Palestine and territories of other Arab states besides, Arab officialdom formulated a common Arab policy at the Khartoum summit conference held in August. The "nos" of Khartoum tersely articulated the precepts that had formed the basis of Arab policy for two decades. By November, however, it had become clear that the brave words of Khartoum were an epitaph, not a program: they expressed the bases of the policy pursued during an era that the June war had suddenly brought to an end, instead of the bases of the policy to be pursued after the June defeat.

Looking back at 1967 with the benefit of hindsight, we can see that Israeli occupation of territories belonging to other Arab states in addition to Palestine could have had one of two effects: it could have joined indissolubly the struggle of the Palestinian people with the struggles of the other Arab peoples for the liberation of all occupied Arab lands; or it could have separated those struggles, focusing the attention of Arab officialdom on the liberation of the recently occupied territories and pushing the original question of Palestine to the background. Security Council resolution 242 served as the catalyst. The decisions of Khartoum notwithstanding, some Arab states—enticed by the promise of Israeli withdrawal from the lands seized in June—acquiesced in the resolution's twin requirements of termination of states of belligerency and acknowledgment of the alleged right of Israel to sovereignty and security, as well as in the resolution's total disregard of the Palestinian factor in the Arab-Israeli equation; and they unwaveringly pursued their diplomatic struggle, from November 1967 until October 1973, within the framework of Security Council resolution 242. Other Arab states demurred; but some of these, too, moved imperceptibly over the years toward declared or implicit acceptance of the terms of that resolution. By 1973, the demand for the implementation of resolution 242 had become the dominant theme in Arab diplomacy. Only a small minority of Arab states continued to reject that resolution—in most cases, perfunctorily.

Meanwhile, the resurgence in the mid-sixties of the Palestinian struggle, which received fresh impetus from the Arab defeat of 1967, began to focus Arab and international attention on the problem of Palestine.

Ironically, it was while the Palestinian smoulder was becoming a blaze, and the international community was beginning to recognize, more and more forthrightly, the national rights of the Palestinian people (as was exemplified by General Assembly resolutions from December 1969 onward regarding those rights), that Arab diplomacy was becoming tied more and more securely to Security Council resolution 242. Differences between one Arab government or another and the PLO over this issue would reach the breaking point whenever the implementation of resolution 242 appeared, either to that Arab government or to the PLO, to be imminent (as in 1970 in the aftermath of the Rogers initiative), only to be papered over when the hopes or the fears, as the case might be, proved to be premature.

The 1973 war, which revived Arab hopes for liberation and also generated a trend toward inter-Arab conciliation and collaboration, gave birth to the new Arab diplomacy of today. Its hallmark was

the interweaving of Security Council resolution 242 with General
Assembly resolutions 2535 B, 2672 C, 2792 D, 2963 E, and 3089
D, affirming the inalienable rights of the Palestinian people, including
its right to self-determination. The magic formula: a dual Arab demand,
for Israeli withdrawal from the territories seized in 1967 and for the
realization of the "legitimate rights of the Palestinian people."

I must confess that I have been baffled by the words *legitimate
rights*. Surely, if the objectives of the Palestinian people are rights
then they must also be legitimate: if they are legitimate, then they
are rights. At best, then, the qualification *legitimate* is a redundancy;
at worst, it conceals more than it reveals. Do the words *legitimate
rights* perhaps mean that there are some Palestinian rights that may—
and others that may not—be legitimately pursued? If so, where is
the line of demarcation to be drawn?

The conclusion is inescapable: when read in conjunction with the
demand for Israeli withdrawal from the territories seized in 1967,
and when viewed within the general framework of resolution 242
(with its clear requirement for termination of the state of belligerency
and acknowledgment of the alleged rights of Israel to sovereignty
and security), the Arab demand for the "realization of the 'legitimate
rights' of the Palestinian people" must be interpreted *restrictively;*
that is, it must be interpreted as confining the *geographic, territorial
scope* of those rights to the Palestinian territories seized in 1967,
namely, the West Bank, Gaza, and El-Hamma, and as limiting their
demographic scope, in effect, to the present and original inhabitants
of those areas only—leaving some four-fifths of Palestinian soil under
permanent and legitimatized Israeli rule and two-thirds of the Palestinian people outside Palestine, as refugees destined to be permanently
resettled and absorbed. The post-October Arab diplomacy has contrived
a reconciliation between resolution 242 and Palestinian national rights
only by shrinking those rights to miniature proportions.

It is as if 1967 has suddenly become the borderline between
legitimacy and illegitimacy, the criterion by reference to which one
determines what Arab rights may legitimately be restored and what
Arab rights may not. Now we are all agreed that the restoration of
Sinai to Egyptian sovereignty and of the Golan to Syrian sovereignty
is, respectively, an Egyptian and a Syrian right. And we all agree
that the struggle of Egypt and Syria for the liberation of Sinai and
the Golan, respectively, is legitimate. But it seems that Palestinians
must now accept the limitation that only those Palestinian territories
seized in 1967 (when Sinai and the Golan were also seized) may
legitimately be liberated.

I submit that the Arab right—and the Arab duty—to liberate *all* occupied Arab territories is one and indivisible. I submit that Acre is no less a part of the Arab homeland than Nablus and Gaza, or Sinai and the Golan. To discriminate between Arab lands on the basis of the date of their occupation by Israel is neither valid nor acceptable, whether from the Palestinian or the Arab standpoint.

The same reasoning applies to *people.* The right of those Palestinians who now live outside Palestine to self-determination in their homeland is not less by one iota than the right of their fellow Palestinians who live now, or who lived until 1967, on the West Bank or in Gaza.

If one part of the Palestinian people remains unable to exercise its inalienable right to self-determination in Palestine, or if one part of Palestine remains occupied, then the entire Palestinian people and indeed the entire Arab nation remain deprived.

The demand for "the realization of the 'legitimate rights' of the Palestinian people"—read in the historical-political context within which it was formulated—is incompatible with the Charter of the Palestine Liberation Organization. It is also irreconcilable with the ideals and principles of Arab nationalism. I lament the acquiescence of the competent authorities of the Palestine Liberation Organization in the proclamation of this objective.

I turn now to Palestinian diplomacy.

"Palestinian diplomacy?" Doesn't the term sound utterly unfamiliar—perhaps ill-fitting? Is not the very concept somewhat unorthodox? *How* can a national liberation movement lacking a territorial base and a governmental apparatus have its own diplomacy? And *why* should a fighting movement want to involve itself in the political process at all? These very questions have in fact engaged the Palestinian mind agonizingly in the course of the past year; and the emerging answers have polarized the Palestinian people. Even though many, including the most crucial, issues have remained unresolved, the year that has just elapsed has indeed witnessed the birth of a Palestinian diplomacy, for it has witnessed both the opportunity for waging, and the obligation to wage, a Palestinian diplomatic campaign. The world-wide international recognition received by the PLO has provided it with the opportunity and the capacity to engage in diplomatic action and to shape a Palestinian diplomacy; and the aftermath of the October war, in which the Arab confrontation with Israel shifted from the military battlefield to the diplomatic front, has convinced many Palestinian leaders that the PLO should be involved in the politico-diplomatic process or else run the risk of missing the boat.

In the "great debate" that ensued among Palestinians of all walks of life there was at times a tendency to confuse the discussion of whether or not to get involved in the politico-diplomatic process at all with the discussion of the respective merits of alternative diplomatic courses. Some were apparently convinced—I believe, wrongly—that becoming involved in the diplomatic process automatically implied acceptance of one or another of the political compromises that were in the air.

The "great debate" was definitively resolved at the Twelfth Session of the Palestine National Council, held in Cairo in June 1974, on the basis of the Ten-Point Program that had been formulated by the leaders of all the commando organizations at their protracted meetings the preceding spring.

As one whose adult life has been spent in academic pursuits, information work, and diplomatic work at the United Nations, I cannot possibly be chagrined by the fact that the PLO has chosen to participate in the politico-diplomatic process. At the same time, I am not entirely without apprehensions about the possibly adverse effects of this decision on the Palestine Liberation Movement.

To be involved in the political process is to agree to play the game in accordance with the established rules. Now, the rules of the game prescribe that a problem receives not a solution but a settlement; and the settlement, in its turn, emerges not from the confrontation of rights but from the confrontation of power, and reflects the weight of power more than justice. Conciliation of positions, not the triumph of a position, is the objective. Compromises, including some that involve basic rights and fundamental principles, are often the end result. And the strange thing about compromises is that the most difficult compromise of all is the first one; from the moment the first compromise is made, the path is downhill, each compromise setting the stage for the next. Acceptance of the first compromise weakens the movement's resistance to those compromises that follow. For the essential thing is the attitude, the posture, the outlook. The moment you begin to approach your problem with the demeanor of one who is willing—however reluctantly—to compromise, you lose the essential integrity of your position. The first compromise is the most difficult. Such a process as I have described may be all right for an established state to engage in when the issues at stake are peripheral and the basic issues of life or death are not involved; but for a revolution and a movement of national liberation the process may prove fatal.

For better or for worse, the PLO decided last June to participate in the politico-diplomatic process. But the Ten-Point Program implying that decision contained built-in guarantees against compromises of principle. In essence, therefore, the program was a victory at one and the same time for those who wanted participation in the politico-diplomatic process and for those who rejected any of the compromises that, according to all available indications, were inherent in the diplomatic framework within which a comprehensive settlement was to be sought. Whether the Ten-Point Program is capable of implementation in all its parts, including the built-in safeguards against compromise, through the diplomatic process, given the international realities that now obtain, remains to be seen. In fact, it is precisely this that constitutes the basic question relating to the prospects of the Palestinian cause in the diplomatic arena today. I, for one, would prefer diplomatic failure to a diplomatic victory made possible by compromise.

Two specific questions preoccupied the Palestinian mind during the "great debate" that followed the October war: whether or not to participate in the Geneva Conference, if and when it is reconvened; and whether or not to strive for the establishment of a Palestinian state in those Palestinian territories from which Israel might withdraw. As I understand it, the Ten-Point Program gave an affirmative but conditional response to both questions. Palestinian participation in the Geneva Conference was to be predicated on its having acceptable terms of reference other than Security Council resolution 242. And statehood in a part of Palestine was an acceptable short-range goal if it did not entail Palestinian legitimatization of the exclusionist, racist, usurper Zionist regime in the remainder of Palestine and if it did not in effect foredoom to failure our continued struggle for the creation of a unitary pluralistic state in all of Palestine.

I believe I am correctly interpreting the thrust of the Ten-Point Program. And I am now, as I was in June 1974, in agreement with it. Such misgivings as I have pertain to the application of the program. For there are certain points of emphasis on which I would disagree with some of those who are entrusted with the task of implementing that program.

Take the question of the terms of reference of the Geneva Conference. Now we all agree that Security Council resolution 242 is not an acceptable basis. But are we all in agreement also on what constitutes an acceptable basis? Or, to put it differently: Are we all in agreement on why resolution 242 is not acceptable and on what it takes to correct it? To judge from some statements made by some responsible Palestinian leaders, resolution 242 is unacceptable because it reduces the problem of Palestine to the level of a humanitarian problem of refugees and ignores the national dimensions of the problem. This is true, but it does not go far enough. It points to only one deficiency in resolution 242. At the June 1974 session of the Palestine National Council, I suggested that resolution 242 sins against our cause both by *omission* and by *commission;* yet the statement that the resolution is unacceptable to us because it reduces our problem to the level of a humanitarian problem of refugees and ignores its national dimensions refers only to the sin of omission, ignoring the deadlier sin of commission. If this were really all that was wrong with resolution 242, it could be remedied by juxtaposing it with the resolutions of the General Assembly which declared that "full respect for and realization of the inalienable rights of the people of Palestine, particularly its right to self-determination, are indispensable for the establishment of a just and lasting peace in the Middle East." Let us assume, for the sake of the argument, that the powers that be are persuaded to accept this addition; will that render the new, expanded terms of reference of the Geneva Conference acceptable? Some Palestinian leaders may say yes. I strongly disagree. For this correction takes care of the sin of omission only; it does not begin to reckon with the sin of commission in resolution 242—namely, its insistence on the requirement of ending the state of belligerency and acknowledging the so-called right of the exclusionist, racist, usurper settler regime to sovereignty and security. The hypothetical correction of resolution 242 about which I just spoke, in other words, only brings the Palestinians into the fold, from the limbo to which that resolution had relegated them, and enables them to be considered as one more factor among the other factors to the equation; but the settlement within which their point of view would be considered along with the others would be the same kind of settlement prescribed by resolution 242 for all the parties, namely, a settlement which trades "withdrawal" from the territories seized in 1967 for "recognition."

The effect of such a limited corrective operation on the terms of reference of the Geneva Conference (assuming that the operation could be performed at all) would be identical with the effect of accepting the post-October Arab formula about which I spoke earlier—namely, the juxtaposing of the demand for the "realization of the 'legitimate rights' of the Palestinian people" with the demand for Israeli withdrawal from the territories seized in 1967.

My other misgivings relate to some interpretations of the provisions of the Ten-Point Program pertaining to the interim Palestinian goals to be sought at Geneva. So far, attention has been focused almost exclusively on the interim objective of statehood in a part of Palestine—a part which, at most, would embrace the West Bank and the Gaza Strip, that is, about one-fifth of Palestine. In so focusing on statehood, Palestinian diplomacy has become—and please forgive me for so saying—"one-track-minded." Statehood is an important goal; but no less important is the exercise of the right to return to their homes and property by Palestinians whose towns and villages fell to the enemy before 1967. This is an important goal for many reasons: because the right to return is an inalienable right which has been internationally recognized as such; because, in practice, the West Bank and Gaza cannot possibly accommodate, in addition to their present inhabitants, all the Palestinians who are now outside Palestine; and because, when Palestinians return to their homes and property in those parts of Palestine that were occupied prior to 1967, the entire Zionist character of Israel—its exclusionist, racist character—will be transformed, and a formidable step will have been taken toward the achievement of our ultimate goal: the establishment of a unitary pluralistic state in Palestine.

The attention of Palestinian diplomacy has been so fully directed toward the goal of *statehood* that little or no attention has been given to the goal of *repatriation*. And this is all the more regrettable because the two goals are not mutually exclusive. They are compatible goals. They are complementary goals. And, in practice, they require one another.

The two sets of misgivings about which I have just spoken are not unrelated. Regarding Geneva, my fear is that we have pursued the goal of gaining recognition for the Palestinian people as a party and neglected the goal of opposing the legitimatization of the exclusionist, usurper regime in Palestine; and, regarding the substantive objective of our post-October diplomacy, my fear is that we have permitted the goal of statehood to overshadow the goal of repatriation (which, I maintain, is a practical means of challenging the continued exclusionism of the racist, usurper regime). My fear, in short, is that Palestinian diplomacy may have permitted itself to be maneuvered into seeking certain affirmative objectives (namely, recognition of the Palestinian national factor and establishment of a Palestinian state) in return for its silence about the issue of recognition by the Arab states of a Zionist Israel in four-fifths of the area of Palestine, and about the return of Palestinians to their homes, which would in itself de-Zionize the usurper regime. These, you will have noticed, are substantially the same misgivings I expressed a while ago in relation to the objectives of the post-October Arab diplomacy.

The only antidote against the insidious danger inherent in a selective application of some of the provisions of the Ten-Point Program is the faithful implementation of that program in its entirety—that is to say, including its built-in safeguards against compromise.

If diplomacy is the handmaid of national policy, which, in turn, is the expression of basic national rights, aspirations, and interests, then the new Palestinian diplomacy must conform in its basic thrust with the rights, aspirations, and interests of the Palestinian people as defined in the Palestinian National Charter. Interim objectives are valid and acceptable, even when they fall short of the ultimate goals, only if two conditions are satisfied: if they do not, by their achievement, create barriers that obstruct further progress toward the ultimate goals; and if they are likely to create new conditions that will facilitate that progress. Otherwise they are at best inexpedient and at worst inadmissible.

In order to meet the objective requirements of its function, Palestinian diplomacy must place special emphasis in the months to come upon three principles that appear to have been underemphasized in recent months.

So far, post-October Palestinian diplomacy has emphasized the following principles: (1) that the Palestinian people is a principal party to the Arab-Israeli conflict, and that therefore full respect for and realization of the national rights of the Palestinian people are indispensable for the establishment of a just and lasting peace in the Middle East; (2) that the direct participation of the Palestinian people, through the Palestine Liberation Organization, its sole legitimate representative, in the peace-keeping process is indispensable; and (3) that the inalienable right of the Palestinian people to self-determination requires the establishment of an independent Palestinian authority in any part of Palestine that will be liberated.

These principles are valid—so far as they go. But they do not go far enough. Unless supplemented by other equally important and equally valid principles, there is a great risk that a settlement which takes into account the three foregoing principles alone may turn into the compromise envisaged in the slogan "the realization of the 'legitimate rights' of the Palestinian people."

To guard against this danger, Palestinian diplomacy must additionally emphasize the following three principles:

1. Palestinian recognition of an exclusionist, racist, Zionist usurper, settler regime in Palestine, within whatever borders, is unthinkable. We must be neither apologetic nor evasive when the issue at stake is none other than the legitimatization of the usurpation of our inalienable rights. To the world at large we must declare that we *do* recognize the right of any state to exist on land rightfully belonging to its inhabitants—but that we recognize no such claimed right to any state established on land rightfully belonging to someone else. (We must remind the world that when Israel was established, only 5.6 percent of the total land area of Palestine was owned by Jews, and that only 0.3 percent of Palestinian land was sold to Jewish immigrants by Palestinians during the thirty years of British occupation. Every other inch of Palestinian land currently claimed by Israel or by Jewish Israelis was obtained by illegal confiscation.) Our refusal to legitimatize the usurpation of our land is an integral part of the world-wide rejection of colonialism, an integral part of the process of decolonization that has transformed the face of the world in the past quarter-century. We cannot under any circumstances purchase statehood in a part of Palestine for the price of legitimatizing the usurpation of the remainder of Palestine.

2. No less important than the creation of a state for and by a part of the Palestinian people in a part of Palestine as an interim goal is the goal of the return of all Palestinians to their homes and property in all of Palestine. I have already referred to some of the reasons that make this an imperative, immediate objective of Palestinian diplomacy.

3. We must continue to proclaim our ultimate objective of a unitary pluralistic state in Palestine, a state in which indigenous Palestinians (Muslims, Christians, and Jews) and nonindigenous Jews can coexist within a democratic system, a state that belongs to all of them equally and to which they all equally belong. It has been said that this objective is tantamount to the destruction of Israel: I maintain that this objective is tantamount to the destruction of the exclusionism and racism and usurpation that Israel represents; that it is tantamount to the transformation, the humanization, of the inhuman situation that now obtains in Palestine. Every step in the process of decolonization throughout the world has involved the destruction of colonial politico-juridical structures and the erection in their place of legitimate indigenous ones. This is the quintessence of decolonization. Destruction is always an indispensable part of the process of corrective transformation. What is distinctive about the Palestinian revolution, therefore, is not its determination to destroy an alien, illegitimate, imposed politico-juridi-

cal structure (something that every anticolonial revolution has done) but the magnanimity that characterizes its ultimate objective. For its goal is not the expulsion of the Jewish *colon* but the elimination of the exclusionist regime that he has set up in the process of his displacement and dispossession of the indigenous Palestinian, and the creation of a new body politic in which the Jewish *colon* as well as the indigenous Palestinian is assured a place. It is not often that the world witnesses a deprived and disinherited people, in the heat of battle, offer its oppressor an equal share in its own patrimony and a chance for coexistence within the framework of democratic pluralism. The Palestinian goal is indeed unique in its humanistic morality, just as the tragedy inflicted on the Palestinian people, and which the Palestinian people continues to suffer until this very day, is unique in its inhuman cruelty.

Tomorrow at Rabat, and in two weeks' time at the United Nations, Palestinian diplomacy will have the opportunity to supplement its recent emphasis on the three principles I mentioned earlier with equal emphasis on the three essential principles that I have just enumerated. Whether or not it will do so may well prove to be the test of its vision and also of its faithfulness to the rights and aspirations and interests of the Palestinian people—of which, after all, it is only a handmaid.